DATE DUE

MAY 1 8 2009			

Demco, Inc. 38-293

Pulpit Politics

Pulpit Politics

Faces of American Protestant Nationalism
in the Twentieth Century

by
Warren L. Vinz

Foreword by Martin E. Marty

STATE UNIVERSITY OF NEW YORK PRESS

Chapter 3, "Foreign Polity Through Benediction," is reprinted from *Religion and Political Power* by Benavides and Daly by permission of the State University of New York Press. © 1989.

In Chapter 2, "Bifurcated Nationalism," portions of the unpublished manuscripts of Walter Rauschenbusch are reprinted by permission from The Ambrose Swasey Library of Colgate Rochester Divinity School, Bexley Hall, Crozer Theological Seminary and Saint Bernard's Institute.

Versions of Chapters 6, "Nationalism and the Sword," and 9, "The Nationalism of Survival," were written previously with Chapter titles, "The Sword and the Lord," and "Christ is the Answer" respectively and will appear with those titles in the forthcoming volume, *The American Conservative Press*, edited by Ron Lora and William Longton, Greenwood Press, an imprint of the Greenwood Publishing Group, Inc., Westport, Conn.

Published by
State University of New York Press, Albany

© 1997 State University of New York

For information, address the State University of New York Press,
State University Plaza, Albany, NY 12246

Production by Christine Lynch
Marketing by Theresa Abad Swierzowski

Library of Congress Cataloging-in-Publication Data

Vinz, Warren Lang.
    Pulpit politics : faces of American Protestant nationalism in the
twentieth century / by Warren L. Vinz.
        p.   cm.
    Includes bibliographical references and index.
    ISBN 0-7914-3175-4 (hardcover : alk. paper). — ISBN 0-7914-3176-2
(pbk. : alk. paper)
    1. Nationalism—Religious aspects—Christianity—History—20th
century.   2. Protestant churches—United States—Doctrines—
History—20th century.   3. United States—Church history—20th
century.   I. Title.
BR526.V56   1997
320.5'4'0972—dc20   96-10703
                                                                CIP

10 9 8 7 6 5 4 3 2 1

Contents

Foreword

Warren Vinz takes considerable care to define most of the terms in this book. He treats key words such as "nationalism" circumspectly, knowing how easily the plot of the book can be set on a meandering course if a word like this is ill-described.

If there is one word that a visitor from a distant shore might find confusing at the beginning, middle, and end of this book, it is "Protestantism." It makes more than cameo appearances on scores of pages that follow. All the lead characters are described and self-described as Protestant. But what is it to be Protestant?

If I suggest that Vinz chooses to point more than to define, I am not saying he is deficient in his duties. Rather, he is true to reality. Some years ago a publisher assigned me the task of writing a book called simply *Protestantism*, to match titles on *Hinduism*, *Buddhism*, and the like. I envied the Western authors who wrote about faiths most of whose millions of adherents lived oceans and hemispheres away. From that distance it was possible to develop some coherence.

Protestantism, to Europeans, Americans, Sub-Saharan Africans, and increasingly, Latin Americans, is too close to home for anyone to sort out or bring simple perspective and definition. There are about 25,000 denominations in Christianity, and no doubt all but a few hundred are some version or other of Protestantism. If they cannot get together, how can an encyclopedist or an historian herd them into one definitional fold?

For the record, having ranged around Protestant historical markers, I have to say that the only thing uniting all these Western Christians is their refusal to be seen as part of the Roman Catholic obedience—the fact that they were not under the authority of the Pope. Many of them see themselves at Catholics; they have bishops; they overlap with Catholicism on many points. Today's Catholics often share what Protestants thought made themselves distinctive: reverence for biblical authority and a stress on grace. But in fact there were more differences among Protestants on these themes than there were between them and Catholics.

The definition I came up with is not very useful to Vinz, since his characters—being Protestants who thrived between 1900 and 1960—were all non- and often quite anti-Catholic, but made less use of anti-Catholicism in Vinz's chosen contexts than one might have expected. Only a fundamentalist of the John R. Rice sort or some end-of-the-world preachers made negations of Catholicism a main theme as they worked on Protestant destiny.

I have gone on so long about one word in a short foreword because the vagueness of definition serves Vinz better than a clear definition would. I would dare a scholar from the south Asian subcontinent to read the stories of the Protestant leaders in this book and find what they had in common theologically. The spectrum from ultrafundamentalists—and there are some here—to modernists—and there is one here—is too broad. The range from ultraconservatives in respect to politics—and there are numbers of them here—to the Social Gospel and political liberals—and you will find several—is also wide. The already mentioned theme of scriptural authority divides those on Vinz's two poles bitterly, but they do not fight much over grace when they take up his themes.

If their Protestantism does not serve to unite the members of the people in the club Vinz forms by treating their themes, what does? I find three themes coursing through the chapters. One is relevant to the Protestant definitional instance: pluralism. Whoever thinks America, American nationalism, Protestantism, or American Protestant nationalism can be squeezed into a monolithic mold and rendered homogeneous will run into a reality that Vinz treats consistently if sometimes casually. There are an awful lot of varieties of Protestantisms and Protestant interpretations running around. If there is implicit advice, let it be: Dear reader, ideologue or not, learn to live with messiness, confusion, chaos, anarchy, surprise. The Protestant tent is big and has many competitive acts in it. Enjoy. But don't run away from the task of trying to interpret them.

A second theme, one that speaks its name here and there, is "transcendent authority." The most fire-breathing fundamentalist or apocalypticist on one end and the most tolerant, wishy-washy some say, compromising and inclusivist liberal on the other, show themselves to be wrestling with the issue of authority. What or Who exists and acts behind the screen of daily existence in the United States? How do leaders evoke such authority? How do they attract followings, make their criticisms, see themselves judged, and provoke hope in a time when so many leaders invoke so many versions of authority? Nothing gets settled on that front.

The third theme is, of course, American nationalism of a singular set of sorts. If Vinz's cast of characters are representative in any way, the one thing with which they all somehow wrestle is the meaning of religious life in America and of the nation's mission and destiny. On one set of terms, such wrestling is natural; all religious movements reflect their environments, whether these be Islam in Algeria or Indonesia, Judaism in Israel or Brazil, Sikhism in India or Canada. But Protestants, who stand in the prophetic and Jesus traditions, are supposed to reflect on a "kingdom not of this world," or to come with a fundamentally subversive word.

This Vinz's characters do not do. A fundamentalist intellectual like J. Gresham Machen, may sound almost anarchically libertarian at times, but at others makes a fetish of an earlier Christian American constitutionalism. Reinhold Niebuhr may have an ironic view of history in which America laughed at incongruity between pretentious illusions of greatness and realities of experience. But he also clearly sees the nation called to responsibility before or under God. These two and all their kin in this book appraise the American past, assess the present, and project a future, all in the name of a transcendent authority that they evoke in different ways, often against each other.

Those who resent pluralism, have transcendent authority all figured out, and know exactly what America and nationalism are, may wish for more clarity than the plot here can produce. Vinz observes too much ambiguity, double-mindedness ("bifurcated minds"), contradiction, and fluidity to be able to make a judgment that this or that is normative. He deals with the leaders of Protestant factions symbiotically. They live off each other and on each and neither kills the other nor can get along wholly without the other. There appear to be genuine contradictions between some of the leaders' theological convictions about transcendence and their near idolatrous attachment to America. Vinz has patience to live with them all, to sort the claims, and to make modest judgments about where the various leaders would lead or have led America.

Because there is so much ambiguity, nuance, and texture on this particular subject, Vinz's book is helpful in impressive ways. Those

who do the sorting and defining after him will neglect this book at
their peril. Those who stumble onto his subjects because they read
this book will have embarked on an adventure that they are as likely
to enjoy as Vinz does his. It shows.

Martin E. Marty
Fairfax M. Cone Distinguished Service Professor
The University of Chicago

Acknowledgments

Work on this volume has evolved over the better part of a decade, beginning with the summer of 1986 at an eight-week National Endowment for the Humanities (NEH) Faculty Seminar on Religious Nationalism hosted by the University of California, Santa Barbara. A colleague and friend Spencer Bennett of Siena College was in attendance at this seminar. It was the long conversations we had during those weeks that served as the spark for this study.

From this point on many colleagues and friends have contributed to this endeavor and have some ownership in this work. Those who have read all or portions of the text include Martin Marty of the University of Chicago, Eldon Ernst of the American Baptist Seminary of the West, and Ron Lora of the University of Toledo. Being privileged to be a postdoctoral fellow at the Institute for the Advanced Study of Religion at the University of Chicago in 1989, my thanks goes to those colleagues who read and criticized the chapter on Rauschenbusch. My sister, Marjorie Turner, former executive at the American Baptist Convention headquarters in Valley Forge, proved most helpful. She not only read the text, but along with husband, Nate, engaged me in long conversations that added to the reservoir of ideas.

Any work of this kind needs the help and support of local colleagues. I am indebted to Milton Small, formerly director of higher education for the state of Idaho, Todd Shallat, historian and colleague, who read the text and offered valuable suggestions, and Errol Jones, department chair along with former Dean Robert Sims and Dean Jane Ollenburger who authorized monetary and personnel support. Special thanks goes to the Idaho State Board of Education for a $32,000 grant that bought time from class, and airline tickets to libraries. Several faculty research grants from Boise State University provided seed money to get the project started.

The following libraries were most gracious in opening up their archives and other sources: the Ambrose Swasey Library, Colgate Rochester Divinity School; Houghton Library, Harvard University; the Mongomery Library, Westminster Theological Seminary, Philadelphia; Liberty University, Lynchburg, Va.; Burke Library, Union Theological Seminary, New York City; the Flora Lamson Hewlett Library, Graduate Theological Union, Berkeley; the Joseph Regenstein Library, University of Chicago; University of California, Santa Barbara; Templana, Temple University, Philadelphia.

Appreciation goes to Greenwood Press for permission to use the substance of chapters six and nine originally prepared for the forthcoming work on *The Conservative Press in America* edited by Ron Lora and William Longton, University of Toledo. Also, SUNY Press has allowed the inclusion of chapter three, "Foreign Policy through Benediction," originally included in Daly and Benevidas, *Religion and Political Power*.

An indispensable component in producing a book is the secretarial expertise which I have been fortunate to have over the years. Marilyn Paterson was secretary for twenty years while I was department chair and worked on my extra secretarial needs along with her busy routine. Karen Kelsch, administative secretary for the dean's office provided valuable assistance in preparing the concluding chapter during the year I was "sentenced" to one year as interim dean. Denise Fitelson-Nelis, department secretary and computer expert extraordinaire, put the final manuscript copy together for the press, after incorporating a multitude of nit-picking changes in the text; Susan Emerson came to the rescue with additional assistance as deadlines approached. Much needed editing was provided by Barbara Valdez. I am also grateful to Christine Lynch, production editor, and the staff of SUNY Press for their attention to various details necessary in helping tranform a manuscript into a book.

Finally, as anyone with family knows, the support of loved ones is essential not only in providing space to think and write, but providing it with grace. Tracy and Jason over the years, now out of the nest, did just that. Of supreme importance, is the extraordinary understanding of professional pressures by my teenage daughter Kati, whose presence is a constant reminder of what is ultimately important in life, and the unmitigated support and love from my wife Ruth, superb scholar, writer, professor, who inspires one to seek excellence in writing and teaching through her example.

With all the help I have received, I am responsible for any inadequacies.

CHAPTER 1

Introduction

Leonardo da Vinci found the study of faces a fascinating and character-revealing exercise. Relying on his observation and subsequent caricature drawings, he declared that some people's faces are good only for passing food. Like da Vinci, political cartoonists make their living from faces, using their medium to reveal character. Even the faces of animals symbolizing a people frequently appear in the press. The cartoon of the "stern eagle looking in the mirror and seeing there a chaste and beautiful swan"[1] reveals a face of American nationalism that is pervasive in the twentieth century.

Without such cartoons, caricatures, or pictures of faces, human or animal, this volume focuses on the faces of individuals and the types of nationalistic expression they represent, both beauty marks and warts. It reveals how exponents of nationalism sought to forge a new religious relevance predicated on the American experience and the extent which these diverse styles of religious nationalism create and reflect the tension in the American experience of the twentieth century. The study reveals the similar nationalistic expressions uttered by unlikely bedfellows within Protestantism. Common theology did not necessarily shape one face of nationalism.

The scope of the study, 1900 to the Vietnam era, can be helpful not only in understanding the present phenomenon of the religious resurgence in American politics, but also because during this period Protestant leadership gave mixed signals as to who the American people are and what they are about as a people, contributing to the crisis of community in this post-Vietnam/Watergate era. Today many conservative religious leaders look to the turn of the century as a glorious time in American history when the United States was emerging as an industrial giant and world power. Those years are perceived as glory days when America began to assert itself in a manner advocated by these admirers of that era for today's world.

1

Other leaders of a more liberal persuasion in the current religious community look to this period, but as a time of shameful imperialism that should not be repeated in our time: they choke on the policies that are reminiscent of earlier gunboat diplomacy mentality. What, then, are the American people to believe about themselves and their mission to the world? To understand this dilemma more fully, we consider the numerous forms of nationalism prevalent in the American Protestant experience and the confusion of identity revealed there.

Since a point of departure in this work considers nationalistic expression as the centerpiece of the inquiry, a careful definition and explanation of the form of nationalism employed is necessary. This is especially important when the term is applied to personalities—as in this study—that are not normally perceived as exponents of nationalism. Some who read this volume may even take offense that this or that person is even included in a study of religious nationalism. This is understandable since nationalism today is normally defined in negative terms. It is often identified as a major incentive for arms races, imperialism, and revolution, emanating from a mindless enthusiasm of fanatical citizens asserting their identity and willing to follow the leader over the cliff of national aggression against other nation-states on behalf of the mother/fatherland. Such has often been the case. But to apply the term "nationalism" exclusively with this connotation would be grossly incomplete as a working definition of the term and hence an inappropriate description of the widely varied nationalistic expressions revealed by most of the subjects of this study. Just a cursory perusal of the enormous amount of the literature on the subject will give one a sense of the variety of nationalistic expressions identified by scholars in the field. Happily, much of the spadework on the varieties of nationalism has been done. Louis Snyder is one example; his summary piece titled *Varieties of Nationalism* elaborated on the American style, which he identified as the nationalism of messianism.[2]

The nationalism defined by Snyder is the belief that the nation has come into existence to mark a new stage in history that will transform the human condition from misery to abundance, happiness, and peace. It is a belief by a people that their way of life is superior and should be adopted by others.

Consistent with this definition early Americans were certain that Europe had sunk into decrepitude and senility. One American hayseed boasted: "We air [sic] a great people and bound to be troublesome to them kings." Noah Webster's spelling book made it culturally official: "Europe has grown old in folly, corruption, and tyranny." And

Jefferson, the opposite in intellect and culture from our "hayseed" ancestor: "We are acting for all of mankind."[3]

That Americans should have felt obliged to be messianic should come as no surprise. At the time of national infancy, Americans were nurtured on a Calvinist teething ring that God had chosen certain people to do His work. For these infants of nation-building, this meant the obligation to establish the "City on a Hill" with the expectation that the rest of the world would ultimately fall into line. The mission of the United States, said Thomas Paine, was to "excite emulation throughout the kingdoms of the earth and meliorate the conditions of the human race."[4] It is unnecessary to go into all the details of subsequent evidence of American messianic nationalism. Merely citing that America entered World War I to make the world safe for democracy, World War II to save it from Nazi and Japanese tyranny, and Korea and Vietnam from Communism, will suffice.

However, while American nationalism has been messianic in style, it has not always presented a consistent face in revealing the object of its messianism. It revealed a libertarianism, a materialism, an Anglo-Saxon ethnocentrism, and an egalitarianism. Obviously, not all these faces were compatible, and when revealed simultaneously created a very confusing and sometimes contorted image of American identity and purpose. Libertarianism was a unifying concept identified with the idea of individual liberty in opposition to the power of the state. It was a prominent sentiment seen in the Articles of Confederation at this country's inception, and later on in states' rights movements at various times in United States history up to the mid-twentieth century. And, Americans liked to tell the world how free they were as individuals in American society even if locked into some corporate juggernaut.

Materialism, a second unifying concept, has always been a major component in American nationalistic expression, reinforced by the so-called Protestant ethic. While on the one hand declaring that money was not everything in life, many Americans, on the other hand, believed that worldly success was a sign of God's favor on individual and nation alike. Whether religious or not, Americans tended to think that the prosperity of the nation legitimated their political and economic system applicable to the whole world.

The American belief in egalitarianism, another unifying concept, is fraught with ambiguity. In one sense Americans found their identity by preaching that the ideal society, their society, was egalitarian, that one person was as good as any other and entitled to the same rights and privileges. This egalitarianism was even expressed proudly that

Americans were made up of all races, creeds, ethnic origins, and cultures. However, this image of egalitarianism was qualified by the insistence that multicultural diversity be Anglo-Saxonized—that the diversity of race, creed, ethnic origin, and cultures was desirable only insofar as the unique characteristics of each were subordinated to a paternalistic Eurocentric core. The many unique cultural traditions in American society were seen as quaint contributions to the cultural mix, especially on parade day when spectators could feel good about seeing the colorful costumes worn by people who would no doubt be expected to return the next day to "normal dress." This subordination of cultures has been euphemistically called "Americanization," and the popular identification of this process the "melting pot."

It must be made very clear at the outset that this is not the sense in which the term "egalitarianism" is used in this study. In fact, that concept of the melting pot and Americanization can evolve into the very opposite of egalitarianism, a view in which all cultural traditions represented in American society are expected to capitulate to the mythical Anglo-Saxon "values of the past." This attitude was even extended to national immigration policy, which in the 1920s favored Northern Europeans since they were considered to be more assimilable into American society than Southern Europeans and Orientals, and hence superior. The concept of racial hierarchy helped to explain levels of civilization. At the top of the hierarchy was the American civilization. Whether it be a Theodore Roosevelt who believed progress comes when the civilized subdues the barbarian, or a Harry Truman who spoke of Eastern hordes vs. Christian morality, the rankings after World War II were similar to the racial rankings at the turn of the century. The terms were different—the rankings the same. Americans knew they were "on top" as Anglo-Americans over what is now called the Third World. "This genteel and patronizing label simply made more plausible the denial of any links to an unfashionable racist worldview."[5] But even with this respectable designation for dark-skinned, backward, and sometimes barbarous people, the real American opinion on race remained amazingly consistent throughout this century.

The bias affected nearly everyone in the American Protestant community—liberal and premillennialist, believer and skeptic. Their attitudes toward ethnicity at home were reflected in the same hierarchy of race on the mission field, "having the practical effect of little distinction between those who went out [consciously] to civilize, and those who felt they were scorning such an approach."[6] They believed the white Anglo-Saxon, Teutonic race was destined by God to Christianize and civilize the world. Yet the white American community stumbled over itself to tell the world how egalitarian it was. The most popular American World War I poster was one by Howard Chandler Christy which depicted a young girl appealing to onlookers to buy Liberty Bonds and pointing with pride to the list of names: "Americans All! DuBois, Smith, O'Brien, Knutson, Cejka, Haucke, Pappaneikopolous, Gonzales, Andrassi, Villotto, Levy, Turovich, Kowalski, Chiczanevicz." What this kind of list meant to Theodore Roosevelt was clear. "We must shun," said he, "as we would shun the plague all efforts to make us separate in groups of separate nationalities. We must all of us be Americans and nothing but Americans."[7] It was a nationalistic rallying cry in spite of the egalitarian label and was characterized by a strong Anglo-Saxon ethnocentrism meant to blot out any unique characteristics of ethnic groups in America, and subordinate them under an Anglo-Saxon core and a messianism that sought to make the world in its own image according to its perception of itself as a superior culture.

In another sense, however, one which represents a genuine egalitarian nationalism, American identity celebrated an ethnic diversity that was seen to actually make the nation stronger culturally, politically, economically, and morally. Rather than the metaphor of the "melting pot" that destroys distinctive cultural uniqueness in the societal soup, a more accurate, but still limited metaphor would be the mosaic, which displays distinctiveness and color, making the total production the more beautiful. Whether intentional or not, this mosaic metaphor was deficient in that it tended to legitimate what was not only multicultural brilliance in America but also economic, political, and social deprivation wherever it existed. However, those who connected American identity with this mosaic perception often portrayed the United States as the greatest and most successful experiment in multicultural diversity by a nation-state in history and a model for the world to emulate. This egalitarian nationalism extended beyond merely celebrating the diversity of cultures within the unity of the American nation to include an appreciation of all cultures in the world as equal under the eye of God. It maintained that each nation must be allowed/encouraged to maintain its own identity and development to its fullest potential.

Two centuries ago Johann Gottfried Herder (1744–1803), known as the father of nationalism, expressed these sentiments in the wake of Napoleon's conquests, which continued to entrench French cultural dominance in all of Europe and specifically in the German "hoi polloi" who were aping French customs and speaking the French language. Irritated by this, he argued that all nations and their cultures had an equal right to exist and should be proud of their respective cultures. Rejecting Enlightenment notions about the ideal man and ideal society, it held that no person was like any other person and no nation like any other nation. All were part of humanity, and all made their unique contributions.

Here was an egalitarian nationalism, that few Americans, given their sense of superiority, could swallow. However, some few did in varying degrees recognize without judgment the uniqueness and legitimacy of all cultures and religions. Celebrating this worldwide diversity of cultures and religions, exponents argued that much could be learned from the diverse peoples of the world as well as much given, enriching all.

While most Americans could not buy into this position of egalitarian nationalism—all cultures being equal under the eye of God—there was one sense in which they bought into Herder's nationalism totally, without knowing that Herder ever existed. It was his emphasis that each people must find its own way, one that fit its traditions, literature, language and customs. In exhorting the Germans to be German, he got downright carried away with "Awake, German nation! Do not let them [French] ravish your palladium! . . . Germans speak German! Spew out the Seine's ugly slime."[8]

Such inflammatory sentiments virtually guaranteed the involvement of politics in defending cultural nationalism, the very thing Herder wished to avoid. It was now only a step to conclude that while all cultures were equal, some were more equal than others. Says Gordon Craig:

> It was Herder's tragedy that the essential humanity of his philosophy was to be perverted into narrow political nationalism by patriotic tub-thumpers, and that his views on the individuality of the nation were to be transformed by philosophers like J. G. Fichte and George Fredrick Hegel into an idealization of the state as a kind of super-personality to which the individual citizen owed complete allegiance, which, indeed, alone validated his existence.[9]

As for Germany, then, the ideas of Herder, this father of nationalism, were contorted all out of recognition, and the Germany of a later century came to wallow in the horror of Nazi German tribalism.

But the ideas of Herder unsullied by tribal maniacs framed a particular face of American nationalism that represented a force for cultural identity. Again, without necessarily having Herder in mind, American artists, writers, philosophers, and theologians of the twentieth century sought to develop a genuine national culture. They continued a trend that began in the early nineteenth century when they became sensitive to their rootlessness as a new nation. Chafing under the sentence of American cultural inferiority from Europeans, these cultural elitists worked for the birth of a genuine American art, literature, and philosophy. Throughout this century some religious leaders also saw the need for a new and unique application of religion to the threat of industrialism. Within the diversity of Protestantism there was emphasis on creating a genuine American religion and an American church applicable to uniquely American problems, an aspect of American cultural nationalism.

The messianic spin-off of this development was particularly interesting in relation to the search for an American church. This search led to either the conviction that the American model be spread through missions or to a contrary conviction that each culture develop its indigenous style of Christian commitment. In either case, a form of messianic nationalism: make them like Westerners/Americans or encourage them to develop their own way.

In defining and explaining American nationalism as used in this study, then, we see a phenomenon that is messianic with variant supporting characteristics that are not necessarily compatible and in fact represent antithetical perceptions of American identity, but are seen, nonetheless, by diverse groups and individuals as the enlightened way to live and worthy of being spread around the world.

But not only was there ambiguity and conflict over about what to be messianic, but also there was sharp difference on how to be messianic. Should America win the world by killing off the wicked, sending them to their early reward, or win the world by killing with kindness? Should the messianic mission be accomplished through the example of a superior way or through leadership in a search for truth regardless of source, acknowledging the mutual exchange of diverse cultural exponents?

Robert Jewett, in his book with the engaging title *The Captain America Complex*, acknowledged the American ambiguity in how to be messianic. Jewett distinguished between "zealous nationalism" and "prophetic realism." These concurrent strands of mission style in American life, both biblically based, feed the American perception of mission to the world. Zealous nationalism is "derived from the Book of Revelation that after destruction of the Beast the world will automatically come under control of the saints."[10] It is the driving force to redeem the world by destroying the wicked and fits with the traditional perception of a nationalism exuding superiority and race and viewing the world in manichaean terms.

Prophetic realism is based on Jesus' rejection of a messianic kingdom of violence (Luke 4:5–8); that evil is not in the enemy, but in the heart of the chosen people themselves (Mark 3:1–6); that zealous rebellion will not guarantee intervention of divine forces: "Those who take the sword, die by the sword." It seeks to redeem the world for coexistence by impartial justice. Being very close to egalitarian nationalism, it differs only in its assumption of superiority, but a superiority to be demonstrated by example rather than by physical conquest.

These two strands, interwoven and coexisting in the American mind, are incompatible in their extremes. The strain alternately surfaces and submerges at varying points in American history. On the one hand, a Timothy Dwight saw the American Revolution ushering in the millennial hope. "Through earth's wide realms Thy glory shall extend and savage nations at Thy scepter bend." On the other hand, "We hold these truths to be self-evident, that all men are created equal." Manifest Destiny justified wars against Mexicans and Indians, while the McGuffy Reader warned of the dangers of zealotry. The "Battle Hymn of the Republic" promised the elimination of the wicked by the "terrible swift sword," while Lincoln urged "malice toward none, and charity toward all." Angels called to battle to rid the world of Kaiserism, overcame the plea for a "Peace Without Victory." On the one hand, Communism and Russia, the Bear of the North, would be destroyed by Armageddon, ushering in the ultimate reign of Christ and his saints. On the other hand, Communism must be overcome by meeting the demands of rising expectations among the underdeveloped peoples of the world. On a continuum reaching from the most militant form of zealous nationalism to the most pacific form of prophetic realism, the variant acts of American mission fit within this broad range of redemptive mission to the world. Though vastly different in styles of messianic mission, these two strands in American history—zealous nationalism and prophetic realism—represented agreement on a central theme. America was great, perhaps the greatest nation-state in history, and it had a mission to the world.

Within these parameters, one can recall the ambiguity of messianic method relative to American foreign policy. As perhaps the greatest nation-state in history, the United States had generally been assumed to have the wisdom and experience to define a good revolution and a bad revolution, as occurred at various times and places around the world, and had acted accordingly. To either aid or hinder a revolution, Americans sometimes acted from motives of morality and sometimes from self-interest. Logically, revolutions subsequent to the American Revolution were evaluated according to the extent they copied the American model. Americans were quick to welcome revolutions "which seemed to reflect the example of their own."[11]

However, by the end of the nineteenth century it became apparent that more was needed than merely serving as an example to the world. All men may be created equal, but certainly not all revolutions. With the concern over suspect revolutions came the call for possible intervention. Should freedom come to danger, "be never wanting there." The mission of America must assist the victims of oppression wherever they may be. As Woodrow Wilson would put it, the American responsibility is "teaching the Mexicans to elect good men."[12] An ounce of prevention would prevent a pound of bad revolution. If the United States had the responsibility for supporting good revolutions then it must certainly assist the victims of oppression wherever they may be, "perhaps even intervening on behalf of justice and liberty wherever it is endangered."[13]

After 1910 this right to intervene was invoked consistently in response to bursts of revolutionary activity abroad, especially in Latin America. Policymakers in Washington examined revolutions to keep them "within safe bounds."[14] Revolutions that merited United States support were to resemble the American Revolution. They were to cause a minimum of "disorder" led by "respectable citizens" having "moderate political goals" that were happily concluded with a balanced constitution "safeguarding human and property rights."[15]

Dangerous revolutions that did not merit American support and perhaps even qualified for American intervention were characterized as social revolutions out of control, driven by the radical doctrines of dictators and demagogues. Such revolutions were extremely violent: destruction of private property, redistribution of land and goods, and merciless violence against the old dominant classes. They were characterized by senseless violence, women violated, "elders slain and children impaled." In short, individual liberty was violated and the revolution ended with "survival rather than liberty the greater good."[16]

A *New York Times* article written by Gary Trudeau has suggested that nothing had changed regarding American judgmental skills. Not only had Americans categorized good and bad revolutions, but now they were obliged to identify villains and heroes from the old world order to the so-called new world order. Bad invasions of the old world order included the Syrian invasion of Lebanon (1976), the Vietnam invasion of Cambodia (1978), the U.S.S.R. invasion of Afghanistan (1979), and the Libyan invasion of Chad (1983). Good invasions of the old world order were China's invasion of Vietnam (1979), Iraq's invasion of Iran (1980), Israel's invasion of Lebanon (1982), and the U.S.

invasion of Grenada (1983). A bad invasion of the new world order was the Iraqi invasion of Kuwait (1990). Good invasions of the new world order included the U.S. invasion of Panama (1989), the U.S.S.R. invasion of itself (1991), the U.S. and allies invasion and Kuwait and Iraq (1991).

American judgments included old world order and new world order leaders. Bad Hitlers of the old world order were Muammer el-Qaddafi, Mikhail Gorbachev, Hafez al-Assad, Ayatollah Ruhollah Khomeini, and Daniel Ortega. Good Hitlers of the old world order included Ferdinand Marcos, Manuel Noriega, Saddham Hussein, and Augusto Pinochet. Miraculously good Hitlers of the new world order included Mikhail Gorbachev, Hafez al-Assad, and Deng Xiaoping. As for bad U.N. Security Council Resolutions of the old and new orders, none existed, since the United States supported all good resolutions and vetoed all bad resolutions such as resolutions on United States invasions of Grenada and Panama.[17]

While Americans had the ultimate wisdom to judge the good, the bad, and the ugly revolutions, from the very beginnings of American national life they did not always agree on what to do about them. John Adams and Thomas Jefferson disagreed, and both had followers from their day into the twentieth century. For Adams, revolutions were "under the direction of all too fallible man—and foreigners at that! The revolutionary impulse was all too likely to degenerate, and unless quickly restrained, to rend the fragile social fabric and destroy liberty."[18] Those adhering to the heritage of Adams were inclined to intervene to stop revolutions.

For Jefferson and his followers into the twentieth century, there was "deep faith in the ultimate triumph of liberty." They were "prepared to tolerate greater excesses because of their conviction that emancipation for all mankind was not only possible, but imminent."[19] Those adhering to the heritage of Jefferson were inclined to intervene in order to guide revolutions.

American policy toward revolutions in the twentieth century represented a combination of both tendencies. Where bad revolutions appeared to get out of hand, policymakers used a variety of strategies to control the given situation, such as manipulation of arms sales, judicious financial aid, diplomatic recognition, intrigue with pro-U.S. factions, coordination with major powers, and if need be, troops.[20] But, regardless of the policy, central at all times was the assumption that American wisdom could determine the legitimacy of a revolution.

Much the same attitude could be seen in Protestant leadership of the twentieth century. Even as the American Protestant mission enterprise served as judge and jury of foreign cultures, so again the theology mattered not. Because Americans were under special obligation to save and renovate the world, they were obliged to evaluate world revolutions with a view to helping those on the straight and narrow and to condemning those not so blessed. Indeed, "post millennial optimism . . . tended to produce more militant images of world conquest than did premillennialism."[21]

These, then, are the criteria by which the faces of American Protestant nationalism are to be recognized with all their warts and beauty marks. The primary focus is to demonstrate that the cacophonous mix of nationalistic expression evident in the Protestant experience throughout the twentieth century enables one to better understand the American struggle to focus on national meaning.

In choosing the faces for this study, I sought to engage representatives in a broad spectrum from separatist fundamentalism to liberalism. John R. Rice represents separatists fundamentalism, which came into its own in the 1940s and 1950s as a result of the more liberal elements of fundamentalism forming the National Association of Evangelicals (NAE). This organization sought to cooperate minimally with theologically conservative Christians not considered absolutely orthodox by the "ultras" of the John R. Rice stripe of fundamentalism. "Be not unequally yoked" in fellowship with those not totally fundamentalist in belief and action was the battle cry of Rice and others like him such as Carl McIntire, founder of the American Council of Christian Churches (ACCC), and Bob Jones, Sr. and Jr. of Bob Jones University. The latter voice expressed separatism in action with the declaration that Jerry Falwell is "the most dangerous man in America" because of his willingness to work with Catholics, Mormons, Jews, and evangelicals through the Moral Majority.[22] Billy Graham also fell from grace because of his willingness to work with the more liberal National Council of Churches (NCC) in revival meetings.

The separatist fundamentalism, sometimes referred to as ultra-fundamentalism, had very clear ideas concerning the proper role of the United States in the Cold War world and an equally clear message concerning their perception of a godly American ideal. Those views of the American role at home and abroad were driven by a dispensationalism that believed the end of time and the Second Coming of Jesus were near. This perception was based upon an interpretation of portions of the books of Daniel, Revelation, and the sayings of Jesus regarding last things. "There will be wars and rumors of wars" seemed to fit the situation around the Cold War world. Reference was also made of the return of the Jews to their homeland as a sign that the end was near, and to the soon-to-be culminating battle of Armageddon in the Middle East, which would involve conflict with the Bear of the North, meaning Russia. Therefore, the United States, it was believed, should not back away from a nuclear fight with the Soviet Union since an engagement of that sort would no doubt be God's way of using America to end the present age (dispensation) and to usher in the millennium of Christ's reign on earth. America would be the agent used by God to cleanse the earth of evil empires. Hence, any move for peace or détente by the United States with the "Evil Empire" would be run directly counter to God's intended design.

Clyde Edminster, survivalist, numerologist, and dispensationalist par excellence, is included in this study since he saw the United States as having cosmic significance. Dividing the ages of the world into dispensations, Edminster paralleled the captivity of the children of Israel in Egypt, delivered after 210 years, with a history of the people of the United States, who had suffered for 210 years in preparation for Armageddon and its deliverance. This "deliverance" was to occur in 1986. In near ecstasy, Edminster stated: "So the more I studied into this possibility, the more I was convinced that Israel's sojourn in Egypt was the pre-written history of the United States of America."[23] In short, America was born as a nation under God, being His New Israel destined to rule the world.

Jerry Falwell, also a dispensationalist of a different sort than Edminster, but similar to Rice, is included because he represents a fundamentalism rigid in doctrine but pragmatic in enlisting any of the socially conservative forces in America regardless of their theology in a drive to lead America back to perceived traditional American Christian values. The Moral Majority of the 1980s was his most public and extensive manifestation of this effort. Falwell is also significant to this study because of his seeming ambivalent perception of the nature of American chosenness in God's scheme. One the one hand America was in danger of losing its status as God's instrument in human affairs because of its moral decay. On the other hand, Falwell believed that God would never allow the Soviet Union to destroy America, since the republic, in spite of its faults, was still a Christian nation.

J. Gresham Machen, a leading fundamentalist intellectual of the early twentieth century, would likely be considered an inappropriate prospect for a study of American Protestant nationalism in this century by those familiar with his life work. When his name comes up among American religious academics and those lay people familiar with his life and ministry, he is usually connected to the Modernist Fundamentalist Controversy in the 1920s and 1930s. Or, he is admired for his New Testament Greek scholarship, having created a standard Greek text used by divinity schools regardless of denominational affiliation or theological tradition.

However, if nationalism includes the intense expression of a nation's identity role and mission, then J. Gresham Machen, who addressed this issue head-on, was a major player in that debate, and his role and influence in that regard are fair game. Furthermore, successive fundamentalists, notably John R. Rice, Jerry Falwell, and others, have looked to Machen as their fundamentalist guru, no doubt ratcheting up the debate to a shrillness that probably would not have been approved by this gentleman scholar. His influence adds a significant face to this study of variant and antithetical perceptions of a proper American identity.

Carl Henry and the journal he founded, *Christianity Today*, were chosen to demonstrate an evangelical perception of a proper, divinely ordained, American identity. Considerable emphasis was also given concerning the extent that America had drifted from its alleged godly motivated beginnings.

Conservative in theology, the journal never displayed the level of shrillness typical of fundamentalist leadership. If anything, it moderated gradually over the years, recognizing the complexity of the geopolitical arena and the increasingly pluralistic complexity of American life. Its thoughtful moderation over the years between the height of the Cold War fifties when it was founded and the latter years of the Vietnam struggle earned for *Christianity Today* the scorn of its fundamentalist critics, especially as it even found itself agreeing with the more liberal *Christian Century* on a number of domestic and foreign policy issues. The scorn it received from fundamentalists compared to that heaped upon Billy Graham, who can be linked to *Christianity Today* not only to the founding of the journal but also in its theology and thoughtful caution of refraining from the temptation to crown every political action or politician with divine approval or sanction. Hence, the journal is portrayed as displaying a nationalism of moderation, declaring on the one hand that America has a divine calling to minister to the lost, both at home and abroad, but on the other hand willing to concede to diversity in fulfilling the mission.

A face of American Protestant nationalism that has proven to be one of the most fascinating and colorful is that of Russell Conwell during the first quarter of the twentieth century. Normally remembered as the Carnegiesque Gospel of Wealth advocate who crisscrossed the country to deliver his famous motivational lecture, *Acres of Diamonds*, over 6,000 times, Conwell offered even more to the subject at hand through sermons and books. Theologically mainstream Protestant, not wishing to get embroiled in Virgin Birth or evolution controversies of his day, Conwell had clear ideas concerning America's emergence as a major world power. He could mix unabashed nationalistic fervor proclaiming American superiority in any and all categories with withering prophetic excoriation of national policies he believed un-Christian. The chapter "Foreign Policy through Benediction" is named, not only because of his famous sermons on national policy, but also because he often confirmed the issues expounded upon in sermon with an extensive benediction that appeared to outline instructions to the Almighty and to faithful listeners. He represents enthusiasm for American greatness when the country was flexing its adolescent muscles in the world, discovering that it had weight to push around.

One cannot treat the subject adequately without considering the work of Reinhold Niebuhr. While he has been considered neo-orthodox in theology, the label does not do him justice. On the one hand he emphasized the inherent reality of human sin and the perverseness of all human collectives. On the other hand, he was intensely devoted to implementing social justice through collective power. The two emphases were not contradictory since for him some human collectives were simply more evil than others, and the responsibility of the less evil collective was to exercise its power for justice over the more evil one. This meant that no perfect justice could ever be fulfilled in this life in an absolute sense. History could be fulfilled only outside of time.

When applied to the geopolitics of the twentieth century and especially to the Cold War era, the United States was seen as the less evil collective which had the God-ordained responsibility of checking the more evil collective, the Soviet Union. Great Britain and the United States also had a godly mandate in thwarting the evil Nazi threat. Along with this divine mandate to use power was the warning that arrogance and pride could lead to misuse of power, which Niebuhr saw the United States guilty of in regards to Vietnam.

Niebuhr applied the same model to domestic politics. Those in power who were oppressive could not be expected to relinquish their hold on the less franchised of society without some domestic collective force, be it labor unions or the church applying pressure for change. This judicious use of power to bring about a better society/world is why Niebuhr's system has been called Christian Realism, and why I have entitled this chapter "Nationalism and Realism."

Theological liberals no less than conservatives and fundamentalists had visions of an ideal American identity, which they strived to bring to fruition. One such theological liberal during the early twentieth century was Walter Rauschenbusch. He is best known as the Baptist minister to the poor immigrants in Hell's Kitchen, New York City, turned divinity school professor-scholar and eloquent exponent of the Social Gospel movement. Emphasizing that sin was social as well as individual, he envisioned a reformed America in which social, political, and economic institutions would provide a healthy, positive environment allowing the disenfranchised the opportunity for the better material life. This, he believed would more likely lead to spiritual salvation of the individual as well.

Optimistically, he saw that some American institutions were already well on the way to reform, such as political, religious, and educational institutions. Business was viewed as needing considerable improvement. While he urged continued improvement of America's institutions through reform, he still viewed the American experience as vastly superior to that in any other part of the world. Furthermore, in expressing an optimism fairly typical of the Progressive era of which he was a part, he believed that the social evolutionary process was at work in establishing the democratic Kingdom of God on earth.

What is puzzling in the total picture, however, were the mixed messages from this Rochester professor. On the one hand, he compassionately advocated social reform for the down-and-outers of society, and on the other hand he harshly judged the Native American in his praise of the "yellow-haired" Custer. Rauschenbusch admirers downplay this unsavory aspect as well as his enthusiastic support for the Spanish-American War, while praising him for his pacifism in World War I. Attempts to explain these discrepancies will be made in the chapter on "Bifurcated Nationalism."

Representing the antithesis of fundamentalism in this study is the liberal idealist, William Earnest Hocking, Congregational layman and Harvard philosophy professor whose life spanned some 92 years with his death in 1962. Hocking represented the best example of what I'm calling egalitarian nationalism described earlier in this Introduction. His consistent theme was to celebrate diversity in unity—that there was much to learn from other cultures and religions in the world— that one's own faith could be understood and enhanced by understanding other belief systems in the world.

Hocking's position, difficult for most Americans to swallow given their sense of superiority, was all the more remarkable given his application of his teachings to the Cold War relations of the United States and the Soviet Union. Writing in the 1950s and celebrating that the United States and the Soviet Union were learning from each other and drifting closer together, the Soviets becoming more capitalistic and individualistic, and the United States more collective, was not a message that most people wanted to hear.

Two decades earlier he had applied the same principle concerning the relationship of Christianity and the other religions of the world in calling for Christian missionaries to seek truth with peoples of other faiths rather than to tell them the truth, as though having the last word on the subject. One need not read about the response of mission boards to this advice to imagine their chagrin.

The significance of Hocking in this study stems from the nationalism he represented that encouraged and celebrated the richness of cultural diversity in the world without any one people imposing on any other people. All cultures, while not equal under the eye of God, had contributions that could add richness to the life of the individual and of the nation, if allowed to do so.

These are the choices and reasons for them. Obviously the list could be nearly endless. Why not a Billy Graham? *Christianity Today* can be seen as generally representing his pilgrimage. Pat Robertson? The study was limited to exclude charismatics. Charles Clayton Morrison and *Christian Century*? It could have been included, but neo-orthodoxy to liberalism was represented without it. Billy Sunday? John R. Rice fits the bill nicely. In point of fact the book contains quite enough cacophony to drive home the theme that American Protestant leadership conveyed confusion, contradiction, and bifurcation in its struggle to define America. Whether leadership led or reflected the populace is a chicken-or-egg question and really does not matter. It is probably some of both. Either case is not pretty, and while one may want to rationalize that this is the free market of ideas in action and therefore good, the fact is that American society is in some trouble with its struggle over values and this is not some recent phenomenon brought on by the "crazies" of the 1960s.

To drive this home further, the sequence of chapters is arranged both chronologically and thematically to cover the century to Vietnam while concurrently showing the varying and conflicting faces within the period. Thus, Rauschenbusch, Conwell, and Machen, in that order, can be taken as a cluster in which all three during the same period demonstrate dramatic differences in their perceptions of American identity during the first third of the century.

The Hocking chapter follows the first three because he straddles the early part of the century and the latter decades into Vietnam during his 92 years on this earth, and was productive to the end. Because of this he can be seen, not only in contrast to Machen of the 1930s (the two infuriated each other), but also to Niebuhr (who also wrote in the thirties and in the succeeding decades into the sixties) and everyone else in the 1950s and 1960s.

The remaining cluster of figures, including Rice, Niebuhr, Carl Henry and *Christianity Today*, Edminster, and Falwell, round out the figures in the remaining thirty years or so into the Vietnam years and continue to demonstrate enormous contrasts among generally contemporaneous Protestant leaders concerning the role and mission of the United States during the Cold War years.

Finally, a word needs to be said about bias in writing history, especially in a work such as this. Roland Bainton's cautionary words in the introduction to his Reformation history are appropriate for a work such as this. In writing about the Reformation (and in this case twentieth-century American Protestant nationalism) "one is not poking ashes with embers." Indeed, this note is perhaps even more appropriate since the issues considered in this work represent more accurately a smoldering, sometimes flaming, controversy that can easily be fed the fuel of discussion that results in a roaring fire of controversy.

Bainton goes on to indicate the direction from which he comes to the subject, which is what every historian should declare as he/she presents to an audience. As I suggest to my students, the only way to eliminate bias is suicide. By virtue of being a human being, with background in race, gender, education, religious upbringing, and a host of other personal experiences uniquely received and uniquely responded to, we are all biased. The difference among the biased is between those who know what their bias is and allow for the biases of others and those who do not know they are biased, and who see the world in manichaean terms.

But this is not to say that fairmindedness is impossible. Objectivity simply means for all to see. That is, in the writing of history there is the stuff out there that anyone can examine, the documents, records, shared interviews, statistics of X number of automobile deaths due to alcohol and whatnot. But one's interpretation of the objective data is done by inference, by an individual subjectively declaring the meaning and significance of the data, and no two historians will ever see all the possible relationships between the collected objective (for all to see) data. There will not even be agreement on which data is significant and that which is not. Two or several historians will often make a larger number of the same inferential judgments on a given set of data. But never will there be total agreement on every possible angle of meaning and significance of the data. But herein lies the key. Objectivity can and does occur to the extent to which one is able to alter one's inferences when exposed to new information, new data, and even new interpretations, new ways of viewing an issue—new to the one who searches for insights and expanded understanding. This means that learning and understanding are very dynamic. The next day's efforts may necessitate altering one's inferences on the nature and meaning of this or that event. Indeed a little "larning" can be a dangerous thing.

And so, the pages that follow represent a piece that poses a particular angle of vision of one raised in a Protestant minister's home that in the 1980s and 1990s would be called evangelical, but in the 1930s and 1940s was tagged liberal, and which was embroiled in the tail end of the modernist-fundamentalist controversy. It is written by one who subsequently became a third-generation minister trained in a "liberal" divinity school by the definition of McCarthy era values and by one whose ministerial cloth has been subsequently devoured by the moths of other interests. Yet the concern that something is terribly wrong with American society is shared with fundamentalist and liberal alike, and the search for answers is an odyssey with an understanding that inferences will need continuing adjustments as new objective realities confront one's consciousness.

Do I have my candidates for warts and beauty marks? One would be brain dead to not have one's favorites and villains. But even at that I found myself actually liking all of the candidates under study. Aside from that, however, the central focus of this piece is an appreciation of the deep fissures in American society, long standing, potentially dangerous, and in need of attention. The concluding chapter attempts to summarize and suggest potential scenarios of resolution.

CHAPTER 2

Bifurcated Nationalism

Providence has endowed us with an unmatched territorial base for a great national life. The labor of four centuries has been spent chiefly in subduing this continent to the needs of man. Every brawny arm that has plied the ax, or guided the plow, or fitted the rafters of a home, or held the throttle of an engine, has helped in that great task of civilization. Men are needed for labor and women to bear and rear the men of the future.

—Walter Rauschenbusch

On the occasion of his 1902 commencement address before graduates, faculty, and friends of Rochester Theological Seminary, Walter Rauschenbusch encapsulated the mission of America. As a former pastor of a small German Baptist church in Hell's Kitchen, New York City, turned divinity school professor, he explained to the faculty and graduates of the seminary the reasons for dramatic American successes around the world resulting from victory over Spain. The focus of the Rochester professor's address was America's becoming a Christian nation along with its success as an emerging world power.

Rauschenbusch believed America succeeded not only because of her access to the unmatched resources of this vast continent but also because this land was largely settled by Teutonic blood destined to dominate and lead. By Teutonic, Rauschenbusch meant England, Germany, and America—the three places where Teutonic blood was most evident: "By the tread of the foot on the soil, by the grip of the strong right arm, and the flash of the blue-eye, we know it to be blood kin to us, the eldest brother of the Teutonic family."[1] In the future, other races would lead, he believed, but for the present it was the Teuton's day with "America as the youngest but sovereign of the richest and vastest continuous empire . . . It is Providential that Teutons hold the larger part of the world's wealth and power in the hollow of their hands, and the larger share of the world's intellectual

19

and spiritual possessions in the hollow of their heads. They are a princely stock, these fair skinned men, an imperial race, as they stand at the forge of time and hammer out history."[2] Emphasizing Teutonic destiny and superiority, Rauschenbusch exposed one face of his distinctive American nationalism.

Thus, Rauschenbusch thought Americans should be thankful to Arminius who crushed Varus and his Roman legions in A.D. 9 in the Teutoburg Forest: otherwise, the Teutons like the Goths, Vandals, and Franks, would have become Latinized, and "the Angles and Saxons would have been civilized vassals of Rome before they crossed the sea to Britain, if they had ever crossed it; and I should not be speaking to you here in a Teutonic tongue and about the Teutonic race." When the Teutons landed in Britain, it became the "nursery for seeding the earth with Teutons "[3]

Contrasted with this blood of destiny and dominance was the perceived danger of alien blood emigrating, multiplying, and/or intermixing in America—French blood in the North and South; Spanish in the Southwest; Slav in the cities and mines; and the Negro everywhere. "Can the racial characteristics of the Teutons hold their predominance against this blending of stock? With the appalling sterility of Yankee families, could the native population do it alone?" he asked. No, but Teuton blood was saving the day. With alien presence on the rise, those who had despised Germans should be sorry and wish for renewed increase in German immigration. "We're getting Bohemians and Poles and Russian Jews and Syrians," he lamented in 1900.[4] But the Teutonic race was the alleged leader of progress. They were strong in education and opposed to slavery. They were fighters of Indians. "Long years after [the Civil War] a detachment of United States regulars fell fighting against the Sioux on the Little [Big] Horn led by a gallant yellow haired soldier. Do you know," said Rauschenbusch, "that General Custer was a grandson of a Hessian officer Kuster, who had settled in Pennsylvania?"[5]

The juxtaposition of freedom fighter and Indian fighter in Rauschenbusch's address gives one an academic whiplash when matched with his reputation as compassionate yet intellectual exponent of the Social Gospel. One does not associate racism and praise for Custer with the man who labored in Hell's Kitchen. Yet what of his own audience, which must have inwardly nodded approval, given the climate of opinion? While Rauschenbusch was revered for the new ground he plowed in social concern and a new theology of the Kingdom of God, such an anachronism necessarily reminds one of the extent to which even a saint can be caught up in the less savory values of the time, and thus gives a lesson on the limits of reforming even for a great reformer.

But while Walter Rauschenbusch was convinced that America's greatness largely depended upon German blood in America, he also recognized German weaknesses that were overcome because of the American environment. Germans, because of their continental origins, lacked a wholesome moral and religious life, participated in drinking customs, and were neglectful of the Sabbath. Religion in Germany, he said, leaves much to be desired: too much ceremony, too little ethics, too much custom, and too little personal and intelligent appropriation. The church was used by the government to suppress the longing of the people for liberty and justice. The minister was a policeman in black uniform "ready to club riotous ideas." People were indifferent, suspicious, and openly hostile. All of this was the result of "the age-long sins of rulers and priests."[6]

Germans coming to America, however, were seen to thrive on American freedom. He observed that whereas arriving Germans were short and stunted, the next generation's sons grew "tall and stalwart" and the daughters "fair and shapely." Teutonic stock needed only a chance, and America had given that. Given America's environmental generosity, Germans produced. Apologetically, this German-American professor torn between two masters said: "Will you blame me if I love both countries and defend each in turn?" Do not ask a German to "blot out his nationality and its characteristics as soon as he steps on your shores, as if it were an evil or contemptible thing, and as if American peculiarities were the only noble and desirable thing in the sight of God and Man. . . . When you say to him, 'Give up what you are' you commit an indignity. When you say 'share with us what you are' you treat him as an equal."[7]

But what Rauschenbusch said of Germans coming to America he would not say to those of "alien blood." Appearing at one moment on the verge of affirming a Herder-like nationalism that believed in the individuality and equality of "all cultures under the eye of God,"[8] he remained firmly ensconced in Teutonic superiority. While rejecting the Social Darwinist yen for brutal individualism with its concomitant trampling of the poor, he did concede that in the evolutionary course of events other races might achieve dominance. He feared that even in his own lifetime changes might occur. But for now, the Teutonic race (English, American, German), in 1902, was the leader.

This affirmation of Teutonic leadership helps to account for his support of the Spanish-American War, and later in his career his distress over American involvement in World War I. American victory over Spain represented victory over an alien blood, whereas World War I could only shatter Teutonic leadership of civilization. What a dichotomous position he placed himself in, yet his blood of destiny doctrine provided the rationalization for both.

In his Thanksgiving Day message to Baptists reprinted in a Rochester newspaper commemorating the American victory over Spain, Rauschenbusch called for the United States to be magnanimous since "God loves and pities Spain, and desires her salvation."[9] He then cited seven lessons to be gained from the war experience, most of which reveal typical racism and nationalism of the day. The war had brought to Americans the feeling of belonging to a "larger whole of the nation as an immense collective life." It had made Americans aware of their reservoir of national strength and vitality under the leadership of "President McKinley, Admiral Dewey, and the quiet courage of the common soldier and sailor."[10] It had called to mind the need for manly self-criticism, "that Teutonic virtue," in contrast to Spain's peculiar inability to see facts.

This lesson in self-effacement is fascinating when one considers that Rauschenbusch was unable to view uncomfortable facts during the war. He passed lightly over such scandals as the "embalmed beef incident," and laid blame for the dangers and scandals during the war on the lack of personal piety of the foot soldier rather than on the corporate and societal evils of the day.[11] The remaining lessons from the war enumerated by Rauschenbusch continued the theme of American greatness. As a result of the war the nations of the world admired and respected the United States for its disinterest in territorial expansion and its generous foreign aid to the vanquished. A new, close relationship with Britain resulted from the war because the British understood American motives, harbored similar values, and kept the sea lanes open for America. How fortunate it would have been, thought Rauschenbusch, if all Teutons had joined in the war: England, Scandinavia, Denmark, Holland, and the United States. What a power for Western civilization that would be.

The war also revealed national, moral, and spiritual strength. In a Bancroftian mode, he believed that two kinds of civilization had been in conflict: the civilization of liberty —which valued freedom of thought, a personal relationship with God, the supremacy of personal conscience, and a sense of responsibility and duty—and the civilization demanding submission to authority and dogma, with a mediation of the church that precluded individual initiative in matters of spiritual growth. In America, Protestant thought, the linchpin of liberty, dominated public life. Even American Catholics were Protestant compared to Spanish Catholics. This, said Rauschenbusch, has made America great—the purity of the gospel it has inherited. And maintaining this would alone "save us from the decline which has overtaken one after the other of the great nations of the past when wealth accumulated and men decayed."[12]

Finally, the war caused a closer contact with God. "We have been on God's side and the Lord of Hosts has been on our side," he said. "American people have responded to the higher command. God calls and we obey. We did not want this new empire. God put it there, and we must accept and obey." God spoke and acted through the events of the war: "As a nation we must learn to walk by faith and not by sight."[13]

Clearly, this Thanksgiving sermon by Walter Rauschenbusch was patriotic, evangelical, racist, and nationalistic. While on balance the Rochester professor never advocated war—"nine-tenths of all wars are immoral"[14]—God could sometimes use war to fulfill His purpose. Even on occasion war was better obedience to God than inaction. When that was so, "the blood of the battlefield is like the blood that stains the surgeon's table. War may be an operation that saves a nation from lingering disease and death."[15] From the Spanish-American War came the destruction of a corrupt empire and the liberation of an oppressed people. As late as 1904 Rauschenbusch was delivering these strongly patriotic speeches, mixing praise for America with warnings and exhortations on the meaning of the nation and God's will.[16]

In sharp contrast to his support of the Spanish-American War and his perception of God's will in it, Rauschenbusch opposed American sale of arms to Britain and, ultimately, intervention in World War I. In a plea for fairness to Germany,[17] he warned about the danger of partiality to England. The disadvantage to Germany was enormous. The German cable was cut; the language of German was different; English poems spoke to us, while German poems did not. The British-controlled press presented accounts of alleged German atrocities; Germany was land-locked, facing a two-front war, and she was a Fredrick-come-lately in the colonial game, needing to make up for a late start. Most of all, the United States was the workshop of death, supplying weapons to England and engaged in trade for profit not for patriotism. It was so one-sided, Rauschenbusch lamented. Instead of favoring England, how much fairer to terminate the sale of arms.

Revealing a nationalistic fervor for American mission, albeit different than expressed concerning the Spanish-American War, he declared that "many of us believe that our nation has a peculiar mission to restore peace."[18] "The United States is the only great Christian power that is detached and really neutral. We may be able to shorten the war by weeks or months, and save millions of lives."[19]

These hopes for American influence for a "peace without victory" did not materialize for Walter Rauschenbusch, or for anyone. While ultimately recognizing the dangers of Kaiserism, Rauschenbusch took the family quarrel extremely hard. It was painful to end his life with physical infirmities, friends who questioned his patriotism, and a broader public more concerned with the war effort and Hun-bashing than with his fervent concern for the Social Gospel.

What is fascinating is not only the stark contrast between his attitude toward a war against Germany as opposed to one against Spain, but the possible reason for the contrast. His biographers generally pass over lightly his enthusiasm for the Spanish-American War and emphasize the pacifist, anti-interventionist stance characteristic of his later ministry. The latest biography of Rauschenbusch by Paul Minus says that the Spanish-American War period is Walter Rauschenbusch at his most jingoistic and drops it at that, apparently because it is an aberration in comparison to the major thrust of his life of leadership in the Social Gospel movement.[20]

Evidence suggests, however, that there is a key common to the Rochester professor's radically different responses toward the two wars. The suggestion is that Rauschenbusch reflects dominant racist, nationalist views of his day which bled through more of his career than is either admitted or detected. His definition of just and unjust wars appears to be highly, though not exclusively, influenced by these assumptions. It has even been suggested that his views on education for social reform were highly influenced by racist, elitist, and sexist assumptions that conflicted with his public assertions favoring democracy on every level.[21] On the one hand, he tried to educate the working class for social change with a "people's paper," *For The Right*. However, this publication did not reach the workers. Instead of using direct address "you" and "we," articles and editorials spoke of "them," "they," and "their."[22] He was not realistic in devising an educational plan for the working class (certainly not as effective as the educational system devised by Russell Conwell through his night schools for the proletariat), yet working-class education was essential in reforming society. How could it have been otherwise when, to Rauschenbusch, the biggest threat to the German idea of education was the "new immigration of inferior peoples to America"?[23] It would appear that his Social Gospel was modified by a commitment to racial theories of Social Darwinism and elitism. Those on top were fittest as a result of God's law of evolution.[24]

In light of this, since he rejected a pro war stance when it came to American involvement in the Great War, it seems fair to ask that if the Spanish-American War were a crusade to end Spanish tyranny, why would a war to end Kaiserism not be equally noble? Approaching the issue with this question, the answer becomes clearer in light of his statements on the glory and destiny of the Teutonic race. Aside from other motives that may have induced him to speak against intervention in World War I, he understandably would be torn asunder when this racial component is understood. One empathizes with and agonizes for this man in his excruciating struggle. Does he oppose American aid to England, and ultimate entry into the War because of an intense pacifism, or because of racism, or for both reasons? Does this frustration over American one-sidedness mean it would be all right if the aid were evened out or swung in Germany's favor? He did concede that if American territory were threatened, intervention might be justified. But then American territory was not threatened by a Spanish presence in the New World, the Spanish empire wobbling like a top ready to tumble under its own de-energized weight. Furthermore, the American people neither spoke Spanish nor cared for Spanish poetry. If a choice were made over which war was justified on the basis of territorial threat, intervention by the United States in the Great War was far the nobler choice given the perception of the territorial threat to the United States revealed in the Zimmerman Note. But Rauschenbusch was worried that Germany would be crushed—an international assassination. He was concerned for the United States, and Western civilization too, since he did not want any member of the family of nations crippled, the context for this concern being a Teutonic civil war sweeping away the flower of the white race.[25] One wonders what his position on aid and intervention would have been had players shifted from being German to being Japanese in the war.

These questions cannot be answered but deserve consideration. Walter Rauschenbusch faced a problem that affected thousands of German-Americans, many of whom responded in the other extreme—outdoing themselves to prove their Americanism. Not so for Rauschenbusch, which in itself may be a credit to his integrity. He really believed that the Teutonic race was destined by the Almighty to lead in civilizing and Christianizing the world, a mission now in jeopardy. In a back-handed way, just possibly this racist nationalist conviction was one force in his move toward pacifism that could intensify as early as the turn of the century when Germany attempted colonial expansion, provoking trouble with France and Britain.

Rauschenbusch revealed another face of nationalism with his democratization of God:

When he [Jesus] took God by the hand and called him "our Father" he democratized the conception of God. He disconnected the idea

from the coercive and predatory state, and transferred it to the realm
of family life, the chief social embodiment of solidarity and love. He
not only saved humanity; he saved God. . . . The value of Christ's
idea of the Fatherhood of God is realized only by contrast to the
despotic idea which it opposed and was meant to displace. We have
classified theology as Greek and Latin, as Catholic and Protestant. It
is time to classify it as despotic and democratic.[26]

For Rauschenbusch, democracy was the finest ideal of American
life, and "Jesus is on the side of America."[27] America's lack of social
classes contrasted with Europe's multiclassed society. He recounted
the story of a German minister in Hamburg who tried to reach people
by social church gatherings. Class differences in the church made it
impossible. The clergyman had to serve three kinds of teas. The first
tea was served in thick cups, the second tea in thin cups, and the third
from a silver tea urn. "Imagine Jesus being invited!" lamented the
minister.[28] In Rauschenbusch's theology, this nonsense was foreign to
America and to his democratic concept of the Kingdom of God.

Consistent, also, with his democratic emphasis was the need for
social redemption and individual salvation. Baptism was individualistic, but it originated in a mass movement of social reform by John
the Baptist.[29] Original sin was given a new significance. The traditional
view did not square with the American view of fairness. How silly in
the American sense to think that the world's ills could be attributed to
the folly of the two originals of humankind. For Rauschenbusch it
made sense to emphasize the social heredity of sin which could be
remedied through social reform. His was a theology of action, and
historically, Americans take action; contemplation was not their style.
Linking a theology of common sense with authority of Scripture,
Rauschenbusch observed that the doctrine of the Fall was ignored by
Jesus and given little attention in the Old Testament.

Hoping to spur American churches into social action, Rauschenbusch believed that as churches adopted principles of religious liberty
and democratic government, they would become more attuned to the
spiritual and social welfare of people,[30] for already democracy had
brought the working class "a great spiritual awakening.[31] Rauschenbusch came to identify Christianity with a form of government, a
cultural form, and to equate democratizing historical forces with the
Kingdom of God.[32]

Rauschenbusch's search for a national religion revealed another
face of his nationalism—an American church capable of effective and
relevant ministry to American problems. With rapid change through

massive industrial development and the inundation of America with immigrants of alien blood and religion, a united American church capable of dealing effectively with these new challenges was essential. If the church were to have positive impact on the problems of poverty, dislocation, and exploitation associated with industrialism and be effective in converting immigrants to Protestantism, it must overcome inefficient and quarrelsome divisions.

While, in his view, denominations had value in the past by producing competitive zeal and loyalty, the circumstances responsible for their creation no longer existed. Yet denominations, most of which had European origins, survived. The questions dogging Rauschenbusch were to "what extent [did] these denominational issues really represent vital and permanent interests of America in modern religious life" and "What denominations [were] genuine historical products of our own people and times?" What is American?[33] These questions frustrated Rauschenbusch because he identified two antithetical categories of denominations and sects in America, making identification of "American" difficult: those from the historic stream of Protestantism, and those outside of the stream yet indigenous to America. The Protestant category, other than the mainline denominations, consisted of many small bodies of holiness persuasion, faith movements, Pentecostal bands—genuine products of American emotional religion, with practical impulses and conceptions of Christian perfection. Included in this category were Negro denominations, which came out of white churches but had their own congregations. Directly out of the American situation, though founded by Scotch-Irish leadership, had come the Disciples of Christ. Their movement was launched against real American evils. Finally, there were the Unitarian and Universalist denominations.

Groups identified by Rauschenbusch from outside Protestantism, but yet American, included Mormonism—syncretistic, "blending the dominant religious ideas, superstitions, the emotionalism, the practical genius, the social ideals and the vices of the American frontier of a hundred years ago."[34] Mormonism "soaked up and amalgamated all that was undesirable and half true in America, and made a very effective religion of it. We cannot blame Mormonism on Europe," he said. "It was 'Made in America.'"[35]

Christian Science, like Mormonism, had Christian elements, said Rauschenbusch. It follows Christ's teachings and the Bible and has other religious authorities. It holds a profound concern for physical well-being while denying the physical. It has a strong feminist complexion, a genius for publicity, a keen appreciation for money, and an ability to create a powerful religious trust that muzzles everybody else. Above all, it is modern and American.

These indigenous American religions created a conundrum for Rauschenbusch. On the one hand, he wanted an American church. On the other hand, the greatest hope for an American church lay with mainline Protestant denominations, which have European roots. Religions that were genuinely American were not only inassimilable in mainline American religion, they were inassimilable among themselves. Roman Catholicism, Mormonism, or Christian Science? "I am hopeless about them," he conceded.[36] In what may have been an inadvertently prophetic statement, he said that our great-grandchildren may see hope of inclusion for these groups, "but for the present we might as well discuss a regular weekly airship line to reach the moon."[37] His resolution? To write off the genuine American religions and hope for union of all mainline Protestant denominations.[38]

Contrary to the thinking of a number of historians it would appear that Rauschenbusch preferred organic unity.[39] True, he knew it would be difficult under the best of circumstances to accomplish union. He cited failed attempts by denominations already close in theology and polity—the German and Dutch Reformed being indistinguishable, and the Congregational, Methodist, and United Brethren attempt failing in 1907. But time heals. History created disunion; history was working for reunion. Time and human necessity were "wearing away the differences."[40] Realistically, he knew unity would not happen in his lifetime. The best he could hope for now was unity of action for utilitarian purposes of ministry. Evolution and organic unity take longer.

In the meantime, he believed an American church lay unborn "in the womb of Time,"[41] powerful in numbers and influence. The main bodies of Methodists and Baptists numbered more than one-half of American Protestantism and have played an immense part in caring for the common people. Add the Congregationalists, Presbyterians, the two Reformed churches, Disciples, and perhaps the Lutherans, to represent the majority of Protestants in America. All had similar historic roots. Together, these denominations constituted the American church. Though foreign in origin, "they have absorbed the American Spirit."[42]

To unify these American churches under a theological umbrella, Rauschenbusch, a Baptist, saw Methodist theology as holding the best promise in a democratic America.[43] Reasons for this choice were very American. Arminian theology opposed aristocratic doctrines of election and limited atonement. Methodism had a more democratic doctrine of Christ's sacrifice for all, and grace to any who accept it. The sacraments were a visible sign of God's grace rather than mere symbols. The Methodist tradition had revivals and emotional religious experiences. It stressed religious education and applying Christian virtues to all of life. Methodists were original in calling for total abstinence and in having a social consciousness that burned with a desire to apply Christian truths in reforming society: "Methodism had harnessed the forces of social consciousness and democracy so effectively that it held the key to successful church union in America."[44]

To see any hope for extending the American church to include Episcopalians, he analyzed the Lambeth Quadrilateral (Episcopalian articles, four of which related to ecumenism). The first article indicating that the Old and New Testaments are God's revealed Word was acceptable to him. The second article based on the Nicene Greed was satisfactory with one exception: it precluded Unitarians and Universalists. The third article on the sacraments precluded the Quakers. The fourth, on the historic episcopate, would be acceptable if interpreted in terms of Methodist utilitarianism that bishops precluded apostolic succession from the apostle Peter. Bishops could be useful, he conceded, if the line of succession from Peter were not taken too literally since "at the year 40 the historic episcopate [was] a shadow."[45]

Rauschenbusch obviously went to great lengths to identify characteristics of an American church. That he concerned himself with integrating episcopacies, sacraments, creeds, lamenting denominational rivalry and its accompanying inefficiencies, carefully detailing how Methodist Arminianism could be the theological basis for an American church, and measuring the possibilities for success by analyzing the failures of the past, attests to the importance he placed upon having an American church. He wanted a functional union of churches able to perform an efficient social ministry which he identified as the central mission of the American church.

The issue was urgent for him because he believed the modern world was losing its religious consciousness by having no clear sense of God or divine law. Thousands of Christian homes have no family worship, he lamented, and young people get either flimsy religious education or none at all. The Roman Catholic Church "looms up strong by solidarity and self-confidence,"[46] and the industrial worker is not connected with Protestantism. Tenant farmers, as a growing class, "are bound to go the same way." When the church needs to be vital and aggressive, it is "becoming a class institution of the wealthy, and not of the needy." Many intelligent people view the church with suspicion because it "does not listen to the grievances or see the oppression of the many." The ethical standard of churches is respectability, not the ethics of Jesus. Many inadequacies of the church exist "because we have done so much of our thinking with an eye on our denominations and not on the Kingdom of God."[47] For Rauschenbusch, "Every denomination has a protective tariff wall and some denominations are rank imperialists."[48]

Fearful that America was losing its religious moorings, Rauschenbusch clearly revealed his nationalistic fervor. Contemporary American problems needed to be solved by a contemporary American church. He was adamant that a just and democratic society was inseparable from a Christian society, and that Protestantism stood for freedom of intellect and democracy, whereas Roman Catholicism stood for medieval philosophy and theology, denying individual freedom through aristocratic and monarchical government.[49]

This urgency for an American church carried with it a price of criticism, inconsistencies and disclaimers. Rauschenbusch's critics feared that church unity would become organic with the resultant loss of denominational distinctiveness and competitive vitality. Disclaiming such an intention he responded that "a leveling uniformity is neither possible nor desirable."[50] Initially, this response sounds incredulous in light of his statements cited earlier, that Methodist theology held the best promise for church unity in a democratic America. But on further reflection, the response makes sense when it becomes evident that without such a disclaimer, his prime concern, church cooperative social action, would be futile. Apparently, criticism of his views on church union forced him to craft a response to mollify his critics. That would have been a small price to pay since those opposed to organic church unity might agree, at the very least, to cooperative social action. That, after all, was Rauschenbusch's central goal regardless of the means. However, it appears that he revealed his true feelings when in the same paragraph he stated that "Actual fellowship alone can furnish an enduring basis for any efforts at formal union, which will be made by us or our children."[51]

Whatever his real preference on the church union issue, Rauschenbusch was so intent on at least achieving cooperation that a de facto Protestant theocracy as a means of accomplishing this was central. This urgency gave rise to a more serious implication with several ironic twists. In his total commitment to the democratic ideal, he potentially exposed his identification of an American church to a tyranny of the majority in matters of religion, the very thing that the founders of the Republic and his own Baptist tradition had sought to avoid. Yet, for Rauschenbusch, the ideal was a "national evangelism which would dominate the society and allow by sufferance [toleration] the existence of various conclaves such as, for example, Roman Catholics, Mormons, and Judaism."[52] David Alan McClintock called the potential tyranny "a noncoercive messianic theocracy,"[53] a clever way to justify a de facto Protestant establishment. Rauschenbusch was "sure that history would bear him out and evolve into this kind of modern Christendom."[54] The irony of this position is extended when we see that Cardinal Gibbon, a contemporary of Rauschenbusch, was just as certain about the destiny of the Roman Catholic Church in America. Both supported religious toleration and freedom of expression in the public forum. Both were sure that in the free exchange of ideas in society the de facto establishment would one day be theirs. Both were sure that when that occurred their respective dominance of government through godly representatives would enable the passage of laws consistent with what they perceived God to be saying to society. Pluralism as a principle was foreign to both.

Even Rauschenbusch's tolerant "messianic theocracy which is universalistic, spiritual, voluntary (non coercive by force or miraculous display), and . . . establishes the value and responsibility of the human personality"[55] was deficient because it was based on tolerance, not religious liberty. Tolerance gives and takes away. That which is tolerated can become un-tolerated should majority power bring about change. Yet Religious liberty does neither; it is an inherent right not subject to human vacillation. Rauschenbusch's Messianic theocracy came "perilously close to draping the eternal cross of Golgotha with the red, white, and blue bunting. . . . [He] was not afraid of the word 'theocracy.'"[56] One of the tricks that history plays on both the living and the dead is that what one may want so desperately—for Rauschenbusch an American church—was what his bitterest critics then and today want—a Christian theocracy. If they only knew what a champion they had.

In another face of nationalistic expression, Rauschenbusch believed in the Christianized superiority of key American institutions—home life, the church, education, and political life—over their counterparts in other parts of the world. Since he was remembered more as a critic of American society in his advocacy of fundamental Christian social reform, the extent of his praise for America seems surprising. The United States had serious shortcomings, cavernous gaps between the rich and poor, corruption in high places, exploitation of the poor, and cultural immaturity, but some key institutions could be praised and emulated universally. He believed that America led the world in home life, the church, education, and political life. While his praise for these institutions is well known and even considered unrealistically opti-

mistic by his admirers, such praise is especially appropriate to his
nationalism and to his enthusiasm for an American Christianized
society.

According to Rauschenbusch, the enlightened American family
resulted from centuries of evolutionary development. In the ancient
past the family had been based on despotism and exploitation. Old
Testament and classical heroes did not receive their sterling reputa-
tions because of familial or marital relations. Not one of the Hebrew
patriarchs or Roman worthies had family relations that would be
acceptable in any "self-respecting church today."[57] But, said Rauschenbusch, "the course of evolution has come to a swift culmination. Our
own generation has witnessed a remarkable advance toward democracy in the relation between parents and children."[58]

Between ancient paternal despotism and his own period of enlightenment, Rauschenbusch traced an evolutionary transition. Gradually
wives were no longer bought outright. Divorce laws became more
humane. A wife acquired property and legal rights. Polygamy ended,
and adultery became a crime for a man as well as for a woman. The
basis had been laid for equality between man and woman. "Within the
last one hundred years," observed Rauschenbusch, "women [have]
risen toward acknowledged equality with swift and decisive steps." In a
burst of nationalistic pride, he continued, "Most other countries are
still far from conceding what our American women have now learned
to take as a matter of course."[59] Happily for Rauschenbusch, these
advances occurred with the hearty approval of the American man who,
"aglow with Christian [pride], describes how wisely his wife manages
the common finances and selects his neck-ties; how he sends his girls
to Vassar, though it ruins his bank account; how fond the girls are of
their dad, and how he would hate himself if he thought that his family
regarded him as a tyrant."[60]

If fathers of the past, speculated Rauschenbusch, had foreseen the
democratic institution of the family, they would consider the result a
tragic loss of power to wife and children, creating disorder in the institution. Conceding a loss of power to the family man, this German-
American professor acclaimed the gain of love for the man as compen-
sation. The mother previously enjoyed all the love and affection from
her children. Now she must share that with her husband. In a glowing
accolade to the American male, Rauschenbusch said, "It is probably
fair to say that American men are more considerate and reverent
towards women than the men of any other nation."[61] Women of other
countries were alleged to feel that America is the paradise for women.
American men were also remarkable for their tenderness toward

children. "All of this," said Rauschenbusch, "is the expression of the saving spirit of Christ, which has sweetened and ennobled our national custom."[62] The professor saw agitation for women's suffrage (1910) as one of the last steps in this ascent which would give women direct political power.

On balance, Rauschenbusch saw American home life as very highly developed, monogamy firmly established, and the society pure-minded enough to allow men and women to mingle quite freely. Young girls could even move about "almost as they please" and nothing in American culture prevented young people from selecting their mates. Rauschenbusch, hinting that familial openness had almost gone to the point of over indulgence, still affirmed that "all of this we can register as social attainment of the first rank."[63] "We can therefore say that the family has been assimilated to Christianity. As an institution it has been Christianized."[64]

The church in America, to Rauschenbusch, was also superior to churches elsewhere in the world. The early modern era saw the church in Europe as despotic and exploitive through its monarchical and aristocratic hierarchy. But "this coercion is in religion what rape is in love." All attempts to reform a commercialized heaven, hell, and purgatory, and the practice of simony and lay investiture were thwarted by "the ecclesiastical Tammany Hall."[65] So entrenched was ecclesiastical corruption in 1500 that if anyone had prophesied that the "lazy and fat-bellied priest" would disappear from literature and the stage and the ministry of the church be wholly free from any charge of general sexual impurity would have seemed an unattainable utopian dream. Inconceivable, too, would be a church without governmental powers or legal privileges, without power to collect levies and tithes or to execute its verdicts by the aid of the state, without endowed wealth, depending on voluntary contributions, without corruption and graft, and clergy hardworking men with few exceptions. Perhaps most startling would be a time without any forcing of religious belief, or if any attempt were made to do so, general condemnation by the populace. "Yet," says Rauschenbusch proudly, "that is the condition actually attained in our country. Our ministers as a class are a clean, laborious and honorable profession." The churches in America enjoy no special privileges except for tax exemption to charitable institutions. Few churches have endowments. All live from hand to mouth and are happy only to end the year without debt. Some Protestant churches have entirely democratized their organizations, and those that still have hierarchies "have at least been steeped in the democratic spirit."[66] For Rauschenbusch, churches in America were Christianized, democratized, and we should add—Americanized.

A third American institution perceived by Rauschenbusch as superior to European and global counterparts, was the public school. Born of the Puritan tradition with "its high estimate of a clear intellectual comprehension of truth," Rauschenbusch said that American education, through the school, spread its influence to Europe. It was a cause of the French Revolution through insisting on the "value and rights of the individual" after first giving the American "nation from the outset a democratic ideal of popular education."[67] Popular education, for Rauschenbusch, was incarnate in the public schools, based upon an essentially Christian concept once articulated by the French socialist Louis Blanc: "From everyone according to his ability, and to everyone according to his need."[68] This lofty principle was evidenced in America where every family was taxed according to its ability yet received the benefits of schools for its children. The rich man contributes heavily but may have no children, while the man with ten children, who is poor, may pay almost nothing, yet have full access to public education for his children. This reality, said Rauschenbusch, can be "justly . . . called a Christianizing of the educational organization."[69]

In Rauschenbusch's view, enthusiasm for education had made up for much that was wrong with America. "It has gone far to redeem us from the charge of gross mammonism."[70] Not only was support of public schools the largest item on our tax bills, but the country, through foreign policy, dedicated its skills of education to Christianizing and civilizing newly acquired colonies. "In sizing up the future of our Filipino brothers, the commercial corporation was our biggest anxiety, the public school our best justification. The school is Christian; the corporation—not yet."[71] The school would follow the flag. A superior American educational system, exulted Rauschenbusch, meant primary education for practically all children. Extension of educational opportunities to the high school and university was massive, making this era "one of the most creditable chapters in recent American history." Additions to the list were night schools, university extension courses, summer schools, and chautauqua circles; all of these showed the American enthusiasm for education.

In contrast to this glowing picture, Rauschenbusch described the European educational scene. There the upper classes were the intellectual elite; the poor had no opportunity for education. In some countries the church blocked the intellect and the free flow of ideas. A believer in the rags-to-riches myth, Rauschenbusch said that the poor laborers in Germany "have become great merchants" in America. Children of these poor workers, who emigrated to America, "shook off the dullness and mental limitations of their immigrant parents and became intellectual leaders. . . . In the common people are the possibilities of uncounted intellectual wealth."[72] If education were not provided for them, "the intellectual life of the nation is the poorer." It takes only two or three generations for descendants of "Germanic stock" to climb to the average of intellectual life around them, given plentiful food, healthful surroundings, a chance to get ahead with moral and intellectual stimulus.[73]

The final institution Christianized and superior to counterparts elsewhere, according to Rauschenbusch, was the American political system. After this country ousted special privilege with the Constitution, she inserted the principle of equal rights and personal liberty.[74] Again, the process leading to American superiority was evolutionary and thus still developing. Inequality existed and still exists where vestiges of feudalism remain. In the past, feudal nobles had the "right of judicature" in their territories. When the peasant was oppressed by servants of the baron and claimed justice in court, the baron or his appointee would sit to decide the case. That, said Rauschenbusch, was like a corporation director being tried only by a jury of corporation officers, or "every public service corporation [having] the right to operate its own court of justice to settle all difficulties with its employees and the ordinary public, and [putting] the offensive citizen who protested against the size of his gas bill into the corporation jail!"[75] This was conceivably not possible in America. But Rauschenbusch, referring to his own time, cited a Russian nobleman and a moujik committing the same offense yet not receiving the same punishment. In Germany two workmen who cut each other up and two army officers who duel are treated differently. In Italy two cardinals claim the right to have their depositions as witnesses taken in their houses rather than in public court as must be done by commoners.

Through comparisons with the past, or outside of America in the present, said Rauschenbusch, we see how far we have come, and have "entered a decisive moral change." We have no king, no landed and hereditary nobility. "So by the favor of Providence and by our political and economic babyhood the principles of liberty and equality got a solid footing in our tradition."[76] He suggested that graft was at least not embodied in our Constitution, and when we backslide it is due to the newness of democracy and the fact that "the State very directly affects the property interests of the country."[77] Hence conflict between Christian principles of democracy, liberty, and equality and the greed of business was inevitable. But consistent with his belief in the evolutionary process, the day would come when business would be Christianized too. And when Christianized "the fundamental Christianity of our political structure will become clearer and more effective."[78]

In spite of lapses into class inequality, corruption, and exploitation, Rauschenbusch believed that America was on a Christian footing constitutionally—that at least inequality was not legalized. Nearly equating democracy and Christianity, he said: "Democracy is the expression and method of the Christian spirit. It has made the most permanent achievements in the younger communities of the Anglo-Saxon group, but it is making headway throughout the world, and is the conquering tendency in modern political life."[79] In a statement of Protestant nationalism, he said that democracy "has been best led in Protestant countries where a free type of religion ranged men of distinctly Christian character on the side of popular liberty." And again: "The more broadly and justly we view the history of the last eight centuries the more influence we will attribute to Christianity in the rise of modern democracy. In the Anglo-Saxon communities, especially, the spirit of religion has blended with the spirit of freedom, or rather, here the spirit of Christianity has been set free sufficiently to work in political life and has found one great outlet for its power in creating a passionate love for freedom and equality."[80]

In affirming America's superiority in these four institutions, Rauschenbusch cited several themes that constitute an American Protestant nationalism. Christianity and democracy were closely linked. Rauschenbusch rejected the idea that they are one and the same but accepted rather that one comes out of the other—that is, that the true Christian spirit is democratic. This superiority, secondly, resulted from centuries of slow evolutionary growth. Not automatic or consistent, but clearly in each of the four institutions cited, the growth began in despotism and ended in democracy—from the dark past to the enlightened present in America. Third, while America was superior in key institutions, she too represented only a link in the chain of progress. For Rauschenbusch, each of the four institutions, to say nothing of those institutions not yet Christianized needed much improvement. In an article, "What is a Christian Nation?" he referred to the process of "becoming." Christian character was not defined by what one is, but in what one is coming to be. Applying this to nations he said that America is a Christian nation but is also "becoming." "Look yonder at the crossroads gallows in England," he said, "where putrid corpses dangled in brutal warning to evil doers. Look here at the juvenile court of Denver, where Judge Lindsay teaches kids to 'switch' on themselves and to transport themselves unguarded to the reform school. Those two pictures mark the progress of nations in Christianity in administrating punitive justice."[81] Of his own analysis, Rauschenbusch said, "If this analysis [of the four areas of society Christianized] is even approximately correct, it ought to create an immense hopefulness in all Christian minds."[82]

Another face of Rauschenbusch's nationalism was his most positive. Born of his obsession to forge a new religious expression endogenously related to rapidly changing times brought on by industrialism, science, and American involvement for the first time in world affairs, Rauschenbusch knew that old theological answers to new conditions would never do. The Church must be the primary catalyst in seeking and applying new theological answers. Thus, the Church would create revolutionary ferment in society.

For those made nervous by talk of revolution, Rauschenbusch said that one's understanding of the Gospel must change to fit new paradigms of life and thought. His words, as quoted by Winthrop Hudson, explain:

> The gospel, to have power over an age, must be the highest expression of the moral and religious truths held by that age. If it lags behind and presents outgrown conceptions of life and duty, it is no longer in the full sense the gospel. Christianity itself lifts the minds of men to demand a better expression of Christianity. If the official wardens of the gospel from selfish motives or from conservative veneration for old statements refuse to let the subject of Christ flow into the larger vessels of thought and feeling which God himself has prepared for it, they are warned by finding men turn from their message as sapless and powerless.[83]

Such a call to forge new theological expressions for new conditions did not mean for Rauschenbush that society should govern or determine the message of the Church. Rather, it meant that the Church must speak clearly to men of the day in terms of their own situations and "so state these truths that men would be deeply stirred and grasped by them."[84] Rauschenbusch again:

> The social movement is the most important ethical and spiritual movement in the modern world, and the social gospel is the response of a Christian consciousness to it. . . . The social gospel registers the fact that for the first time in history the spirit of Christianity had had a chance to form a working partnership with real social and psychological science. It is the religious reaction to the historic advent of democracy. It seeks to put the democratic spirit, which the Church inherited from Jesus and the prophets, once more in control of the institutions, and teachings of the church. . . . The social gospel seeks to bring men under repentance for their collective sins and to create a more modern and sensitive conscience.[85]

Rauschenbusch complained that instead of religious expression of
new conditions, the ordinary hymnal had only two or three hymns of
social hope. Liturgies and devotional manuals offered little. Even men
who had absorbed the social ideals still clung to traditional verbiage in
their prayers. "The old language of prayer clings to the antique for the
sake of dignity, and plain references to modern facts and contrivances
jar the ear." So we follow the old.[86]

A new form of worship was needed—a form "unknown to our fore-
fathers [which] kindle religious passion of wonderful intensity and
purity."[87] New religious emotion ought to find conscious and social
expression. "We need to blaze new paths to God for the feel of modern
men."[88] A new form of prayer should express a new set of conditions
and needs.

A moving example of this new theology in action is seen in his
book of prayers for social action.[89] The table of contents reveals an addressing of the new condition with new solutions.

Prayers for:

Children who work
Children of the street
Women who toil
Workingmen
Immigrants
Employers
Men in business
Kings and magnates
Discoverers and inventors
Artists and musicians
Judges
Lawyers and legislators
Public officers
Doctors and nurses
Writers and newspapermen
Ministers
Teachers
Mothers
For all true lovers
Idle
Morituri Te Salutant

In this face of Rauschenbusch's nationalism several themes consistently occur. Religion must be made in America. That is, it must fit

American conditions—needs, local and national. While the heritage of the past—both American and European—was important, the religion of the past was not sufficient for the needs of the American present. Therefore, the religion of the past must be reshaped to be a potent force in regenerating American society.

Religion must also have emotion. Rauschenbusch even said that if there is a choice between genuine emotion and religious work the choice is "genuine emotion with little intellect rather than the reverse." Religion without emotion is "value less," having "no saving power."[90] A religious message that does not instill a passion for social action lacks relevance to current human need. Individually, a test for religious truth, said Rauschenbusch, is whether it unsettles one with divine dissatisfaction, impels one with longing for holiness and God, lifts one beyond the fear of men, and gives the taste of joy and peace of eternity. If so, religious truth is sanctifying. "If not, it may be religious truth, but not religious truth for you."[91]

What is one to make of the faces of nationalism in Walter Rauschenbusch? Certainly students of his career will identify for themselves what they perceive to be his strengths and weaknesses revealed in his varied nationalistic expressions. Whatever those individual judgments, he was clearly a child of his times. His enthusiasm for democracy is a page out of the book of Populism with its lead in achieving the initiative, referendum, recall, and direct election of senators. His call for social reform reflected not only the Populist program but also the era of Progressivism, with its regulation of big business, its monetary reform, and prohibition. It is noteworthy that his blind spots on reform generally paralleled those of Progressivism—a slowness to recognize women's rights, traditional treatment of blacks, and racism in general.

He owed to the times his utilitarianism in attaining short-term goals of church cooperation to bring about social change and in his faith in the evolutionary process to explain progress and give hope for needed changes. He was generally in step with racist views of his day, though not a pernicious racism. His views on race allowed for ultimate elevation of less developed peoples, given proper education and Christianizing. The differences did not represent inherent inferiority of the non-Teutonics, rather environmental inferiority, which could be corrected.

What may surprise admirers of Rauschenbusch is that he was on the left wing of Protestantism and of the American political spectrum—not a Socialist but a socialist—who on occasion sounded like a tub-thumper for American and Western civilization. The coming of Western civilization was like the plowing of ground followed by sowing new thoughts. America's task as part of this was to sow. Time was of the essence in such sowing since conditions would harden again. Sowing meant occupying the ground with schools to win youth and penetrating the national life with Christian ethics and literature. American history revealed God's plan for the human race.[92] "Whenever any other nation is stirring uneasily under despotism or is trying to break the strangle-hold of ancient tyranny, an instinctive thrill of sympathy runs through our American people showing that we have not forgotten our divine calling. . . . As far as our religion is concerned the passion for freedom is a distinctive mark of genuine Christianity."[93] These statements were made throughout most of his professional life and generally reflected American values throughout this century. America was superior and hence had a responsibility to civilize and Christianize the world.[94]

Walter Rauschenbusch also represented a microcosm of international Socialism that declared war obsolete since the workers of the world would not produce the materials of war. But when push got to shove between nation-states, reluctant though they were, workers produced war material for their respective father/motherlands. After accounting for the inequities to Germany's disadvantage, the craftiness of the British, and the greed of American merchants of death, Rauschenbusch came to understand the threat posed by unchecked German militarism. Ironically, he could have said with Cardinal Gibbon, "America, with all thy faults, I love thee still."[95]

Observing how Rauschenbusch has been viewed by friend and foe is instructive too. The religious Right, including fundamentalism and early evangelicalism (1940s–50s), dismisses him out of hand as a liberal, socialist, Commie. For the religious Left he practically walks on water. Variant perceptions of Rauschenbusch reveal a clinic on what Martin Marty calls the two-party system in American Protestantism.

Even more fascinating may be not how Rauschenbusch was viewed in his own time, nor how he has been traditionally viewed since then, but how he could be viewed today were he seriously studied by the whole spectrum of extreme Right to extreme Left. Present-day fundamentalists (I am not including evangelicals here) would discover a champion of a near Christian theocracy. They would be surprised at his strong emphasis on emotional fervor and the need for conversion in religion, and perhaps most of all his strong sense of divinely ordained national mission to Christianize the world. They would delight in his concept of proper family relations between husband, wife, and children, which to the liberal ear sounds patronizing. Their rage at his Social Gospel, some of it misunderstood (his emphasis was evangelical, not humanistic), has blinded them to these other aspects of the man and his ministry. They would continue to be disgusted with his diminution of conversion for individual salvation and bliss of heaven, although they would not reject his deference to a personal conversion that compels the individual to help change the social order. The difference might be on the focus of reform, although both would agree on the need for Prohibition.

Evangelicals over the past twenty years have combined the social aspects of the gospel with their evangelistic and revivalistic fervor—a combination insisted upon by Rauschenbusch as essential.[96] The evangelical community would be comfortable with his belief in the American mission to Christianize the world through education, technology, and medicine. Some would like his use of the word "conquer" in the process. They would be nervous with his call for organic church union, though themselves constituting a movement that transcends traditional denominational lines.

Liberals hold Walter Rauschenbusch in awe because of his leadership in theory and practice of the Social Gospel and the tremendous impact he and the movement had on shaping denominational and interdenominational structures to institutionalize social Christianity. His admirers would not support him on his church, state, theocratic leanings, would be mixed on the church union issue—again over concern of "to be, or not to be" one church—and would be embarrassed, hostile, or mute on the issues of his nationalism, racism, and elitism. His defenders insist that these minor aberrations are not worthy of much consideration compared to his overall contribution. It might be noted in response, however, that these expressions were more pervasive than admitted by his admirers, and in any case are part of his career, however extensive. Had he so chosen, he would have had company in opposing the Spanish-American War and subsequent territorial acquisition. The presence of the American Anti-Imperialism League, which formulated a platform opposing American intervention in Cuba that sounds like something written in the Vietnam era provided impressive support for a non intervention position. Ironically, William Graham Sumner supported the American Anti-Imperialism League, and attacked annexation of the Philippines.[97] As for Rauschenbusch's elitism, there was enough pedagogical research to support a more liberal, democratic approach to education more consistent with his democratic Social Gospel theory.[98] In other words, Rauschenbusch was not locked into his times.

This analysis suggests that within one man, Walter Rauschenbusch, resided issues that bitterly divide American society today. He revealed nationalistic expression and fervor with racial overtones and yet was the brilliant, compassionate exponent of the Social Gospel. How could this dichotomy reside in one man? Sidney Mead observed this phenomenon in the average American citizen, which he called the bifurcated mind, whereby the normal church-goer believes, on the one hand, that his religion is the revealed religion—"no one comes to the Father but by me"—and on the other hand, ascribes to the religion of the Republic, or in its lowest common denominator, "all religions lead to the same place"—mutually inconsistent propositions.[99] Charles Dunn describes a similar tendency within the American national experience in his book, *American Political Theology*. Inherent in American history is the nurturing of mutually inconsistent themes which intermingle, coexist beneath the surface, but, occasionally surface and separate into bitter polarization.[100] The Civil War is the obvious example of separation, and John C. Calhoun is an excellent individual example of bifurcation before the war. He was a nationalist and a states righter all in one and maintained this uneasy alliance within. But the homogenization ended with the Civil War and one then was either a states righter or a nationalist.

This bifurcation existed in Walter Rauschenbusch, who epitomizes Protestant liberalism at the turn of the century. He seems to be the least likely candidate to demonstrate nationalist, racist, elitist tendencies alongside his Social Gospel. He is the hero for liberals. That he would have these seemingly inconsistent attitudes testifies to the pervasiveness and depth of such conflicting values in the American fabric. These inconsistencies in Walter Rauschenbusch have coexisted throughout the twentieth century.[101] What happens when they no longer peacefully coexist in a people?

Today the separation is apparent again, and a study of Walter Rauschenbusch helps us to understand the depth of the problem. We can perhaps appreciate how fundamental these inconsistencies have been in the American experience, unchallenged seriously until Vietnam and Watergate. The study was certainly not done to denigrate Walter Rauschenbusch. His contribution in terms of the Social Gospel stands. Perhaps paraphrasing William Hutchison should be the last word. That Walter Rauschenbush had a nationalist, racist side must not necessarily denigrate his contribution anymore than the abolitionist efforts of the nineteenth century should be denigrated because of the "racist frame of much abolitionist thought."[102]

CHAPTER 3

Foreign Policy through Benediction

"And now oh God! wilt thou save Mexico! Wilt thou use the United States of America as thine agent to save those millions of people to civilization and to thee. We ask it in Jesus name—Amen."[1] Such was the benediction intoned by the Reverend Russell Conwell, minister of Temple Baptist Church, Philadelphia, following a stem-winding sermon oration on a Sunday morning in late 1919. He implored the congregation to support mission efforts to send teachers, build schools, and invite Mexican teachers to the United States for training in order to "change the nature of the Mexican people through education and good deeds."[2]

Not normally remembered for sermons and benedictions of this sort Conwell is known instead as the cleric who delivered his famous lecture "Acres of Diamonds" over 6,000 times across the land. Conwell, builder of a great institutional church providing a total daycare program for children of the proletariat and educational programs for people wanting to earn a better living; Conwell, founder of Temple University and three hospitals; Conwell, the exponent of the gospel of wealth declaring that material fortunes are a trust from God for the benefit of humankind or, more crudely, if realistically put, that the wealth of the entrepreneur trickles down to the masses through established institutions; this is how the Temple Baptist minister is normally remembered.

But Conwell was much more than this. He produced a couple of sermons each week, spoke to civic groups in Philadelphia and around the country, was a political activist and world traveler, wrote thirty books including biographies of the presidents, and was confidant to senators and representatives and educator to his flock on issues of national and international importance in an age of burgeoning industry, big-time military power, and domestic and international political and economic hardball.

43

He also reflected his times in sharing the ambivalence with which America enters the modern industrial world, as described by Henry May's *The End of American Innocence*—an age into which America enters with a guilty conscience for leaving the Arcadian existence of the clean-living agrarian life for that of the sinister, corrupt, big time of modernity. And yet the guilty conscience is salved by an optimism that America with its newly acquired power emerges on the world scene in the nick of time to begin democratizing and christianizing America and the world. The text of Esther seems appropriate for America and the times: "Who knows but what you have been raised for such an hour as this."[3] Henry May again: "Together, most social conservatives and most social reformists perceived their century as a triumphant march forward of American society and American religion."[4]

So on balance, Conwell, reflecting the times with its uncertainties yet exuding optimism was especially outspoken, if sometimes peripatetic, on America's role in foreign affairs.

In keeping with this vacillation, Conwell displayed nationalism in the center of two extremes: on the one hand, at his most bellicose, he was not a rabid advocate of expansionism and empire; on the other hand, at his most nationally repentant, he was not a pietistic preacher condemning any intervention in world affairs.

On the one hand, hear his nearly unbridled huffing and puffing for the nation-state then muted by prophetic warnings and criticism of American pride and greed for empire. On special holidays—Memorial Day, Flag Day, Fourth of July, Labor Day, and Thanksgiving—the sanctuary was decorated, festooned with draped flags, the worship service ringing with patriotic songs by the congregation and choirs, veterans organizations invited and sitting in a body. To rally the people to the Cuban cause, the Young Men's Congress, one of several Temple patriotic organizations, called on Congress to "recognize Cuban rights to belligerency as soon as it may be done according to international law."[5] Organizing a pro-Cuban rally as early as October 1895 to influence the government, with Conwell the featured speaker, the Young Men's Congress arranged an audience for the Temple minister that included the governor of Pennsylvania and the mayor of Philadelphia. The Temple Guard, another of the Temple's patriotic organizations, performed rifle and machete drills to the thrill of the crowd.

On the other hand, as though the hyper rallies of the day would have no lasting impact on the media and the people, the Temple minister warned of dangerous pride and journalistic boasting of national power. Acquiring the Philippines so easily, we have lost our balance of judgement, he declared. Boasting to be the greatest naval power in the world, we have forgotten the poor, and afflicted Cubans, "acting more like Bonaparte."[6] Moreover, in our greed we must not take territory: "Shall we govern the Cubans, the Philippines or Puerto Rico, tell them they can't have privileges we have? Or shall we look on our history and remember that God has prospered us when we have adhered to Christian principles? Never must money be a consideration in determining our policy toward the Philippines and a stepping stone to dominate China,"[7] he said.

In perhaps his sharpest criticism of American foreign policy, Conwell excoriated the government for passing the Platt Amendment. "Cuba must obey or starve," he thundered. "Is that freedom?"[8] Accusing the United States of pretending brotherhood to liberate the island, he saw American policy as intending to dominate the island. Still fuming he remarked: "I have never been so disturbed or indignant over anything the nation ever did as I have been over this wickedness and foolishness concerning the Cuban tariff."[9] As for Puerto Rico, Conwell was adamant that this small island not be dominated by the Screaming Eagle either. Rather, America's providential role should be to help and then withdraw.

Emphasizing America's humble yet influential beginnings, Conwell on numerous occasions reminded his audiences that the United States had more influence in the world during the years before its big armies and navies. With a navy of only five vessels and a meager army of 18,000 men, the United States was alleged to be more powerful in world affairs than ever since, "unless it be just at the present time [1919],"[10] he conceded, the inconsistency of his argument hardly registering. His romantic perception of the American past oozed throughout the Temple on a Sunday morning as he described the presence of only six million Americans scattered in the woods in 1800 and in back of them "the great enemy, the North American Indian."[11] In spite of being at such a disadvantage, this grubby and newly independent nation forged a constitution with democratic ideas—people willing to die for the principle that "all men are created equal—no high, no low, rich or poor, every religion tolerated, working together as brethren,"[12] while in contrast there was Spain with its aristocracy, titled nobility, hierarchy of the church, its decadent and superstitious religion, and its expulsion of Jews. And while the Spanish were rotting silently, the United States was winning the moral battle. "Little United States, six million people quietly chopping wood, hewing timber, engaged in their own occupations singing gladly the joy of liberty. Those men unshaven, those men in skins of animals, those men meeting the forest at its very edge and fighting the wild beasts and the more wild Indian."[13] Those American patriots, intent on building their utopian republic, minding their own business, were alleged by the Temple minister to know nothing of the rest of the world. Yet in their simple and pure life they were winning the battle for the mind around the world, unaware of either the battle or the winning. Furthermore, the witness of two Christian American businessmen in Chile around 1800 Conwell perceived as leaven leading to Chilean overthrowal of Spanish rule, and disavowal of the Church of Spain and the Inquisition. Venezuela, Haiti, and Mexico followed suit. They all copied the American Constitution with Mexico "taking only eight hours to draft a constitution"[14] because of such pilfering. Such defections occurred from Spain, which had a powerful army and navy, whereas the United States, whose influence was pervasive, had no military.

Stretching to absurd limits the theme of America's humility, Conwell perceived the United States as getting Panama without using military power. Once again American moral leadership in the Western hemisphere allegedly induced Panamanian loyalty. In what would be considered sickening patronization in some quarters today, Conwell cites "Little Panama" with only 31,000 square miles, two-thirds the size of Pennsylvania with 221,000 people or nine people to every square mile. "One would think that President Roosevelt would need a small pen with which to sign the treaty with such a nation as that and require a microscope with which to read the treaty."[15] How could this happen?—such a small country coming over on its own to the United States, Conwell asked. Why was Panama in such a hurry to get United States recognition? "I do not believe they are in such a hurry simply for the ten millions of dollars. I cannot feel that, because Panama fifty years ago adopted the American Constitution and determined then to imitate us in the common schools."[16] Incredible naiveté concerning Panamanian motives and American "success" by the Temple minister! America's power was moral and the greatest and most successful power on earth—not needing armies and navies to achieve it.

Shifting, however, to emphasize America's military power and influence, Conwell displayed great pride in American military might. For rhetorical purposes America may have been more influential in the days before her armies and navies, but Conwell knew better and on most occasions praised the American military as indispensable to freedom for its people and essential in liberating oppressed peoples everywhere. In one of his great sermons on the flag, Conwell declared that it not only represents the great wisdom of the American people— a people with greater intelligence than any other nation in the world, an educational system for all citizens, religious progress and equality, but also *power*. Go anywhere in the world—Turkey, for example—and if a Pasha arrests you "immediately a mighty Navy is at your command and within five days you could have the forces of this government to your aid to demand your freedom because that flag now represents power, power!"[17]

What stark contrast with his words proclaiming the United States the most powerful and influential when least powerful militarily. But more than mere starkness of contrast is the deeper significance of the inconsistency. The United States had it both ways. It was influential in the world without military might—a pure and simple characteristic that seems the reason for becoming a world power in the first place— with armies and navies developing later and having the added task of making the world safe for democracy. The Weberian model explaining the relationship of the Protestant work ethic and capitalism is useful. Even as hard work and saving one's earnings accumulates capital which can be invested in business enterprise resulting in even greater wealth, so America was humble, hardworking, not needing armies and navies, which resulted in prosperity invested in armies and navies to defend, protect, and spread great Christian moral principles. In both, success was not only a sign of God's favor but also a Divine mandate of moral responsibility to the world.

In this light it is understandable that Conwell is haunted by the fear that America would misuse her newly acquired power and Americans would become vainglorious brags gloating over their elevated position in the world. His concern, mixed with unabashed pride in American power, was consistent with an era seeking focus in the face of dizzying change—a people told on the one hand that their real power and influence in the world was moral but invited on the other hand to be inordinately satisfied watching the Spanish navy (symbol of an arrogant wealthy, powerful and decadent society) gurgle helplessly to the bottom.

But if a substantive portion of Conwell's message was peripatetic, a greater portion was resoundingly unequivocal. America's superior morality as exemplary to the world was one unmistakable theme. When the *Titanic* went down the alleged cry was to get the women and children off to safety in lifeboats: great Christian heroism, said Conwell. Moreover, in the Temple minister's mind such male bravery would never occur in Turkey or China or in any of the "heathen" countries of the world: "On the contrary, they throw their children into destruction. They kill their children and the women are the last thought of, and always sacrificed for the safety of the men. But Christianity changes this."[18]

In Conwell's vision, America not only cared for its women and children, but also was magnanimous in victory toward its defeated enemies. Indeed, the humane way the Americans allegedly treated the vanquished Spaniards was more important than the victory itself. Americans treat defeated enemies like honorable men, giving them the utmost comfort, "better than you and I enjoy," providing them food and the privilege of communicating with their families.[19] Some prisoners were even invited to dinner. Moreover, Americans in victory do not extract reparations or demand that Spain pay for the war. Rather the American government said "to this ignorant and benighted nation, 'If you will make these people [Cubans] free for whom we are unselfishly contending, we will take upon ourselves our great debt and all its hardships and pay it ourselves.'"[20]

This perception of American moral superiority was extended to American admirals and generals. Commodore Schley, after the victory at Santiago says, "Three Cheers for the Men Behind the Guns," a "peculiar American sentiment," says Conwell, whereas Europe's generals say, "Three cheers for the King or officers." This simple illustration demonstrates that in a Christian democracy, as America was perceived to be, even in the military the same honor was given to the commoner as to the generals and admirals. Indeed, to Conwell, the average American foot soldier displayed superior intelligence and moral fiber. Consisting of college graduates, educators, business leaders, and most of all Christians, "these men—foot soldiers—privates have the intellectual power to so control themselves as to adjust themselves at once to all the needs of war." Such superior background made them magnificent soldiers contrasted with "the ignorant dummy in all other armies who simply obeys the commands of his superior."[21]

Moral superiority and purity of motives were attributed to Theodore Roosevelt and his open door policy toward China. Roosevelt allegedly engineered this policy because he was concerned about the ignorance of the Chinese and their seclusion with no chance for exposure to Christian civilization. Even his Panama policy was graced with halo and wings. Quoting Roosevelt to prove the assertion, Conwell said the Panama Canal "shall be for all the nations of the world. America is not doing this for ourselves; it is a work for all mankind and consequently a work for God."[22] In a moving sermon titled "The Saviour at the Panama Canal," Conwell spoke of the Christian influence of America on the world in creating the canal—an engineering feat greater than the Pyramids, Karnak, Baalbec, Babylon or medieval cathedrals. Said he, "We have done the greatest thing in the history of the world in building that Canal."[23]

But more than material witness was the Christian witness in the construction of the canal. In Conwell's mind labor was treated as the Bible teaches it should be, with some 50,000 workmen being given more in wages than requested,[24] and hence there being no labor troubles in the project. Additionally, workmen were allowed to earn overtime: "Who would have thought that in working for the government a man would ask for more working hours?"[25] Such employee-employer harmony was perceived as unique and directly attributable to Christian flexibility. The Temple minister exulted that the Christian employer "does not, like Shylock, demand the exact pound of flesh to the closest items; he does not like some men, with mathematical exactness come down to the fifteen millionth of an inch, but always allows a space for adjustment." Therefore the construction of the Panama Canal "holds up its banner to the sunlight and proclaims to the nations of the earth the greatest accomplishment of any age of the world."[26]

More dramatic still was Christ's healing influence in Panama. Whereas the French were driven out of the canal zone by disease and serpents, "the Christian government of the United States went down . . . where there lurked in the swamps the most poisonous of serpents; where malaria lurked in every breath, and fevers were scarcely ever escaped by the healthiest men and . . . changed it into the healthiest place on the face of the entire earth."[27] Under the banner of Christian civilization the swamps were cleansed.

Moreover, with the construction of the canal came Christian education to Panama. Panamanian children were perceived as having a better opportunity for education than any other children on earth. Schools were operated on the American model. Entertainment furnished by Christian America was uplifting and wholesome, movies "high and elevating," music and musicians "of the finest," plays in theaters "uplifting and pure." "Oh it is a blessed, ideal, Christian state," says Conwell. "It is the ideal city they have there; the ideal village; the ideal land, and the reason it was possible to bring it about was because it was under the paternal Government of the United States; a government that loves God and loves mankind."[28]

America's superior morality was demonstrated further through the integrity displayed by the presidents. "Not one president," declared Conwell triumphantly, "was ever elected to that office because he could play a good game of cards."[29] Rather, Washington was known for his purity, Adams his honor, Jefferson a love of humanity, Madison, purity; Monroe and Lincoln, honesty; Pierce, morals; Harrison, bravery; and Jackson, love and respect for pure womanhood. Such good choices for president made by the enlightened American electorate were also seen as evidence of God's direction for His Chosen.

Along with American moral superiority, Conwell was convinced of the moral inferiority of foreign lands. His harsh words and patronizing attitude toward Mexico typified his position toward much of the world, Western and Eastern. Mexico's moral, social, political, economic and religious depravity was to be expected since they had no experience in democracy, no school system like that of America, and no privilege to worship God freely. Mexicans lacked "the intelligence, and the patriotism, and the generosity, and the Christian knowledge of the people of this country,"[30] so it was unfair of Americans to judge negatively the Mexican government. Although Mexico copied the American Constitution, it wasn't likely to work for them since they "are largely savage people, uncultured, and they have not the intelligence to follow that Constitution even though they copied it."[31] Consisting of twenty-seven different states and fourteen different languages, and characterized by hopeless political and cultural division, Mexico most of all, was "yet an adulterous country, given over almost completely to the worship of wood and stone, as though it were in the interior of India or the farthest islands of the sea."[32]

Conwell's worldview was hardly more optimistic as revealed in a major sermon on the League of Nations titled "An Unfair Partnership."[33] "Shall the United States join the League of Nations?" Conwell rhetorically asked. To help the congregation decide on its own "without being told how to vote," the Temple minister loaded the decision-making deck with an illustration that not only revealed his adamant position concerning the League but laid bare his conviction of the moral depravity of the world. Framing the illustration was the story of an Englishman in Victoria, Australia, needing $7,500 to buy mining machinery to mine gold. The five investors of this enterprise were the usual stereotypes associated with ethnic and racial backgrounds. The Negro invested $1,000 and his labor, the "Chinaman" $2,000, the Irishman $1,500, the Egyptian $1,500, and the Jew $500. All contributed different talents to the enterprise. The Negro was athletic, having little education, the Jew had contacts to sell the product, the Englishman was skillful in the wise purchase of goods "and desired, of course, as is natural to Englishmen, to conduct the whole affair and get the profits out of the whole business."[34] However, according to the original agreement all were to share equally in the profits. The man who invested $2,000 would get the same as the man who invested $500. The result of the arrangement was predictable; the Jew realized that if he owned the whole enterprise he could make all the money by selling to people he knows personally. The Englishman was skillful and knew he was more valuable than any of the rest, and hence should have a greater salary than the others. The Negro contended he should have an advancement beyond the Irishman, and so on, leading to a disintegration of the enterprise.

That, said Conwell, is the structure of the League of Nations. Smaller nations having as few as two million people have the same vote as any nation, except for Britain, which having five great empires combined in one, has five votes. American shipping interests would be at the mercy of the British, and the large, wealthy, and well-educated United States would be an equal partner with "one of the South American states or with Mexico or with Japan or some of the smaller states of Europe in our voting power."[35] But more serious than the voting discrepancy would be the moral and religious discrepancy. Basing his position on St. Paul's warning, "Do not be mismated with unbelievers. For what partnership have righteousness and iniquity?,"[36] Conwell in turn warned that Americans must not be unequally yoked with Moslems. Moreover, all Christians believe they should live the Great Commission,[37] meaning that all Christians must insist that all nations become Christian. "That is our duty! . . . Then shall we join a League of Nations and go into a partnership with Turkey with all their extreme ferocities; with all their dreadfully extreme doctrines?"[38] Extending the condemnation, he asserted that the German Christian religion was inferior, that Jews, if ever getting political power in the United States, would impose their religion on everybody else, and the "Chinaman's" worship of Buddha was obviously blatant paganism. Therefore, "If this nation is to be Christian we will build a Christian navy . . . and we will have a Christian army . . . that shall ever set its face against the infidels and against the heathen, and never, never permit them to weaken us."[39] Conscience tingling a bit, Conwell acknowledged how unkind this proposition seems at first but quickly recovered to reminisce on his travels in those Eastern lands where they have "deep and severe . . . prejudices." Hence the great barrier to the League was not so much difference in skill or capital but in religion, precluding any contract with nations having different religions since such arrangements implied to the Temple minister's mind approval of those religions, (a logic no different than that which is inconsistently displayed by the American government towards communist governments unworthy of diplomatic recognition). In a parting shot in his sermon Conwell asked, "Shall we encourage the Buddhists, the Moslems, giving them equal chance with the rest of the world and let them get great sums of money so that they can build their mosques and armies to conquer the world? No—never. Christ is the only king and he should be recognized by every nation on earth."[40]

In view of America's moral superiority contrasted with the rest of the world's moral depravity, the obvious solution to the discrepancy given adherence to the imperative of the Great Commission, was to democratize and Christianize the world. American responsibility to the world made up the bulk of Conwell's sermon themes on foreign policy. Like Israel, America is a chosen people not to bask in luxury, power, and greed, but to serve mankind, and spread the good news of the gospel, preferably through education, medicine, and technology, but through the military if necessary.

America's responsibility to the world included an obligation to defend people who suffer oppression anywhere in the world. As such, the United States should have entered World War I upon the German invasion of Belgium, or if not then, with the sinking of the *Lusitania*. Turkey should have been "wiped off the face of the earth as a political power . . . or exterminated for massacring ten of thousands of Armenian Christians by the Kurds, drowning more than 3,200 in a day in 1894."[41] Such treatment, reasoned Conwell, was appropriate since one could not expect anything else from an infidel Sultan.[42] The best solution for the Turks, were it ever possible, would be to give them schools and a new religion.

Another responsibility placed on America's shoulders by God was to preserve the peace of the world. This preoccupation of Conwell's seems inconsistent when considering his extreme solution concerning the Turks. However, coming from Conwell's perspective, one can see how he resolved such a conflict. He believed that war is sometimes needed to bring peace. Indeed, war is inevitable even as a surgeon's knife must draw blood to effect a cure. Since backward countries do not know better than their pagan ways the United States may need initially to compel them through force of arms or other pressure to change their ways, wean them from their pagan past, and set them toward a Western future, ultimately releasing them for self-determination within democratic and Christian parameters. Only then would peace on earth be possible.

Conwell also felt that American responsibility to the world included an educational mission. He was always quick to follow up a call for military action with a call for pedagogical action. As necessary and as successful as World War I was in accomplishing the goals for which it was fought, more than armies was needed. Democracy can not come up with laws or armies, he said. Rather, democracy comes through education, and education of a particular sort. The Germans, for example, were educated in technology, music, and philosophy, having their schools and universities: "But they are still the most ignorant people of the world in politics unless it be the Russians, and their religion is vastly inferior to religions in America."[43] And obviously peace was impossible with Mexico or Turkey or any uneducated or uneducable nation. Therefore, America could conquer the world for Christ only by establishing educational institutions around the world and sending missionaries—an army of missionaries—teachers for the "preservation of democracy of the world." We must go to China and help the ignorant and "Americanize them."[44]

Curiously, for Conwell an excellent means of spreading Christian education appeared in a bill in Congress to subsidize private enterprise in purchasing surplus ships from World War I. Such purchases could promote trade and spread the gospel of Jesus Christ. Conversion of sailors was also seen as essential so that they would truly represent the American nation.

The particular educational message was that a Christian democracy, which America had, was the best form of government. Moreover, a Christian democracy was a theocracy of the holy whereby the majority will was the will of God. This form of government was the wave of the future. Indeed, God was establishing this form on earth. Even as churches were turning to a congregational form of government , so enlightened, educated people were insisting on a congregational form of government for their nation-states. Conwell could not have said it more clearly: "The voice of the people is finally the voice of God."[45] "The only true democracy is a theocracy," and "the American democracy stands for that ideal."[46] Conversely, a rule by majority of non-Christians was logically impossible within Conwell's scheme.

Conwell not only dramatized America's responsibility to the world in grandiose terms but also exhorted concerning American responsibilities to specific problem areas of the world. Mexico for example, was a major frustration to him: "Poor Mexico is a disgrace," he said in 1913. "It would be well for Mexico . . . if we had a protectorate over it long enough to compel them to recognize the great Christian brotherhood of man, enough to accept the rule of the majority, which is, after all, the rule of God."[47] After the World War his frustration was still virulent. If the Mexicans were doing right "their present condition would not exist,"[48] he fumed. But since they were not doing right, the United States should intervene and straighten them out. Intervention was also seen as protection from foreign exploitation in their weakened, depraved condition. However, justification for intervention always carried with it a warning against American exploitation. Said he, we must go to Mexico "with the same altruistic spirit with which we went to Cuba,"[49] after the Spanish American War and with the same spirit allegedly manifest in the Great War. Indeed, it appeared that the time was ripe as never before to send the gospel to the "heathen in Mexico."

Conwell's central focus toward Puerto Rico and the Philippines was to insist ultimately on Christian home rule. "The only thing the American nation can do," he said, "is to let every people govern themselves by a principle of Christian home rule."[50] Concerning the Philippines specifically, he warned that Americans must not exploit them. Rather, "We can only generously say, 'now you are free, make the best of it yourselves. You may have the same liberties we have, and the same education we have, and the same freedom of religion we enjoy.'"[51] With vintage "white man's burden," however, Conwell was not ready to throw the Philippines to the wolves of international greed or the cannibalism of tribal political factionalism. "Shall we abandon them now like cowards and sneak away from the poor people we have encouraged to seek their liberty?"[52] Never. How long the United States should remain in the Philippines for their own good was never explicitly spelled out by the Temple minister, but his conviction that America should never consider ownership or control of the Philippines for commercial or profit motives was consistent. And Conwell was certain that Americans as Christians ascribed to these high and noble motives making America the first nation in "the pages of history willing to do that."[53]

Cuba was another matter for Conwell. Whether because it was seen as potentially less adept at self-government, or because of its proximity to the United States mainland, Conwell seemed to advocate ultimate statehood for the island. "Do we let an ignorant people flounder with local quarrels and allow them to select officials who are unfit for positions, thereby wrecking their newly discovered liberty?," he asks. "Or shall we accept them as a state in our government?" A third alternative solution, one Conwell implicitly rejected was to "establish the simple protectorate over it and spend millions more in caring for it."[54] Conwell's position concerning Cuba did not change over the years. By the end of 1901, he still felt that the island was too small to maintain independence—that it was easy prey for expansionists. Germany in particular was seen as the potential predator. But if Cuba were to become an American state this danger would end.[55]

Especially fascinating was Conwell's opinion of American immigration policy. One would naturally assume, given his harsh attitude toward Roman Catholic countries as being especially ignorant, that he would wholeheartedly support strict immigration quotas for south-eastern European countries, to say nothing of the quotas and restrictions of the pagan Orientals. Quite the opposite was the case, however. Conwell enthusiastically supported open immigration and scathingly denounced American immigration policy. A member of Congress apparently asked the Temple minister to critique current immigration laws. Conwell did not write the booklet but did deliver sermons on the issue. The immigration laws at the time (1923) had limited foreigners of every class and origin all of which Conwell opposed. Not only did Conwell see quota restrictions denying America the larger labor force needed for its burgeoning industrial capacity, but he believed they shortsightedly kept out good men and women regardless of origin who would be useful to America. Moreover, quota policies were perceived as selfish. While restrictions would temporarily raise wages of the laboring class by keeping labor in short supply, they would in time force a rise in costs and hurt production. Such restrictive policies made no sense to him since the country was in a growth cycle with a need for millions of immigrants. America could support "at least two hundred million more inhabitants,"[56] he said. The only legitimate immigration restrictions would keep out the evil, the diseased, the beggars and bring in "only the righteous and the helpful ones."[57] Conwell also criticized America's unwillingness to treat Japan and China as equals in immigration laws. Such discrimination was seen as detrimental not only to the labor needs of America but also to the missionary enterprise because such a policy engendered ill-feeling in foreign Orientals who were potential candidates for Christian conversion.[58] Unlike many of his ministerial colleagues and thousands of Protestants, Conwell did not share the paranoia over the influx of pagans and Catholics (and many didn't make that distinction) into America. Rejecting the fear of those who believed that immigrants served as a fifth column for the papacy he was disturbed to hear "the severest and harshest language used by members of my own denomination [Northern Baptist] concerning the Roman Catholic Church."[59] Such denominational behavior was "un-American and un-Christian and un-Godlike." Roman Catholics in the military had heroically participated with the Protestants in the Spanish-American war, planting the American flag on Cuban hillsides. Hate campaigns against Roman Catholics could only serve to weaken and destroy the American influence for good in the world.

The only immigration issue that concerned Conwell was the number of immigrants in the United States at the outbreak of World War I: fifteen million foreign born in the United States with twenty million children totaling thirty-five to forty million people who had allegiance to some other country. Compounding his concern was the poor economic and social condition of the immigrant, which implicitly could give rise to disloyalty to the United States or at least apathy toward ones adopted land. Not knowing English, confronted with strange customs, living in disgraceful, overcrowded dwellings and segregated in the cities, the poorest classes of Europe came with higher expectations than could be met. These were the conditions that worried Conwell, conditions not the fault of the immigrant. The solution? Each state should allow no more than can be assimilated and cared for but again welcome with open arms, hearts, and minds "every man, woman and child from any foreign land, as long as they can comply with American institutions, as long as they understand American liberty, and American responsibilities."[60]

Conwell's liberal view of immigration at first glance is puzzling but makes considerable sense when one considers his pro-business stance and its thirst for cheap labor. As for the influx of "ignorant" Catholics and pagans, Conwell still assumed the optimistic stance of Protestants that these immigrants would be converted and absorbed into a Protestant America. Moreover, even though poor and Catholic, any immigrant willing to endure the risks and hardships of immigrating to America was made of the stuff this country desired.

These were the foreign policy issues of concern to Russell Conwell. But what is the significance of his delivering his perception of proper foreign policy through benediction? Surely the pulpits across the land heralded much the same message. The attitude of the Protestant clergy in general concerning foreign policy issues is well documented. What is so special about Conwell?

Viewing another dimension of Conwell's ministry is instructive. He was a prisoner to the fame of his "Acres of Diamonds" lecture. Consequently, historians overlook not only the much broader message that he conveyed, including his foreign policy opinions in his sermons, but also the influence of this broader message by virtue of the name recognition he enjoyed due to "Acres of Diamonds" fame. While his influence on shaping popular opinion on foreign policy issues cannot be quantified, one can note that he was in the vanguard advocating American intervention anywhere in the world, motivated by his conviction that the United States was obligated to aid the oppressed wherever they lived. This call to arms, motivated by altruism, was commonly heard throughout the Protestant press of his day,[61] and it is likely that Conwell's influence played a role in shaping Baptist opinion in particular, and Protestant opinion in general because of his prestige.[62]

Temple Baptist was turned into a center of agitation for intervention on behalf of Cuba. Conwell made several visits to the island, established a Cuban Relief Fund, and members of his church volunteered to help with the National Christian Relief Association organized at the Philadelphia YMCA.

Edward O. Elliott, whose tenure as church trustee spans the ministry of Conwell, felt that the Temple minister pioneered the way to United States intervention in Cuba and occupation of the Philippines.[63] Indeed, Conwell's activities in the 1890s on behalf of Cuba have been compared to Henry Ward Beecher's agitation against slavery in the 1850s. Both used their churches as centers of activity for their crusades; Beecher using Plymouth Church as a site for a mock slave auction, and Conwell using Temple Baptist not only for massive rallies but for a reception in honor of Evangeline Cisneros, the daughter of the Cuban leader rescued from a Spanish prison.[64] Before her arrival Conwell prepared the way with the sermon, "The Escape from Cuba." Once the Spanish-American War was won, and so easily, he believed it was the enthusiasm of the clergy and religious press to "uplift, civilize and Christianize the Philippines" that, along with other pressures, caused President McKinley to go along with the tide and take territory.[65]

The Temple minister is interesting also because he so mirrored the times. Whatever criticism one may level at the man, he was acting in character and should be interpreted and enjoyed in that light. Perry Miller's words to those who habitually excoriate Puritans for prudery apply to those who scorn Conwell. Only one thing is worse than praising the Puritans as harbingers of religious liberty, said Miller, and that is to berate them for their intolerance. The Puritans came to this country because they knew they had the Truth. For them to be tolerant was to be theologically wishy-washy and unfaithful to the Call. Similarly, one might say that worse than to give blanket praise to Conwell for his attitude toward the poor is to berate him for his unabashed nationalistic fervor. The marvel is that he was as moderate as he was in the jingoistic context of his times. The Temple minister fit comfortably within two moods of the country as described by Richard Hofstadter. On the one hand were protest and humanitarian reform, populism, and utopianism; on the other were national self-assertion, aggression, and expansion. The motif of the first was sympathy, the second power.[66] As described at the beginning of this chapter, Conwell expresses both moods with some exceptions. His humanitarian impulse justified aggression on behalf of the oppressed. Of course, the residual benefits of material prosperity, power, and prestige of the nation sweetened the pot and indicated the blessing of God upon these holy ventures.

Furthermore, a study of Conwell's foreign policy opinion through sermon is useful because he represented a strong voice that was in the center. As such he moderated two extremes. Rejecting the expansionism of a Josiah Strong on the one hand and denouncing the do-nothingism of an Anti-Imperialism League on the other, he consistently called for intervention, housecleaning, and withdrawal for the sake of self-determination. Clearly, America was to be the moral policeman of the world. And, while his enthusiasm for American power, technical expertise, education, and moral soundness knew no bounds, his nationalism was not a blind fervor devoid of the prophetic. Conwell praised and damned heroes and villains alike.

Finally, Conwell's foreign policy opinions are worth remembering since they expressed values to which much of American Christianity can relate today. Curiously, he advocated such a diversity of foreign policy attitudes that both fundamentalists and liberals today would be able to find points of agreement with him. This is not to say that all of American Christianity can relate to all of Russell Conwell. But there are Conwellesque opinions that will warm the cockles of any New Right adherent, and opinions which even liberal Protestantism and Catholicism will cheer. This might be considered a rather remarkable achievement were we considering the ability to stretch. Since that is not the case, suffice it to say that Conwell represented significant rootage.

The New Right, including fundamentalists and many evangelicals, would admire Conwell not only as the precursor of the power of positive thinking ministry for which he is best known but for some of his values perceived as lost today and needing to be rediscovered by America. Conwell's anti-League of Nations posture, based on the belief Christian America should not be unequally yoked with unbelievers, is a page appropriated by the fundamentalists of the New Right in its opposition to the United Nations. Other pages from Conwell taken by the New Right would be his emphasis on peace through strength and on American responsibility to make the world Christian and democratic, thereby becoming again the Christian moral leader of the world. Until this day occurs, fundamentalists in particular, like Conwell, see the rest of the world as pagan and hence depraved.

Mainline Protestantism and Catholicism would be comfortable with Conwell's belief in close interdenominational cooperation, including working with Roman Catholics for peace in the world and to apply pressure and influence on governments regarding foreign policy issues. Conwell's caution about not being unequally yoked to nonbelievers applies only to non-Christian religions, certainly not to

Roman Catholics. His adamant opposition to expansionism would be applauded by mainliners as would his emphasis on the need to provide education, technical assistance, and food to parts of the world in need.

I suspect also that upon further investigation Conwell represents a ministry that attempted to fuse individual salvation with broader Christian social concern. Conwell could be seen as being sympathetic to "the camps of both the Moodys and the Rauschenbusches."

This, as well as his middle-ground position on foreign policy issues, is significant, it seems to me, for two reasons. The first comes from a common observation that during Conwell's lifetime the Social Gospel movement, which in the 1890s had enjoyed support from both conservative and liberal clergy, split asunder following the Great War on the issues of evolution and biblical inerrancy. The fundamentalists, who formed out of this controversy, showed their aversion to liberals by rejecting not only evolution and biblical criticism but any social teachings of the gospel in deference to an emphasis on individual salvation. It seemed that there was no middle ground any more. It is my observation, however, that Russell Conwell came close to representing a continuation of this middle ground well into the 1920s, at least in his foreign policy statements, and perhaps even in his social philosophy. Martin Marty observes the growing gap between fundamentalists and liberals when he states that nobody tries to stand in the camps of both the Moodys and the Rauschenbusches with the exception of Benjamin Fay Mills, whom he cites as the last of those who try "to follow the joint vocation of evangelist and agent of social change."[67] Benjamin Fay Mills died in 1916, Conwell in 1926. It could be that a significant Protestant voice extended this dual emphasis as well as a moderate foreign policy voice throughout the heart of the fundamentalist movement and controversy of the 1920s.

A second reason this study seems significant stems from a recent observation that the camps of both the evangelist and the social reformer were coming together again as during the Social Gospel heyday in the current Protestant evangelical movement. Such a movement in the 1960s and 1970s was marked by a middle ground position between the ravings of extreme fundamentalists on the one hand who would bring on Armageddon, and the seeming "peace at any price" accommodationists on the other hand. These Evangelicals, represented by *Christianity Today* as one evangelical voice, were distinguished not only by their fusion of evangelistic fervor with calls for significant social change, but also by their moderate position that was horrified by the thought of Armageddon yet still advocated a generally hardline stance against the Communist world. This evangelical position is considered in detail in Chapter 8, "The Nationalism of Moderation."

Perhaps Conwell represents another link in that thin middle ground during a time when most of Protestantism was either in the Moody camp or the Rauschenbusch camp. Perhaps his middle-ground stance in foreign policy helps to explain why at one time he had a foot in America's more bellicose side and at another time lashed out at inordinate pride, calling for national repentance and humility. And perhaps Conwell represents that thread nearly connecting the Social Gospelers of the 1890s in all their breadth of emphasis with the evangelicals of the 1980s.

Russell Conwell's ministry may surprise those who have viewed him narrowly. Moreover, while on balance he leaned on the political continuum a bit to the right, he showed surprising flexibility and good sense for his day, and understanding him helps us to understand ourselves just a little bit better.

CHAPTER 4

One Way, One Truth, One Life

She was "intelligent, beautiful, exquisite."[1] This is how J. Gresham Machen described the one woman in his life whom he might have married—but she was a Unitarian. This metaphor reveals a lifetime mentality of consistency with the perceived Truth.

Whether this mentality represents foolish consistency—said to be "the hobgoblin of little minds,"—or a trait to be honored as representing theological correctness is not the subject of this chapter. Rather, it is to declare that J. Gresham Machen displayed a unitary face of Protestant nationalism—unambiguous, uncompromising, unequivocal, regardless of public or private cost. Ned Stonehouse, Machen's sympathetic biographer put it: "He [Machen] could be counted upon in the public and conspicuous arenas of conflict but also in the utterly private relations of life to be true to his dearly-bought convictions."[2] His convictions cost him ministerial standing in the Presbyterian Church, and probably a marriage, and led to his resigning as professor in 1929 from an increasingly liberal Princeton Seminary.

His fundamental convictions were certainly not from any ignorance of liberalism. He faced the best that liberalism could throw at him. A very significant part of his education included study at Marburg and Göttingen universities where he was immersed in Higher Criticism under such liberal theologians as Adolf Julicher, Johannes Weiss, Wilhelm Herrmann, and W. Bousset. His German experience represented a veritable theological earthquake of near catastrophic proportions. It took him eight years to rebuild the structure of his shattered worldview edifice. However, this time the rebuilt structure was more like an indestructible blockhouse (and some would say, about as aesthetically pleasing), impervious to any future assault.

When Machen recovered from German influence (he always admired German scholarship), he came to realize the devastating effects of Higher Criticism on biblical infallibility. Accordingly, he was obsessed to vigorously defend the Scripture through "historical sources and a 'common sense' interpretation [to him] of their statements."[3] Through this process he became convinced of the historical reliability of the biblical record, and he dedicated his life to criticizing the modernist position.

Upon resigning from Princeton, he and some colleagues established a new seminary in 1929 at Philadelphia, called Westminster Theological Seminary. He served there as a professor of New Testament until his death on 1 January 1937. Two cardinal principles of the seminary were: final authority of the Bible, "a plain book addressed to plain men and . . . it means exactly what it says," and Reformed Theology as expressed in the Westminster Confession of Faith.[4]

While intelligent, Machen was also predictable. Were America to buy into his perception of its role and mission there would be no crisis of identity, no ambiguity, no complicated formula to deal with the reality of pluralism, no question on how to address the world's great religions—which to him were not religions to begin with.

Not as overtly political as the Radical Right of the 1950s and 1960s or the current New Right, which all give him reverence, he still gave a clarion warning that the America of the 1920s and 1930s was moving headlong in an un-American direction. His consistent message to America was what today we would call libertarian. Decentralization, whether for the nation, state, or church, was the American way spawned by the American Revolution.

He displayed a curious mix of accepting the inevitable diversity of thought which comes from pluralism and noncoercive decentralization, and an open advocacy of intolerance and disassociation toward wrong political and theological thinking. He favored decentralization to ensure freedom to believe and to propagate the one, true, correct way that should be accepted by all—all people; Americans, Chinese, Japanese, Australians, Hotentots—*all*. Like the Baptist Walter Rauschenbusch, and the Roman Catholic Cardinal Gibbon, Machen, the Presbyterian, supported freedom of expression in the public forum and religious toleration. And like them he was hoping and expecting that in this free market of ideas the Truth—God's Truth as revealed through the Westminster Confession—would be accepted by all and become the standard for all. The only problem—Machen could not get along with his own Presbyterian Church.

With clear opinions on American values and how to preserve them, Machen excoriated Franklin D. Roosevelt and the New Deal program as representing the antithesis of American values. The president had sent a letter dated 24 September 1935 "to representative clergymen" around the country, which included Machen, addressed with his misspelled name, requesting information about local conditions in the community, and how the government could better serve the people. The letter also expressed hope that recently passed Social Security legislation giving aid to crippled children, unemployment insurance, and old age pensions, be carried out "in keeping with the high purposes with which this law was enacted." The letter further expressed hope that the "Works Program" provide employment at useful work, to the benefit of the unemployed and the nation.

Machen's response was instant and unequivocal. In a lengthy letter dated a mere four days later (28 September 1935), Machen expressed opposition to Social Security legislation "and to the other distinctive features of your program" because they are "inimical to liberty and honesty." As for being inimical to liberty, "you [Roosevelt] have used the distress of the people in order to sell them into slavery by placing them under a permanent system of government supervision and conflict." Compulsory government insurance was alleged by the Westminster professor to make paupers of all. On the contrary, argued Machen, the American way would be to assure the individual citizen "that if in good times he lays by a store, for himself and his family, against evil times to come, such savings will be kept intact and the distinction will never be obliterated between the man who has saved and toiled and man who has not."[5]

Machen seems to have been oblivious to the megamillions lost in savings leaving helpless those millions of people who had in good times "stored . . . against evil times." He did concede support in emergencies for the destitute, but far better from the community or state than "from a remote and centralized bureaucracy." Such government support was to be avoided "with might and main."[6]

As for Social Security and the New Deal being inimical to honesty, Machen accused Roosevelt of breaking down the sanctity of public and private contracts and encouraging the view that obligations are to be kept only when convenient. Rather than declaring openly and honestly that the government could not meet its obligations as an individual does in an honest bankruptcy, the United States government repudiated its debts through the "might makes right" principle. Such behavior, said Machen, has caused the far greater injury of "depriving our country of its reputation for honesty" to say nothing of the "reckless waste of its material resources."[7] The greatest of all injuries perpetrated by the New Deal policy was moral injury when "dishonesty is officially declared to be the policy of the government. . . . The people will naturally be encouraged to think that an equal dishonesty is allowable also in private life."[8]

In an Open Letter to the President, Machen elaborated even more on the moral peril facing the United States, declaring that the country "stands morally upon the brink of an abyss" and that moral decay is far more perilous than decay of potatoes, corn, cotton, or slaughtered pigs. And, Mr. President, apart from God "no such thing as living morality, integrity, goodness or truth" is possible. No other way to God exists than "through Jesus Christ, His Son, Our Redeemer, Who shed His blood and poured out His soul to save us from the very thing that now spreads ruin about us: the consequences and the pollution of moral evil, and more shortly, simply sin." Of course, conceded Machen, the human objectives of the New Deal to relieve distress and care for the aged "are shared by all right-thinking men." But the method, Mr. President, to do this is wrong. The right method, sir, is to lead the American people to repentance for from repentance comes forgiveness and from forgiveness comes strength and grace for the good life. "Call upon our nation, yes, in spite of its diverse inheritance of races and creeds, to join you in a return to God through the shed blood of the Cross. Lead our nation back to God, so that we shall again be a truly Christian Nation!" If you do this Mr. President, you will have a place in history above secular statesmanship. You will be considered the greatest leader the American people ever had. "To lead us thus in national repentance would be a glorious act. But better still it would be right. Will you do it, Mr. President?"[9]

No ambiguity here. The message transcended the pluralism of the society, and clearly linked uprightness and prosperity as the solution to relieve the distressed and care for the aged.

Machen's response to the president's request was greeted with a hail of letters and editorials uttering excoriations and praise for the Westminster professor's position on the New Deal. Heywood Broun's editorial in *The World Telegram* proved to be among the most scathing. Said he, "J. Gresham Machen is no doubt benevolent even though he would rebuke the sales girl for failing to amass her pennies against a rainy day, after the manner of Miss Barbara Hutton. But still I seem to see the kindly cleric in smug surplices beaming upon the Daughters of the King while they prepare mixed pickles for the poor on Christmas."[10] Accusing Machen of ignoring the teachings of Jesus on the responsibility of the wealthy to the poor, Broun continued: "According to the economic theology of J. Gresham Machen, it should have been the first duty of the state to protect this admirable young fellow [Story of the Rich Young Ruler, Mark 10:17–22] in his property rights and to assure him that no matter how great the distress about him his own wealth would be kept inviolate lest class distinctions be diminished."

If J. Gresham Machen had been in Judea beyond Jordan, "he would have sent the young man away rejoicing. But another preacher back then said, 'Go and sell all that thou hast and give to the poor.'" Machen, said Broun, apparently feels, like Cain, that he is not his brother's keeper, and there is divine sanction for vast inequalities of wealth. Then, Broun's final salvo, that since Machen was a New Testament professor at a seminary "I trust that there is someone. . . to point out to the young theological students that they must make their choice between the words of Jesus Christ and those of J. Gresham Machen."[11]

To Machen's credit, he faithfully responded to all correspondence, most in person, and did so with patience toward his enemies and genuine gratefulness to his supporters. His responses revealed his politics, his view of America, and his prescriptions for its betterment. To Mr. Broun the response was crisp and to the point in suggesting two ways to get rich men to give to the poor: one, force them, and two, induce them to give through love. Arguing that the latter was the way of Jesus, Machen reminded Broun that the Rich Young Ruler was told to "sell all thou hast and give to the poor"; that Jesus did not say to the poor, "Take the goods of that rich young ruler by force, sell them and distribute them among yourselves."[12] We have here, said Machen, the difference between the ethics of Jesus and the ethics of Communism.

Responding to a woman who had experienced undeserved misfortune and who excoriated him for his position, Machen expressed sympathy for her plight but maintained that a New Deal program would create far greater injustices and tyrannies in the society than current conditions. "Because one thing is bad . . .," said Machen, "is no reason why we should rush blindly into something that is vastly worse. . . . Despite all the injustices that prevail in civilized society . . ., they do not begin to be so bad as the hopeless treadmill of the collectivist society."[13]

Responding to his supporters, Machen wrote that FDR was a dangerous man who was plunging the nation into bankruptcy, that his (Machen's) position was biblical, and that the Social Gospel orientation of the "so-called Federal Council of Churches of Christ in America . . . [was] very harmful in many ways."[14] Somewhat surprisingly, in response to persons who accused him of being a Republican, Machen declared himself a lifelong Democrat because the party had favored states' rights as opposed to centralization. "The very thought of the Republican Party," wrote he, "has been abhorrent to me all my life. I have been a lifelong Democrat. That is the reason why I am so much opposed to President Roosevelt. He seems to me to stand for the direct opposite of everything the Democratic Party properly stands for."[15]

Machen's consistent call for decentralization and individual responsibility as the American Way was seen in his vigorous opposition to the proposed Child Labor Amendment of 1924. The amendment was alleged to empower Congress to control all labor of persons under eighteen years of age whether in factory or on farm, home or school, paid or unpaid labor. Worse still, it allegedly authorized the government to take any child away from parents who violated the law to "see to it that its 'labor' in connection with education or otherwise is in accordance with the provisions of whatever law might be passed."[16] It would control the most intimate details of family life and in a few years would be in the hands of a centralized Washington bureaucracy. It would, said Machen, "threaten the U.S. with tyranny similar to Russia." It would place power in the hands of a remote and irresponsible bureaucracy which "is not philanthropy but the coldest and most heartless cruelty."[17]

Supporters of the amendment indicated that no court would so interpret the law. Moreover, they observed that the Child Labor Amendment authorized no more power to the federal government than that which already existed with the states.[18]

Such assurances were no comfort to Machen. No state, said he, had the right under the Constitution "to prohibit all labor of all persons up to eighteen years of age." And even if the courts were unlikely to interpret the law as they could to give the federal government and the courts such power was too great a risk and inappropriate. Still further, to place such power in the hands of the federal government violated the autonomy of the states which "is at the very foundation of our American freedom."[19] If the Child Labor Amendment is passed, mused Machen, the Constitution would be destroyed. But what else could one expect since the Roosevelt administration treats the Constitution of the United States as a "dead letter."[20] And, so much of our constitutional system of government had been to all appearances jettisoned by Congress and the federal administration. Lamenting the alleged moral breakdown found in FDR, the Supreme Court, and Congress, a discouraged Machen wrote: "No substitute has been found for honesty."[21]

An organization dedicated to defeating the Child Labor Amendment and other federal proposals, to which Machen gave time and money, was the Sentinels of the Republic. Machen served as a member of the Executive Committee of the Sentinels which claimed a national audience with the central office in Washington, D.C. The stated purposes of the Sentinels readily revealed its libertarian bent along with claims of having true knowledge of constitutional principles. Implied was that those not in agreement, specifically New Dealers, were less intent on preserving a free republican form of government in the United States.

Specifically, the purposes of the Sentinels of the Republic were

> To maintain the *fundamental principles* of the American Constitution; To oppose further Federal encroachment upon the reserved rights of the States and the individual citizen; To stop the spread of Communism; To prevent the concentration of power in Washington through the multiplication of Administrative bureaus under a perverted interpretation of the General Welfare Clause; To help preserve a free republican form of government in the United States.[22]

The Sentinels acknowledged deep divisions in American society between those who supported the New Deal and those who believed economic and financial reforms "should be accomplished only within the frame of our system with its basic guarantees of local self-government, personal liberty and private property."[23] In a somewhat surprising statement, but consistent with a libertarian philosophy, the Sentinels said: "We have with difficulty freed ourselves from the prohibition of the Eighteenth Amendment and should have learned our lesson never again to surrender to Congress the power to invade the rights of States and their citizens, especially in a matter of such local and parental concern."[24] In keeping with their strict states' rights advocacy and their sensitivity to criticism that only a cruel scrooge would oppose protecting children from abuse, the Sentinels declared that the issue was not whether to protect children but who should do it (not the federal government) and how extensive the authority (not over the home, farm, or nonpaying jobs).

Machen not only publicly ascribed to the tenets of the Sentinels but also gave cosmic and ethnic significance to it, warning that the "planned" society had been the foe of liberty for over two thousand years: "Against it stands our Anglo-Saxon tradition with its guarantees that the individual possesses inalienable rights and shall never be made a mere means to the ends of the race or of the State."[25]

Machen traveled to various states on behalf of the Sentinels to aid forces opposing the Child Labor Amendment. Concerning the Pennsylvania fight over that state's ratification process of the amendment, Machen in a losing cause wrote 164 individual letters to State Senate and House members, most sent by special delivery, and he sent nearly 100 individual telegrams to legislative members.

A losing battle, also, was fought with the Presbyterian Church, U.S.A., which supported the amendment. Sadly the Church is so un-Christian, he said. If adopted by the nation the amendment will "go very far . . . toward the destruction of the home and of the wholesome and delicate things that remain in our life in this country."[26]

The Princeton professor expended similar energy against the proposed federal Department of Education, although with a slightly different rationale. While he opposed the Child Labor Amendment on the grounds that the federal government was intruding upon state authority, to say nothing of private family affairs, he especially opposed a federal Department of Education whose standardization of education would allegedly carry with it violence toward tolerance, diversity, and the voluntary principle.

In a speech before the Sentinels, Machen declared his opposition to such a centralized system because it represented the ancient principle in Plato's *Republic* that education is an affair of the state, that it should be standardized for the welfare of the whole, that children belong to the state, and that the state must provide education for the survival of the state. Said he, this is inimical to liberty and contrary to the principle emanating from the genius of the Anglo-Saxon idea of government, which provided for voluntary association, meaning the right of people to join groups that propagate their own views "however erroneous they may be thought by others in the field of religion or in other spheres."[27] This meant "the most complete tolerance on the part of the state over against all other bodies, religious or social or whatever they may be, no matter how deleterious to the common welfare some men may think that they are."[28] This was a very strong, clear statement for tolerance in a pluralistic society.

It seems somewhat ironic, however, that a man so insistent on absolute Truth in Jesus Christ only, the acceptance of which was essential for a person's salvation, and applicable to all people regardless of culture, should argue for tolerance, diversity, and the voluntary principle in education. Yet that is precisely the message he conveyed as the American way, any digression from which would subvert the Constitution.

Such a position, while surprising to some, was not necessarily inconsistent with his insistence on narrow absolutes. While urging government-protected tolerance for all views, he urged intolerance toward those not in accord with beliefs within a voluntary organization. Writing in an incredulous voice, he noted that people seem to think a voluntary organization does not have the right to exclude people who hold principles opposed to the organization. Yet to have this right of exclusion was for him "at the very roots of human liberty."[29] He hoped that all men everywhere through persuasion would come to see the Truth as revealed in Jesus Christ and expressed in the Westminster Confession. Since that was obviously not going to occur in his lifetime, he clung to the American way of tolerance, which would give voice to the Truth as he was convinced of it, while conceding that all "false" ideologies and theologies would be heard as well.

A federal Department of Education, then, was seen as threatening to tolerance of diversity in education, including his variation in diversity. Even federal aid to the states for education would threaten tolerance. With federal money and a department would come federal control, a secretary at a salary of $15,000 with a host of officers, and a drive for standardization in education "which would be the very worst calamity into which this country would fall."[30]

Machen saw federal control and standardization of education not only as threatening liberty but also as bad education. Not one to apply business and industrial efficiency (the rage of the 1920s), to education, Machen reminded his audience that standardization was good for making Ford cars, which lamentably were not standardized enough. "Some start, and some don't, and giving a Ford that won't start some spiritual advice won't help. Making every Ford just like every other Ford, if it includes starting, is a good thing."[31]

On the other hand, said Machen, standardization in education was not a good thing. People were not Fords—not mechanical objects. But many denied the distinction between a Ford and a person. They were like H. G. Wells in his *Outline of History* who said a problem of state could be solved with education by doing it more efficiently, increasing ease of communication, thereby being able to accomplish what the Roman Empire could not.[32] Further, they were like the behaviorists who believed "that the human race has found itself out, that it has succeeded in getting behind the scenes, that it has pulled off from human nature those tawdry trappings in which the actors formerly moved upon the human stage, that we have discovered that poetry and art and moral responsibility and freedom are delusions and that mechanism rules all."[33]

Testifying against establishing a federal Department of Education before the Senate Committee on Education and Labor and the House Committee on Education, Machen used homespun humor to discredit applying standardization and efficiency to the education process, which he believed would surely occur with such a department. Efficiency, like standardization, had its inappropriate applications as seen in the story of the tramp who wandered to the fourth floor of a department store only to be unceremoniously bounced to the third floor by the floorwalker. Very soon history repeated itself as the third-floor bouncer sent him headlong to the second floor. Sure enough, within seconds the second-floor attendant propelled him to the main floor and quickly thereafter he was thrown out on the street on his back side, whereupon he said in a tone of deep admiration, "My! What a system."[34]

For Machen, a veritable litany of disaster would befall the nation and its youth were a standardized, mechanistic system applied to education. There would be intellectual and moral decline. "If everybody could be like everybody else, if everybody came to agree with everybody else because nobody would be doing any thinking at all for himself, if all could be reduced to harmony—do you think that the world would be a good place under those circumstances? No my friends. It would be a drab, miserable world, with creature comforts in it and nothing else, with all the higher elements of human life destroyed."[35]

Machen thought that education was already too mechanistic. "Poetry is silent; art is imitative or else bizarre; [and] if you examine the products of present-day education you will have to search far before you find a really well-stocked mind." And, students had no world to unify in the professor's mind. "They have not acquired a large enough number of facts even to practice the mental business of putting facts together. They are really being starved for want of facts." Education taught an "absurdly exaggerated emphasis on methodology at the expense of content."[36]

To correct the perceived malaise of education, Machen called for unlimited competition between state education systems and competition between state schools and private schools.[37] This call for "unlimited competition" even included his opposition to federal help to states to create equal opportunity—equal schools for all. (I found no record indicating Machen's view of *Plessey v. Ferguson* concerning the issue of equal opportunity.) "I am dead opposed to it", said Machen. "Ought you to tell the people of that state that it does not make any difference because if they do not do the thing somebody else will do it for them? I think not."[38] State schools, according to Machen, should have to face competition from private and public schools. That would keep state schools healthy. In the sphere of the mind Machen affirmed belief in unlimited competition. Education should not "conform human beings to some fixed standard, but [should] preserve individuality, to keep human beings as much unlike one another in certain spheres as they possibly can be."[39]

The phrase "in certain spheres" was the catch. While Machen appeared to advocate unlimited competition in education, he clearly hedged his bets to give his agenda for America an advantage on the competition. Apparently exempt from nonconformity of individuals was the Westminster Confession. Everyone accepting this confession would be desirable. While Machen was open to intense study of positions contrary to his own, seen in his immersion in German form criticism, and encouraging his students to do the same, such a recommendation was not for all students, but only for those thoroughly grounded in Reformed Theology.

Machen's advocacy of competition between public grammar schools and private Christian schools was likewise less than even handed. He made no secret of his preference for the private Christian grammar school. Accordingly, he always advocated policy that would automatically place the public school at a disadvantage, stating that the role of the public school "ought to be diminished rather than broadened."[40] By that he meant it "ought to pay just a little bit of attention to that limited but not unimportant function which it . . . is now almost wholly neglecting—namely the imparting of knowledge."[41] Conversely, it ought not to do those things that parents should do, such as provide moral instruction and the like. Said he: "I am opposed to 'morality codes' in the public schools . . . they are vicious." They were acclaimed by Machen to be not only faulty in detail but wrong in principle. They based their morality upon experience rather than on absolute distinction between right and wrong. Despite good intentions "they undermine the sense which children . . . ought to have of the majesty of moral law."[42] Therefore, since the public school was inherently incapable of providing the proper basis for morality it was judged inherently inferior to the Christian school.

Given this alleged inherent inferiority of the public school, Machen's call for competition between public and private Christian schools was absurd. Competition was obviously not for sifting out the best. The best had already been determined. Machen's real concern was that the public school not intrude in what he perceived to be the realm of the parents and the Christian school—the imparting of the Christian religion on a "solid basis." This goal would be thwarted by creating a federal Department of Education and standardizing education.

Machen's views on the superiority of the Christian school were hardly subtle, and they reflected a nationalistic fervor about the role and mission of the Christian school he envisioned for the health of the nation. Writing in 1934 he stated two reasons why "The Christian school is to be favored." It was important for American liberty and for the propagation of the Christian religion. As for enhancing American liberty, Machen cited the then current worldwide attack on civil and religious freedom in Mussolini's Italy, Hitler's Germany, and Stalin's Russia, the last example allegedly being the worst that the world had ever known. Linking these heinous worldwide developments to trends in the United States, Machen warned that people in America were valuing principle less and insisting on creature comforts more, which was resulting in rapid growth of centralized bureaucracy embodied by a proposed federal Department of Education. Such a monopolistic system of education controlled by the state was seen as far more efficient in crushing liberty "than the cruder weapons of fire and sword."[43]

Addressing the second reason for the superiority of the Christian school, the propagation of the Christian religion, Machen first elaborated on the inherent shortcomings of the public schools. While the secular public schools were good in technical education, they were producing a horrible "Frankenstein" devoid of sound Christian instruction. Recognizing that defect, education experts were trying to cooperate with Christian people. But this kind of cooperation, said Machen, was not possible or good. Even if moral instruction in the public schools were based on a law of God and not on human experience as the humanists want, Christians could not support such a program. It would be impossible because if the law of God were proclaimed in public schools to people of different faiths, "it is bound in the very nature of the case to be proclaimed with optimism; and if it is proclaimed with optimism it is proclaimed in a way radically opposed to the Christian doctrine of sin." Furthermore, the fundamental notion by students would be that "if they know this [law of God] they know all that is absolutely essential." But a law proclaimed to "unredeemed persons with such optimism at best [is] only an imperfect, garbled law."[44]

For the same reason Machen opposed Bible reading in the public schools. Recognizing his agreement with atheists and liberals on this issue, albeit for opposite reasons, Machen in a tone of horror exclaimed, "What could be more terrible than . . . reading the Lord's Prayer to non-Christian children, as though they could use it without becoming Christians, as though persons who have never been purchased by the blood of Christ could possibly say to God, 'Our Father, which art in Heaven'? The truth is that a garbled Bible may be a falsified Bible; and when any hope is held out to lost humanity from the so-called ethical portions of the Bible apart from its great redemptive core, then the Bible is represented as saying the direct opposite of what it really says."[45]

As would be expected, a study of comparative religions in the public schools was to be forbidden. To suggest any positive attributes in other religions of the world alongside Christianity, as would be necessary in a pluralistic public school setting, would be tantamount to opposing the Christian religion itself.[46] Not even designating a religion as superior, adequate, or less adequate should be allowed. The issue was between true and false. When a "Christian," said Machen, "admits that he can find neutral ground with non-Christians in the study of religion in general, he has given up the battle, and has really . . . made common cause with that syncretism which is today as it was in the first century of our era, the deadliest enemy of the Christian Faith."[47]

Realistically, Machen knew that the Christian school was not always available to people. In that case he advocated released time for the study of the Christian faith. But this was considered a miserable makeshift since it assumed the public school would take care of one part of life, and for a couple of hours the church would deal with the other part. The true solution was the Christian school, which unified all of life. Acknowledging that "truth is truth however learned, the bearings of truth, the meaning of truth, the purpose of truth, even in the sphere of mathematics, [was] seen entirely different to the Christian [than to] the non Christian; and that is why a truly Christian education is possible only when Christian conviction underlies not a part, but all, of the curriculum of the school."[48]

Noticeable by its absence was any advocacy of or statement concerning tax credits or subsidies to private schools. This is not surprising given his outspoken opposition to most state or any federal involvement in education.

Accompanying Machen's speeches and articles on the necessity of the Christian school for American society was his expression of love and concern for America. "When I utter the word 'America'," said Machen, "I am uttering a word which still has to me a sort of precious and homelike sound. I am hopelessly out of date in this matter . . . but I cannot help it."[49] But this love for America turned to sorrow because of the alleged deterioration of principles upon which America was founded—principles of personal freedom, property, privacy of home, freedom of speech and press, and the integrity of the states "each with its inalienable rights, each with its distinctive features, with its own virtues . . . with its own defects not to be remedied at all unless remedied by its own citizens."[50]

America's turning away from God was Machen's perceived reason for these calamities. The "decay of free institutions" in America was similar to a comparable decline of liberty from the Roman Republic to the Roman Empire two thousand years ago. Clearly, the nation that trampled upon the principles of God was headed for destruction unless it repented. Free institutions were based upon "belief in the living

God" as made known through revelation in the Bible. Belief in God was the only sure and lasting foundation. So went the Machen argument. Incredulously, however, the glory of the Roman Republic was never based upon Machen's living God but rather upon pagan deities. And the final meltdown of the empire occurred with Christianity as the state religion. That anomaly somehow got lost in Machen's argument, as it usually does in similar contemporary arguments.

This aside, to implement these laws of God was to implement the Constitution as interpreted by Machen. This meant that the federal government should be carefully limited to "powers expressly granted it by a Constitution which was not of its own making," with a Judiciary independent of popular clamor interpreting the law alone, upholding the high principles of the Constitution through fair weather and foul. Government was negative power. God did not intend it "to produce blessedness or happiness but . . . to prevent blessedness or happiness from being interfered with by wicked men."[51]

To save the nation, the Christian school was the key. It was the nursery of decency, freedom, gentleness, honesty, bravery, and peace. Christianity should have an education system of its own. Machen admired the Roman Catholic school system because it informed and molded human life. At the same time he predictably condemned their "false" theology. A system like the Roman Catholic's, stripped of its bad theology and replaced with "true" theology, was "the hope of America."

Machen applied his opposition to the centralizing trend in government and education as un-American to the Church Union movement of the 1920s. The Plan of Union, 1920, proposed a federation of churches, "The United Churches of Christ in America." Only churches classified as evangelical were invited to join. Member churches were to retain autonomy, including respective creeds, and to have a supervisory council to deal with questions arising between constituent denominations. The ultimate goal of the plan was organic church union. Such a union would have contained for Machen the same negatives attributed to a federal Department of Education. Yet the Assembly of the Presbyterian Church adopted the plan, much to Machen's dismay.

Machen opposed the movement, not only on organizational grounds—being the libertarian that he was—but on theological grounds as well. Bluntly, he stated that the proposed plan was "anti-Christian to the core,"[52] and if ratified would mean "that the Presbyterian Church will have given up its testimony to the Truth."[53] This plan of diversity within unity would have placed the Westminster

Confession on an equal basis with other confessions represented under the Plan of Union. "Is the Westminster Confession a purely denominational affair [as the committee had so indicated]?" he asked. For Machen it was not a purely denominational affair, but rather a confession that was true. Those who believed it to be true, said the Westminster professor, will never be satisfied "until it has been accepted by the whole world and will never consent to be limited in the propagation of it by any church or union of churches whatsoever."[54] Cooperation, he continued, was possible "even with those who are in serious error with regard to many important matters. But cooperation under the present plan involves unfaithfulness to our Lord."[55]

As for membership in the plan being limited to evangelical churches, Machen scoffed. The definition of "evangelical" was in his view too broad and hence meaningless. It was merely a manifesto of "naturalistic liberalism" failing to affirm the "atoning death of Christ and the supernaturalism of the New Testament as represented in the Virgin Birth and the resurrection of our Lord."[56] Were the committee on Church Union to express a belief in the atoning blood many would withdraw. Those remaining would be the true church. Since all statements of belief since the Reformation among the so-called evangelical participants were seen as contradictory it was "impossible to accept all of them as true."[57]

Clearly, Machen feared a loss of identity of the Westminster Confession in a super church just as he feared loss of identity for the Christian school should education become centralized nationally. In both cases the only hope he had of keeping distinctive truths of the Christian faith (as he saw them) before the populace as to education, and before the apostate portions of the church as to church organization, was to insist on decentralization. He could only hope that in a competitive context, truth would win out. One can only wonder what his views would be on decentralization and competition, were his goals of a Christianized America achieved.

Consistently libertarian throughout his life, Machen displayed similar tendencies before and during World War I. This was rather remarkable given the frenzy of the American populace in general and of the American clergy in particular—both being swept up in the emotions of the time and being willing to centralize government for the wartime effort. While recognizing that in wartime under certain circumstances it might be necessary to conscript for the military on a temporary basis, Machen opposed permanent compulsory military service, and he opposed temporary conscription for World War I since the United States was not being invaded. A resident of Europe for some years, he "came to cherish America all the more as a refuge from the servitude of conscription."[58] And, Britain, which had a voluntary system, proved to him that the United States did not need conscription. After all, their voluntary system built the greatest empire in the world and was sufficient for defense. In short, "Americanism" he said, "is in danger—American liberty and the whole American ideal of life."[59]

Although Machen admired the British resistance to compulsory conscription, he was not impressed by arguments urging Anglo-American solidarity as a rationale to enter World War I. Especially, he was galled that the United States allowed its ships to be stopped and searched by the English. "Alas," he wrote, "The Spirit of 76 seems to be dead at last now in this time when America is tamely submitting to the curtailment of the liberty of the seas for which in better ages she bravely stood, but submitting when not war but merely a threat of trade reprisals would conserve the great principles at stake." The sacrifice of principle for dollars? "It is a far cry from the Boston Tea Party."[60]

As for Germany, Machen had a greater appreciation for things German. Before studying there he had perceived Germany as a government system whose aim was crushing out any democratic tendencies. Upon living there in 1906, he came to appreciate the unique problems Germans faced in maintaining their existence. While repulsed by the way Germans repressed the Socialists, he could see Germany would not support them and their international, nation-destroying goals. Their anti-nation stance, for Machen, was wrong "in the sense that it discourages the old fashioned love of country without which the soul is dead."[61]

Love of country for Machen included the love of landscape. It is perhaps no accident that Machen had a soft spot for Germany since the love of landscape and the fatherland was so much a part of German nationalism. Machen spoke of his love for the American landscape and at first actually commended government management of the White Mountain Reservation wilderness in New Hampshire. He delighted that the region was accessible to lovers of nature without the scars of road building, but by plenty of trails through the forest not "ruined by landscape gardening."[62] But then government will be government, as it proceeded to overmanage the likes of Lafayette National Park on Desert Island with too many roads and scarred hillsides.

Seeing the strengths and weaknesses of both the British and Germans, he liked Wilson's "Peace without victory" speech. "I am opposed to *all imperial ambitions*," he said, "wherever they may be cherished and with whatever veneer or benevolent assimilation they may be disguised."[63] As the United States moved toward war, Machen did not quite keep pace with Wilson, perhaps disliking Britain more than Germany. Speaking of Princeton at the time, he said, "Princeton is a hot-bed of patriotic enthusiasm and military ardor, which makes me feel like a man without a country."[64] Yet, observed Ned Stonehouse, while avoiding the "jingoism and other manifestations of narrow nationalism," his patriotism was "robust and unselfish, single-minded." As such he served his country through the YMCA in France.[65]

As for the post–World War I period, Machen was disturbed at the "vindictiveness and unfairness" toward Germany in America. "The war for humanity," he complained, "looks distressingly like an old-fashioned land grab." He was dismayed even more when the report of the Reparation Commission became known. Fuming, he remarked: "The settlement [Treaty of Versailles] is the result of the devilish French policy of obtaining security by keeping the rest of Europe in starvation. It is a dangerous game."[66]

Curiously, the League of Nations is not mentioned in Machen's articles, correspondence, or biographies of his life. On the one hand, one might expect that he would have supported the League given his approval of Woodrow Wilson's Peace Without Victory speech and the Fourteen Points. On the other hand, it may be that he was reticent to support the League given his consistent and adamant opposition to centralization of authority.

Concerning the whole pre–World War I period and into the 1920s, Machen was disturbed by "a feverish outbreak of '100% Americanism.'" His defense of alien rights was especially noteworthy on the heels of the frenzy of the Red Scare when the United States adopted a hardline position on immigration. Machen again bucked the trend by opposing the enrollment of aliens. Such a policy he believed would lead to "full-fledged European police system established almost before we know it."[67] His opposition to this policy, however, does not appear to have been motivated by any humanitarian motive for the alien, but rather because it would increase the "already alarming bureaucratization of the United States" and require citizens to carry papers and show them at checkpoints to authorities in order to prove that they were not aliens.[68] Similarly, Machen opposed compulsory fingerprinting. Proponents argued that such a policy would knit people together and ensure an orderly life. Quite the opposite, argued Machen. It would extend the bureaucracy, destroy moral fiber, liberty, and choice. The concept was un-American. Europe had done it, especially Germany.[69]

The remedy for the superpatriotism of the era was "the Gospel of Christ . . . a blessed relief from that sinful state of affairs commonly known as hundred per-cent Americanism." The church was as guilty as the society at large with its "greater emphasis upon Americanization than upon salvation in the modern missions program."[70]

Like the nation rejecting the values that had made it the greatest nation on earth, so the church was losing its way with modernism at home and on the mission field. Focusing on the growing modernism of his own Presbyterian Church, Machen in a detailed expose excoriated everything from application blanks for missionary candidates to top denominational executives. The complaints roughly paralleled those leveled at the nation and federal government. The application blanks were raked over the coals because they required the candidate to articulate evidence of being tolerant and flexible toward others with differing views and toward "progress in spiritual truth." Such questions, thought Machen, represented "clearly a high mark with respect to those qualities . . . in the candidates' favor."[71] Missing in the application blank were questions on what one should be intolerant of, such as

> holding fellowship with those who are opposed to the gospel of Christ as it is set forth in Holy Scripture, and whether he himself is clear in his understanding of the great issue between supernaturalism and naturalism, between evangelical religion and non-doctrinal religion. Such a questionnaire, authorized by the Mission Board, because of the choice of questions, creates very plainly the impression that "tolerance of opposing views" includes tolerance for views like those of the Candidate Secretary himself and other signers of the Auburn Affirmation, and that such tolerance is far more valued by the Foreign Board [of the Presbyterian Church] than loyalty to the whole Word of God and unswerving opposition of unbelief that is now so uncommon in our church.[72]

Another inadequacy in the questionnaires to missionary candidates was omission of any reference to eternal punishment for those not saved. "The very mention of eternal punishment," lamented Machen, "is practically unheard of and the motive of fear is regarded as unworthy."[73]

Beyond application blanks and ordination statements, Machen was especially critical of the Presbyterian Board of Foreign Missions and its director Robert E. Speer. Pearl Buck, board member, former missionary to China, and famous novelist, also came in for withering criticism. Machen was not only critical of the board appointing alleged modernist missionaries, but was critical of Speer's alleged waffling on the liberal, conservative dichotomy in Presbyterianism, attempting to mollify conservatives and liberals in order to receive broad financial support for the missionary enterprise. Pearl Buck was excoriated for being a rank modernist, which for Machen was tantamount to paganism. In an article "Is Pearl Buck a Christian?," Machen made it clear that she was not, regardless whether she or the board thought she was. The basis for this judgment was Buck's assertion that belief in the historical Jesus was not an essential prerequisite to being a Christian. Rather, Christ was an ideal and the words and deeds attributed to Jesus retained their value with or without the historical Jesus.

Although Buck's position in this regard apparently made even the board uneasy, it was not about to dismiss the famous personage. Rather, the board apparently expected, perhaps hoped, that Buck would resign on her own. Disgusted with the board's "policy of hoping Mrs. Buck will hang herself seems to me," said Machen, "to be thoroughly dishonest. . . . If the Board is really Christian and desires to remove Mrs. Buck it will not only do so but refuse the money from modernists as well."[74]

When Mrs. Buck did resign from the board, Machen could not leave well enough alone when the board, in accepting Buck's resignation declared her an exponent of Christianity. "On the contrary," said Machen, "it is the most complete negation of Christianity that could possibly be conceived."[75] Reiterating what he had said on other occasions, Machen declared that the doctrines of Presbyterianism or "Reformed Faith" are true, not only for Presbyterians, but "true for all men everywhere since they are taught in the Bible . . . the only infallible rule of faith and practice."[76]

Another issue which set Machen off against the board, Speer, and Buck, was the response these three gave to a highly controversial report, *Re-Thinking Missions*, prepared by lay representatives of seven mainline Protestant denominations headed by Professor William E. Hocking of Harvard, and funded by John D. Rockefeller, Jr. The report, which initially sought to understand why interest and contributions to the foreign missions enterprise were falling off, set out to analyze the nature and effectiveness of Protestant missions in China, India, Burma, and Japan. The study raised such issues as principles upon which the missionary enterprise proceeded; the quality and preparation of missionaries; the relation of Christianity to other religions; evangelism as a technique of soul-winning in relation to schools and other institutions on the mission field, and cooperation and consolidation of administrative agencies at home for greater efficiency. As a cardinal criterion by which to evaluate the missions enterprise, the report stated that the aim of missions should be "To seek with people of other lands a true knowledge and love of God expressing in life and word what we have learned through Jesus Christ, and endeavoring to give effect to his spirit in the life of the world."[77]

That the goal of missions should be to seek the truth with believers of other religions rather than to present "the truth which God has supernaturally revealed and which He has recorded through the Holy Spirit in His Word" was anathema to Machen.[78] The statement simply reflected the "Modernist missionary work [which] consists primarily in sharing an experience, while Christian missionary work consists primarily in proclaiming a message."[79]

Among the ten grave shortcomings listed in the report, four are especially germane to this study. The report advocated "the obscuration or obliteration of the line of cleavage between Christian and non-Christians." It dismissed as antiquated in Christendom the belief that there is no salvation for those who do not receive the gospel and that they face eternal punishment. It advocated centralized control of missions, and it declared that there is truth in every religion calling for Christians to listen sympathetically to adherents of other religions.[80]

While the report caused reactions from dismay to concern to acceptance in the Protestant denominations, any equivocation that there might be some value in the report was roundly condemned by the Westminster professor. Only categorical rejection was acceptable. The reaction of the Presbyterian Board of Foreign Missions to the report was judged by Machen as "woefully insufficient and unsatisfactory" because it registered no ringing disapproval of the report, said that many recommendations of the report were sound, failed to excoriate the report for its omission of mentioning Christ as Savior, His Virgin Birth, substitutionary atonement for mankind, physical resurrection, Second Coming, and miracles.[81]

Machen's criticism of Speer's response to the report demonstrated how utterly unequivocal and uncompromising Machen could be toward anyone who deviated in the slightest from his own position. In a lengthy pamphlet titled *"Re-Thinking Missions" Examined* Speer was quite critical of the report on many of the same issues as Machen. The difference was Speer's attempt to steer a middle course, on the one hand attacking the report to satisfy conservatives, and on the other hand specifically citing issues with which he agreed that also gave comfort to liberals. Like Machen, Speer was critical of the report's omission of the power of prayer or supernatural forces of the Gospel. The report did not state a commitment, positively or negatively, to the deity of Christ, his death, resurrection, or incarnation. There was no avowed acceptance of Christ as God, Redeemer, or Savior, and no consideration of the Apostles' Creed. Speer sounded nearly as categorical as Machen when he stated: "For us, Christ is still *the* way, not *a* way, and there is no goal beyond Him or apart from Him, nor any search for truth that is to be found outside of Him, nor any final truth to be sought in Him who is the Way, the Truth, and the Life."[82]

Speer continued to express that Christianity was not only what Jesus said, but what he did. The life, death, and resurrection was not "to us obscurely figurative or 'unexplained symbol'."[83] This position obviously disagreed with Pearl Buck's liberal statement on the historical Jesus being unnecessary for the Christian faith. Speer went further, declaring that Christianity "is not a religion in the sense of non-Christian religions. It is not a search of man for God. It is God's offer of Himself to men in Christ who was not a fellow seeker with us after God, or a founder of a religion like Buddha or Mohammed, but 'the fullness of the Godhead bodily.'"[84] And still further: "there is nothing of good in any non-Christian religion which we do not already have in Christ."[85]

These statements were not good enough for Machen. In a letter to a Rev. Clarence E. Macartney, Machen expressed his frustration with Speer. He was called "wishy washy," allowing the board to commission "modernists" in the field while at the same time expressing true Christian beliefs personally. As chair of the Board of Foreign Missions, he was trying to mollify both conservatives and liberals for purposes of getting money from both ends of the spectrum to run a missionary program.[86] For Machen, this was unacceptable compromise.

But the career of J. Gresham Machen and his face of American Protestant nationalism were significant on a deeper level. His was a face less ambiguous than most in this study, but still there was some ambiguity. He did have an egalitarian nationalistic side not often recognized, especially in liberal circles. He was, for example, unalterably opposed to any imperialism. There was no such thing as good and bad imperialism as a Reinhold Niebuhr would have it. For Machen it was all bad. This position was clearly revealed in his analysis of J.A. Cramb's *Germany and England*, a gift received from a friend. To Machen that book was shallow, vicious, and cynical in its glorification of British imperialism. The book recommended that all men be given an English mind, an immoral recommendation, thought Machen, in which "the world would be the loser." Further, "Imperialism, to my mind is satanic, whether it is German or English." Broadening the scope of his analysis he saw the ideal among nations to be one of mutual respect and confidence which "has been realized in smaller spheres many times in the history of the world. . . . Why not work to make it universal?" But, alas, such would never be realized "if men like Cramb are allowed to mould public opinion. . . . And despite all ridicule of peace movements," said he, "I cherish the hope that the gospel is going to win."[87]

Also, Machen revealed an egalitarian bent when he expressed outrage at Italy's forced "Italianizing of the Germans in Tyrol."[88] Egalitarian in spirit, too, was his opposition to the Vestal copyright bill making it virtually impossible for scholars to import books directly from abroad. Let the ideas flow freely. And, his opposition to registering and fingerprinting immigrants showed a similar spirit of openness. Clearly an element in him welcomed diversity and debate.

On the other hand, Machen set a framework readily useable for his fundamentalist successors to express a militant Protestant nationalism. Not given himself to bellicose huffing and puffing for the nationstate, his rhetoric, tailored to address the ills of the nation and church, was easily racheted up to levels of shrillness and behavior that probably would not have been acceptable to him.

While Machen categorically rejected coexistence of Christianity with the "pagan" non-Christian religions of the world, his successors rejected coexistence with the Communist world, upping the ante in zealous nationalistic fervor with the call to send the reprobates to their early reward in nuclear holocaust. If not so overt a call to destroy the wicked, others who saw themselves in his train added a premillennial theology (which was rejected by Machen) to proclaim the end of the world imminent in a final battle with the Bear of the North.

While Machen categorically proclaimed the Christian faith as revealed in the Bible and expressed in the Westminster Confession to be the one true revealed religion for mankind, his successors not only perpetuated this perception of their mission but included democracy along with true Christianity as exportable to the world. And, while Machen declared that the Christian faith must be untied from culture, the de facto fortunes of the nation and the church made the separation no more possible than separation between civil and church covenants of American colonial days. Finally, declaring the Christian faith the only true faith for all mankind it was but a mere half-step to declare Western culture in general and American culture in particular as superior to the non-Western world.

Machen not only set up a rhetorical framework readily useable for extension beyond his probable intent, he had his own militant Protestant nationalistic face as well, which has been carried to this day intact. The overwhelming emphasis in his career left no doubt as to his perception of American greatness in the past, what was central to losing this greatness, and what was needed to restore it in the future. He addressed the very same issues regarding the church, with the illness and remedy virtually the same. In other words, the religion and the culture were not separated in the least. America must return to the principles of the Constitution with strict constructionist interpretation, and the church must return to the Bible with literal constructionist interpretation. Constitutional and biblical values worked in harmony, but traditional values and correct theology were being forsaken to the peril of nation and church together. The true American nation and the true church should be decentralized, allowing for local governance and uniqueness. Competition was the biblical and American way—competition in business, ideas, and between schools, Christian and secular—competition in ideas and schools as long as a plural society embraced secular schools and incorrect theology—competition that would enable Christian schools and theological correctness to win the day—tolerance that would enable correctness on that glorious day to be intolerant.

It is perhaps no accident that Machen did not mention religious liberty as the ideal, but rather tolerance. The difference is significant. The former sees diversity as an inherent value. The latter sees diversity as an opportunity to ultimately win over diversity. Religious liberty cannot be given or taken away. It is an inherent right. Tolerance can be given and taken away depending on the conditions of power. Machen, like so many Protestant leaders of the twentieth century, liberal and conservative, preferred, if not a theocratic state, a de facto establishment enabling it to grant tolerance if it felt like it.

I said earlier that Machen had his own militant Protestant nationalistic face carried on to this day intact. Indeed, his writings on public versus private Christian schools were reprinted in 1982 by the Christian School Movement. He was and is looked to as the conservative guru by fundamentalists from Carl McIntire to Wilber Smith to Francis Schaeffer to Jerry Falwell. McIntire was admired by Machen in a letter of June 1934. Much correspondence flowed between Machen and Wilber Smith as "Bible Believing Christians." And Machen made an indelible impact on Francis Schaeffer, who in turn was idolized by Jerry Falwell. Schaeffer was dismayed when Machen was defrocked and hence saw himself as continuing Machen's fight against liberalism and modernism in the Church. He picked up Machen's theme that American Christianity in general, Protestant churches in particular, and the Presbyterian Church specifically "from 1900 to 1936" were drifting from their Reformation source toward liberalism and modernism.[89] Also perpetuated by Schaeffer was Machen's dismay at the deterioration of American civilization in its alleged drift toward socialism and moral corruption. An extended emphasis of Schaeffer's was his warning that Western civilization was losing its battle against Communism because of its moral deterioration. Schaeffer's respect for Falwell was apparent in his citing the Moral Majority as an example of appropriate action to reverse the moral and economic deterioration of American society.[90] And, Falwell's "God Bless America Survival Kit" included Schaeffer's *A Christian Manifesto*.

For these three, Machen, Schaeffer, and Falwell, an essential article of faith was to be born again. As Walter Capps observed, this was a prerequisite to being fully human if "life was ever to possess substantial and enduring worth. . . . And the world itself must be reborn too if it is to become the occasion for any genuine satisfaction or pleasure."[91] Such a prerequisite poses a serious danger to any democracy. The supreme irony of it all is that the man J. Gresham Machen and his followers who loudly proclaimed the benefits of democracy exportable to the world should embrace centrally in their worldview "One Way, One Truth, One Life," which inherently denies democracy or pluralism as a national identity for which to strive.

CHAPTER 5

The Face of Egalitarian Nationalism

"State governments express in group form through their laws and deeds the characters of their members. Their histories are histories of individual state experiments in living which have their own continuity. And no one of these can substitute for any other."[1] These words penned in 1932 by William Ernest Hocking, Harvard philosopher and Congregational layman, affirmed the state to be important, potentially a force for good, with each state being unique in the world. Its power over its citizens enables it to use this power for its citizens, "making achievable the essentially democratic impulse, every man a whole man."[2] The state has the power, rightly used, to enable each citizen to achieve wholeness as a human being. It has the ability to motivate its people to creative activity and on occasion has been a harbinger of liberty.

In preserving its uniqueness each state engages in exclusion and limit. Cultural uniqueness requires "a semi-privacy in the world" to attack "invadedness, [a] chronic condition of modern life."[3] The first duty of the state is self-preservation, and to ensure this it tends to monopolize individual loyalty and to embody the universal in itself. Feelings of exclusiveness are natural. " 'This is friend; this is enemy.' It is futile to decry the moral elevation of such experience."[4] Preserving uniqueness was seen as positive for Hocking as long as the state recognized that as a national ego it resides among a group of contrasting egos (other nations) requiring of each self-respect.

But Hocking recognized that this national self-respect and individuality could easily turn into vicious self-assertion, which gives nationalism an automatic negative connotation. National power had "an extraordinary capacity to mislead its holders."[5] Though written in the early 1930s, this description of nationalism gone awry could easily fit national paranoia anyplace, anytime in the twentieth century. In fact, Thucydides would nod knowingly. There is testing of one's neighbor for 100 percent loyalty, "making life hell" for those who "lack the plumage or disdain the parade." Falsified teaching is fed to children. Teachers and writers are "pilloried who reach out for just truth or better brotherhood, and who admit national error." Immature nationalism regards "criticism of one's country and its laws as treason instead of true patriotism. International relations has no reality beyond polite cover for profitable gain." There is the "specious pursuit of peace for warlike purposes." The "halo of virtue" is used by public officials to obscure all vices from deception to disloyalty.[6]

Even the specific examples Hocking gives of nationalism gone ugly engender a cold sweat. Austria thinks Bosnia would "digest well." The United States "swallows" Texas, and Disraeli takes Cyprus. While these performances were called the "workshop of existence," the means were wretched and indicated incidents of political egoism and the failure of reason to deal with the rights and wrongs of existence, growth, and decline of states. Beyond this, Hocking observed problems of the modern state which flawed its performance. One serious trend he observed as early as the 1920s was a growing selfish pluralism—one that "runs the danger of basing its theory on a social disease"—the social disease being a "multi-headedness" of self-willed segments "which can cause the community to drift into social palsy." It is a pluralism which destroys cohesiveness of the unit, destroys its identity, and shatters the simple unifying essence of a society, institution, or community. It is a "struggle of interests for possession of the instruments of coercion; groups of various sorts getting authority from the factions of human nature which they satisfy, set up as so many wholes and seek public control not as ideas but as private I-wills."[7]

While the drift to selfish pluralism was understandable what with the obstructions, eternal delays, "and the frittering efforts in dealing with wool-headed officials," such stupidities need not be seen as inherent in the state and as justifying multiheaded self-willed pluralism. "Nothing is gained," said Hocking, "by postulating these vices and stupidities as inherent and erecting the answering social malsanity into a social standard."[8] Rather, a sound pluralism values varieties of thought within a society whether expressed by the state or by the church. It is open to discovery of new values, rather than being bound by a legal system "derived from a presumed omniscient absolute." The cause of pluralism is the common cause of all. "It requires an alternate strengthening of the whole and part, not a relative weakening of the whole. . . . They must grow and grow diverse, but they must not grow apart."[9]

What Hocking wrote in theory he applied with remarkable consistency. Acknowledging and celebrating the uniqueness of each state, he applauded the many different nation-states and their contributions to the family of nations. He favored the purest form of egalitarian nationalism considered in this study. While not affirming like Herder that all nations are equal under the eye of God, he came close to it. All had contributed to the whole, some more than others, and each could learn from the others. In no case was any nation-state justified in imposing its will on any other. The individuality of each nation-state was natural and sacred, and hence it was morally wrong for any person to live under a government whose will was alien to his own.[10]

Suppose, suggested Hocking, that a colonial dependency is undertaken in which the economy is improved, order restored, regularity of accounts achieved, and a modicum of Western education provided. Such an achievement would allow any official annual report to "bristle with proud points of progress." But suppose in achieving this, a national art is killed, a culture undermined, and a customary moral life of a people contaminated. Would such circumstances likely be entered into the annual report? Not likely. Yet if governments refused to consider such issues on their inherent value, then governments would be forced to consider them because ignoring them would have worse consequences. Englishman Lord Cromer's frustration over British colonial relations with Egypt in the 1920s served as a case in point. Commenting on the different experiments in living represented in the two cultures, Cromer observed that "Neither by the display of sympathy, nor by good government, can we forge bonds [with Egypt] which will be other than brittle." The conclusion was obvious. Egypt must say of British rule: "These are not my doings, but the doings of alien rulers."[11] With the hindsight of history we know this position to be a central and legitimate motivation leading to Third World nationalism and the end of Western territorial colonialism.

Even culturally similar nation-states, Hocking affirmed, were to be honored, preserved, and celebrated. The laws of England could not fit the German, and vice versa. Swiss codes could be adopted in Turkey, Egypt, or Japan, but they would need to be adapted to indigenous conditions. They could not ever be bodily transferred, in fact, or imposed. The individuality of each nation-state was natural and sacred, and was to be afforded to all other nation-states.

But, while on the one hand rendering one world government a false ideal because of the plethora of unique and legitimate national cultures, Hocking on the other hand emphasized the growing interrelatedness and interaction between the culturally diverse nation-states in the world. Since, in his view, the primary standards of reason and right were universal, he was not surprised to see internationalizing occur in many aspects of human activity. Philosophies and religions born in a corner of the world spread, not because anyone willed it, but because metaphysics is not local. Art starting as provincial, too, had "a spirit which wanders, makes alliances, and begets offspring," becoming the property of all nations. Communication, transportation, the network of international finance and geographical knowledge, all "have brought a shattering, penetrating force to bear on all excluding walls." Elements of world civilization had arrived. Every civilized spot on earth owed most of its "light" to the French or the British. But is it destined to remain only French or British light? he would ask. No, it becomes simply "light," or made into "local light." No more French or British, but Syrian, Egyptian, or Turkish "light." "Ingratitude and plagiarism are, in a sense, the completest success of the international mind."[12]

While Hocking's examples of the "giver" and the "receiver" of "light" invariably reflected his Anglo-Saxon ethnocentrism, his central message must not be lost. The vast increase in international commonwealth confirmed, not obliterated, the separateness of nations. Diversity within unity: both must grow proportionately. The international spirit must grow strong in proportion to its national spirit growing strong. The international order must not diminish the value of the strongly separative national mind, nor must egoism of the state be sharpened to the extent of creating national policy for itself alone. Opposition between the national and the international engages only diseased forms of both, bringing moral impoverishment to both.

Hocking applied his perception of the proper balance between the nation-state and the international community similarly to the proper relationship of Christianity to the other world religions—that is, diversity within unity, Christianity maintaining its distinctive character while interacting, cooperating, and giving and receiving insights. While examining this aspect of Hocking's writings takes us away from the matter of the nation-state and its relationship with the international community and focuses on the proper role of Christianity with the non-Christian world, it is relevant as will be seen to his concept of the nature of the American mission to the world, a mission that was similar in style and purpose for both the United States government and the Protestant missionary enterprise.

In describing a proper relationship between the Christian religion and other world religions, Hocking urged Christians, in their attitudes toward other religions, to withstand the temptation to call good evil or evil good.[13] Gandhi was good, even if a Hindu, possessing the spirit of Christ as evident in his relation to friends and enemies alike. Clearly there could be no sweeping repudiation of the world religions as fake, even if Hocking's way of stating the issue gave Christianity an edge on the other religions of the world. There was increasingly "little disposition to believe that sincere and aspiring seekers after God in other religions are to be damned."[14] No doubt he was addressing J. Gresham Machen's habit of refusing to recognize that the other religions of the world were religions at all. In calling good evil, said Hocking, some think Christianity is the only way—an easy conclusion for those not interested in knowing about other religions. But that is dangerous in being ignorant and overlooking that which is good. Mental isolation leads to misrepresentation.[15]

To recognize good in other religions for Hocking was not to suggest a universal religion reduced to things which religions have in common. Such reduction would lack vitality "and is essentially hopeless" even as one world government was "a false ideal." Nor did it mean the kind of syncretism whereby a religion takes over that something in another religion which does not take root on the original stem. "It is pernicious when it becomes eclectic and characterless as if we were to propose to take a part of Christianity, a part of Hinduism and of Buddhism and constitute a religion. That kind of loose and easy appropriation is no solution of any problem."[16]

But on the other hand a good syncretism was seen as combining the individuality of the religion and a unity with other religions consistent with the original principle. For example, Hocking observed that while variants of mystic experience occurred among the great religions, they were not incompatible. All religions, including Christianity, call for certain discipline. All call for removal from the immediate strain of affairs. All bring a healing gift, recovering a sense of proportion, a certitude of will, a re-creation. There is a tendency, said Hocking, of mystics in various traditions to understand one another.[17]

Having said this, Hocking also tried to reassure his readers that recognizing a core of religious truth in all religions entailed "no loss of the historic thread of devotion which unites each to its own origins and inspirations,"[18] that Christianity had the right and obligation to maintain its essence, to declare what it perceives as true and false, and to be clear in condemning things it does not believe in. At the same time, Christianity must "listen to teachings of other religions with open mind for suggestions toward a better grasp of its own truth." Furthermore, "we have no right to assume that our Christianity is the final form of Christianity and the end of its insight." We will find persons in the Orient "who will teach us much which belong to the growth of our faith."[19]

Hocking maintained that the same kind of diversity in unity should prevail within Christianity. He was consistent in perceiving the limits of pluralism, which paralleled his view of pluralism in the state. His concern over schismatic diversity in the American church was especially apparent; he identified it as a critical problem characteristic of the modern period of Christian history. The Protestant movement had "opened a gate to another freedom far more questionable—the freedom of anyone to identify what he personally sees as the content of his own faith—to identify this with Christianity forthwith."[20]

This modern tendency toward schismatic diversity did not negate for Hocking the essential need for freedom in religion and expression of personal faith, which Protestantism enhanced. In fact, he recognized the need for reforms advocated by most of the sects in contemporary society. But the function of reform "should be a function provided for within the church, not calling for schism, but for self-searching and reconception." But, unfortunately, differences became splits when "those who hold the prior faith think they have the whole truth. . . . On this score I am of the opinion that the variety is far in excess of what is necessary." On the other hand, "variety of expression which is not hostile to the essence may contribute to the life of the church."[21]

To solve the nitpicking embarrassment of schismatic diversity that Hocking saw plaguing the church, a united church was needed in America—not organic union, but rather diversity in unity. Conformity was not desirable but diversity was tragic when "one side claimed infallibility and bitterness and hate emerge."[22]

Remarkable and gutsy, Hocking even applied the principle of diversity in unity to Cold War adversaries during the height of tensions in the 1950s. Anyone who lived in that decade knows firsthand the paranoia pervading American life, from the State Department to the local water department, and how McCarthyism played on suspicion and fear. The United States and Soviet Union were mortal enemies, and some demented minds in America hoped that conflict would lead to Armageddon; the rest of humanity experienced the fear of Damocles' sword and the prayer that it would not fall. Yet in this context Hocking was writing about commonalities between antagonists that could not be obliterated. Even in the dichotomies of capitalism and communism, tyranny and freedom, right and wrong, there were identities that could begin to repair "a seemingly hopeless cleavage." And, to affirm those identities *"Can be neither appeasement nor rigidity."*[23]

Beginning at the most basic level of commonality between the United States and the Soviet Union, Hocking included the desire of being alive "rather than blasted to atoms," of enjoying order rather than chaos, of experiencing full human development, and of participating in a history having significance. Universal, also, was aversion to futility, the demand to know full scientific and beyond scientific truth about the world in which we live, and the place of common human values in a noncommittal universe. These fundamental, common aspirations could serve as a springboard for further understanding between Cold War adversaries, leading to ultimate acceptance of diversity with unity.

As for the divisive issue of communism versus capitalism, Hocking argued that the label was misleading—a phony dichotomy not consistent with the facts. There could be no clear "versus" since each economy clearly contained significant elements of the other. In the so-called Communist bloc there was no such thing as a society of pure communists having everything in common "like Plato's guardians, or some early Christian communes." If they could write to set up a "working tool-using industry," the tools, workshops, materials finished goods "would constitute a common capital. . . . They would thus become a capitalistic communism or a communistic capitalism."[24] If the economy were to move beyond the most primitive agricultural manual labor, there could be no such thing as a non-capitalist communism.

Similarly, a capitalist society did not exist without an element of communism. There was no society without a community of goods and common concern of the whole for the individual. The U.S. economy in particular "has as its background a vast commonwealth, a public domain, a far-flung system of roads, harbors, national forests and parks, reserves of natural resources, a shared general welfare (including with an immense credit an immense debt), all severely limiting the possible results of a free-running private competition." Additionally there was a heavily graded income tax, a tax on corporate profits paid into the public purse implying a compulsory sharing of material fortune. Without calling this condition good or bad, Hocking proved "that we have in neither economy a pure example of its professed type."[25]

The same coming together was apparent in the issue of private versus public property. The Soviet Union, which was supposed to be the first modern state founded on public ownership of property, also found itself "affected by private interest." The United States, having much private property, was "affected by public interest." It ceased to be that a person could "do what he will with his own" in any absolute sense. For each person, argued Hocking, some experience with common property and private ownership was essential for normal growth. Every economic system would find itself under pressure to find room for "*both types of property.*" All ownership societies were compelled to check private exploitation of natural resources. All communal societies were compelled "to alter their collective farming plans to the extent of providing 'home plots' and to revise their communal domestic architecture in order to make place for the mine-not-yours requirement of a healthy domestic and individual mentality."[26]

A mixture of communism with capitalism was inevitable. The proportions of the mixture varied to be sure, and the "versus" existed because the "isms" were used to identify the component of choice. "But if the issue were merely one of proportion it would hardly justify the gravity we attach to it." How much better it would be to listen to Confucius, "giving things the right names."[27] So went the Hocking argument urging diversity in unity.

In Hocking's view, the liberty (U.S.A.) versus nonliberty (U.S.S.R.) dichotomy was also misleading. To be sure, the Soviet Union was more regimented than the United States, but for Hocking the issue was as much one of understanding why the Soviet Union was more regimented as it was the fact. Critics, of course, would say that one can be just as restricted in a regimented society whether or not one understands the "why" of regimentation. But for Hocking the understanding was essential to a sound United States policy that should help massage the Soviets toward less regimentation over time. The key to understanding the Soviet Union's regimented society rested with appreciating the differences experienced by the two superpowers in their respective revolutions, and subsequent reactions of the world community toward these revolutions. On the one hand, the American Revolution was accepted and even admired by most of the world, and therefore the new nation did not experience prolonged external hostility. Only with occasional fears of subversion were normal freedoms of speech, writing, and travel curtailed. The Bolshevik Revolution enjoyed no such acceptance. The Soviet Union from its beginnings had been on the defensive in a hostile world, and with this defensiveness came the corresponding call for incessant loyalty and regimentation.

In time, argued Hocking, as the Soviet Union feels less threatened by the outside world, she will become less repressive toward her citizens and satellites. The bottom line for Hocking was that tyranny was on the way out and would continue to be so, barring war. In the meantime, Hocking perceived the Soviet people to expect and welcome regulation—that a substantial portion of the public was with and for the government's visible and tangible objectives. To that extent the populace welcomed regulation, and to that extent they were *"free because they are regimented."* Recognizing the boldness of such a statement, Hocking hedged his hunch with, "This is my guess, not my dogma."[28]

In spite of these apparent and real differences and his own doubts, Hocking preferred to emphasize existing commonalities, demonstrating that the direction of the antagonists revealed potential for reducing world tensions. He consistently argued that the glib dichotomies drawn between "them and us" were not only inaccurate but needlessly dangerous. He would say the so-called "realists" of the world who dichotomize everything, "twiddling [their] thumbs over the analysis of words and sentences—shrinks from the task of meeting the factual world head-on."[29]

Given these stated assumptions, Hocking had clear ideas on the American mission to the world: a mission of healing. In defining this, Hocking again demonstrated, not only an egalitarian nationalism, but also applied the concept equally to Protestant Christian foreign missions and to the American political mission in Cold War affairs of the 1950s. In both cases his standards proved to be bold, courageous, and very controversial.

Hocking's application of egalitarian nationalistic style to American Protestant missions was best seen in the Protestant laymen's report, *Re-Thinking Missions: A Laymen's Inquiry after One Hundred Years*, 1932, chaired by Hocking. A penetrating analysis of Protestant missionary activity in Asia, it threw the whole Protestant missionary enterprise into an uproar. The report not only evaluated the effectiveness of missions over the previous 100 years but recommended sweeping changes in Christian missions of the future.

The past motives of Protestant missions were judged mixed at best—"noble if not legitimate." Even at that, the appraisal emphasized original motives less than the results of those motives. Initial motives for missions included the spiritual welfare of the Orient with vivid images of a Niagara of souls otherwise going over the edge to eternal destruction, a moral unity of the world achieved through the appealing vision of a worldwide church, and maintenance of inner health and truth in the existing church. Mixed with these were motives less noble, including the love of adventure, ambition, the impulse to dominate, and the will to power, laced with a predatory temper.

Activities of missionaries consisted primarily of preaching and teaching to indoctrinate. These activities were conducted generally in buildings, mostly Western style, and too expensive given the economic conditions of the country. Worship was Western style and hence too alien. Encrusting it all was the high compound wall separating the

Christian enterprise from the community at large. Techniques of conveying the gospel often included deprecating the religion of the host country and dwelling on the unfavorable aspects of its culture. In ignoring or putting down native racial habits, ethical and religious culture, family customs, clan life, art and worship forms, the missionary often put down the nobler traits of the indigenous religion. And, holding "fake" religions responsible for "defects in Oriental society and custom," missionaries compounded the error by linking Christianity to "all the advantages they felt in Western life."[30]

Missionaries, according to the report, should have taken more account of family life as a unit, of the aesthetic appeal so prevalent in Japan especially, and the significance of the existing community. They needed to recognize that "the surrounding religions were religions, and as such were ways of God" and a base from which to build.[31] When conversions did occur, converts were uprooted from the rest of society, making their position the more unhappy since their tutors in the faith were seldom inclined to admit them to full equality. The "clean breach" approach of missions was clearly a mistake. "Its uncompromising attitude toward local tradition, social scheme, religion required heroism in the convert. . . . But the cost in human suffering was like the cost of medieval surgery."[32] Serious, also, was the effect on village life "when interpretations of Christianity by immature minds" tended to sharpen the cleavage between Christian and non-Christian, leaving "a legacy of division in the community."[33] If a new idea were to take root it could hardly do so with an amputation.

A significant reason for "the noble if not legitimate motives" and the clumsy conveyance of the Christian faith by many missionaries was the unreasonable expectations of mission boards in the United States, which in turn were under pressure from church members wanting quick results for the missionary dollar. Americans wanted statistics to show growth—now! This locked the missionary into subservience to the organization which was "dominated by expectations of the board."[34] Also part of the problem of previous missions was the major scandal of Christianity—the confusion due to squabbling over nitpicking issues. Defects on the mission field could be accounted for by the defects at home. The solution? Leave sectarian baggage at home. Reform at home and engage in interdenominational cooperation in the missionary enterprise.

If past motives and strategies of mission were seen as inappropriate, necessitating change, the present (1930s) mandated change even more. The move toward a "world civilization" necessitated changes in foreign mission strategy. The maturity of science dispelled superstition better than did the missionary. More sophisticated minds in foreign parts, not intimidated by authority, emerged with the challenge of critical thinking. There was no important idea that was not now world knowledge. Nationalisms originally hostile to the West were developing in the context of world civilization and culture. These "new nationalisms" were inclusive in learning to take for themselves the universal—not Western— as their own. On this basis "new nationalisms" cultivated distinctive traditions and arts. Orientals were becoming self-conscious and self-directing members of the world community. Still supersensitive to any formal dependence on the West, their cry was to stimulate local goods, philosophy, arts, and religious literatures, to recover some losses due to initial Western depreciation. Additionally, the "new nationalisms" were aware of Western deficiencies and hence more critical of Western institutions and democracy. With the failure of Christianity to Christianize Western economic and political life it was especially important for the missionary to disconnect Christianity from Western culture.

With such momentous change in the world, the question was whether Christian missions were justified at all. The answer was, "Of course." But that was similar to the question, Is America great? or, Does America have a mission? Yes, but in what sense is America great and what is the mission and how is it to be accomplished? The issue required sharper definition of reasons for Christian missions and higher standards of qualification so the missionary could deal with increased sophistication. It also required a rationale devoid of the arrogance, as implied in the declaration of greatness and the call for mission.

Nowhere does Hocking's commitment to egalitarian nationalism show more convincingly than in his rationale for Christian missions. It was a rationale he applied to all proselytizing religions, Christian or otherwise. The justification for sending thousands of missionaries was "to communicate a spiritual value regarded as unique and of supreme importance," to promote "world unity through a spread of understanding of the vital elements of *all* [underlining mine] religion," and to assist the human being "in every way to realize [the] longing for peace, tranquility, beauty and affection." Christians, Buddhists, Shintoists, or members of whatever faith, had "much to learn from each other and much to contribute to each other."[35] This was an obligation, not a choice, for all men.

It followed from this that if foreign countries allowed entrance of Christian missions, the United States should welcome missionaries of other religions. For Hocking, the issue was one of liberty of conscience which sliced both ways. And if conscience were to be alive it must be challenged by opinions that may not be valid. It was "never to the advantage of the state to hold its members to a fixed confessional uniformity nor to protect them from strange ideas."[36] The danger from this was not that people would throw off traditional beliefs but that "they will hold nothing at all except under dead momentum." Religious life is more vigorous "when there is friendly rivalry. . . . Sectarian hostilities strengthen no community." The value to any nation was variety of preaching and teaching and a variety of movements. "Challenging ideas from the outside have an intrinsic and irreplaceable value."[37]

But not all cultures valued liberty of conscience in the Western sense. Nor were all cultures moved by the individual who felt called by God to be a missionary. Rather than consigning such individuals to join the "Jonahs of history," Hocking believed the right to propagate a faith might more effectively be made not on ultimate grounds but on grounds of social welfare. Did the proposed activity in question help or hinder the society? This was a question in which any state would have more than a passing interest since "it is the destiny of the religious impulse to permeate and mold the society, and to become a self-preserving and self-propagating organism in that society."[38] And with permeation came the possibility of injecting both the good and the bad into the host society. Science and technology, a gift from the West, belonged to mankind in the world civilization. But with it came social and philosophical diseases—materialism, for one. For that reason, said Hocking, it would be to the great advantage of any community into which the missionary penetrates to consider what may also be universal in the religious message which had been meeting and curing these evils. "By their fruits" was the pragmatic, legitimate test, making universal acceptance of Western cultural values unnecessary as a prerequisite for mission activity.

Justification for missions carried with it very specific guidelines concerning goals and techniques that revealed again Hocking's egalitarian nationalism recognizing the legitimacy and contributions of world religions. If the objective of missions were total conversion of Asia to Christianity, the objective was inappropriate. The objective must be to plant the seed and leave the rest to the locals.

The process of planting the seed called for effectively using the language and symbols of the local culture to convey the Christian faith. A special learning was also needed to determine when to turn a mission over to locals, given the tendency of mission professionals to indefinite expansion. Ideally, Christianity would allow indigenous institutions to receive and develop the Christian message instead of imposing Western-style institutions.

A practical pitfall of missions was what one might call the technique of killing with kindness, that is, using the ministry to human physical and social needs as leverage to convert the "heathen." Hocking called such a technique "stupid, for it confesses a lack of faith in the power of a genuine religious spirit to make itself manifest without words. . . . Let the mission-giver do his own worshiping and let that attitude of his excite where it will."[39]

Especially difficult for the missionary to accomplish, yet of central importance to mission, as cited in the report, was the ability to learn from and recognize the best in other religions as well as to convey the essence of Christianity. The art of meditation from Hinduism and Buddhism could enhance the Christian experience. But since these religions relied too heavily on meditation, from Protestantism could come activity, mission, and the social gospel. Perhaps Protestantism had relied too heavily on activism, making "too little of the concrete and poetic elements of religion conveyed through all the forms of art; through local setting and ritual expression."[40] Great religions such as Buddhism and Taoism in China had borrowed from each other in the past showing strong resemblances. Christianity adopted the Christmas tree, the yule festival, imagery from the mysteries, and philosophy from the Greeks. And, much of Christianity had been assimilated by other religions not only in modes of worship, hymns, and popular fables, but also in aspects of God, ethical notions, and the honoring of Christ, all without calling it Christianity.

Christianity had a special mission to help end superstition in its own system as well as in other religions by promoting the scientific habit of mind and demonstrating its fearlessness in the presence of science. It could contribute to world religions by adding the element of value and meaning through science. It could work with enlightened members of all faiths to develop a nonsuperstitious conception of providence and prayer. It could in a nonsuperstitious manner even be "prepared with the polytheistic faiths to see God in varied aspects." While God was everywhere, He was also One as Christianity stated.[41]

The best mission style to convey the essence of Christianity was action without words, whereas missions had emphasized words without actions. Rather than some doctrinal formulation of the message spoken from a sectarian view there must be conveyance of an "Eternal Gospel" emancipated from "unalterable dogmas." The standard of preaching was far too doctrinal , a "complicated system of ideas instead of a thrilling way of life." The uniqueness of Christianity was its simplicity. If a Christian theology were too complex it was "too little Christian and too much the artifacts of our Western brains."[42] Any words used must be based on experience rather than on dogmatism or theory. Propaganda had to end, but this did not mean surrendering one's faith or softening convictions. On the contrary, one must be outspoken and sincere in holding what one believed to be the truth yet maintaining a tolerant and open mind. These were hard conditions to fulfill since many had been raised to believe only-way Christianity, the custodian of ultimate and exclusive truth without need or benefit from other religions in the world. Hocking's perception of mission represented the ultimate in an egalitarianism that celebrated diversity in unity.

The implications of egalitarian mission were institution-rattling, goal-shattering, and technique-altering. Mission boards experienced near apoplexy. This reconception meant the riddance of 9-1-1 emergency religion inherently noble in motive to "rescue the perishing" but pathetically lacking in the joy of good tidings. Scarier yet, "Christianity as an organization would lose motive for propaganda based on special access to the 'keys.'" Gone would be the superstitious idea that there is "One divine-human administration of the entrance into life, open to variation by plea, performance, or penance. . . . But it would realize a far more convincing universality based on applying to itself its own maxim 'He that loseth his life *for my sake*, the same shall find it.'"[43] Untouched would be the symbols of historic faiths, but a bonus would accrue with the "growth in awareness of a unity more significant than the remaining differences."[44]

Emerging, too, would be Christianity as a universal religion. Not that all men everywhere would become members of the Christian church as traditional mission goals envisioned, but rather, as in the parable of the leaven, the Kingdom of God is like leaven which a woman hid in three measures of meal till the whole was leavened. With such homogenization the specific name of Christian would not be insisted upon in a coming world civilization.

Christianity's experience with Western modernity had qualified it and required it to take the leadership of leaven in the world. But further leadership depended upon Christian humility, the recognition that as a religion it had not arrived as infallible but was always becoming. This entailed a continuing need for "reconception, learning from other religions and calling for a heightened severity of self-consciousness on the part of all religions."[45] This universal need and universal response by historic faiths "will therefore promote the silent rapprochement of the great faiths, without conceding the differences in historic rootage."[46]

What Hocking advocated in rapprochement among the world's great religions, he advocated between the world's two great superpowers. If his advocacy of diversity in unity between the world's great religions all learning from each other created an ecclesiastical earthquake, his urging for the same rapprochement between the United States and the Soviet Union in the 1950s exposed him to peril from a far larger audience.

In urging rapprochement between the United States and the Soviet Union, Hocking displayed his most idealistic and optimistic self based on his faith in the inevitability of change, the necessity of accepting stages in change, and the conviction that more issues unite people than divide them. Given the historic Soviet distrust of the West, her stated goal of conquering the world for Marxist Leninism, if not through military conquest then through peaceful competition, what should be the United States' mission in the Cold War world? Further, given the assumption that the yearnings of people are basically the same the world over and that there is plenty of space in the world for two superpowers, what should be the United States' strategy to maximize its role in the world?

The role for the United States in the Cold War world for Hocking sounded very much like the role he saw for Christianity as the initiator of rapprochement among the world's great religions. Even as Christianity had the potential to initiate this rapprochement, so the United States was uniquely qualified and obligated to initiate rapprochement with the Soviet Union.

To accomplish this rapprochement called for American humility, understanding, and acceptance of diversity in unity. Humility did not mean giving up right for wrong, but rather having humility in accompanying an *a priori* certainty that might allow a truer perspective of right and wrong. Understanding entailed gaining knowledge of world history and world needs, breaking out of self-absorption. Accepting diversity in unity meant applying excellent general resolutions to particulars. For example, Hocking asked: "Is it not conceivable that the Soviet dream of world-domination, pernicious in its possibilities, *calls equally for reinterpretation rather than for blank repudiation* of its limitless capacity for world benefit? There could be no greater challenge to the latent moral strength of America." Indeed, the real test of national strength was the willingness to "break through vicious circles by acts of creative risk." No nation other than the United States was "so fully qualified in terms of the moral resource demanded for this formidable task."[47]

Clearly, Hocking's perception of the American mission was to break the ice, end the vicious circle, and lead in helping, encouraging, and massaging the Soviet Union to redirect its vast resources and energy in a positive way. The United States role could compare with that of a guidance counselor that attempts to redirect the energy of an unruly, misdirected individual with enormous potential for doing good in the world. "The act [on the part of the U.S.] must be one expressing good faith, and tending to elicit good faith, presumably an act of confidence where confidence has had no prior rights."[48]

Hocking recognized that breaking the cycle of suspicion entailed a risk. But the idealism that motivated the risktaking was predicated on the realism of the alternative. So why not take the risk on the side of good? Placing the alternatives in crystalline form, he declared that American policymakers, with the support of the populace, are either going to have to accept as reality the "cruelties of frightened despots [who are] unable to stand without the support of terror," work around these regrettable realities, and agree where agreement is possible, or *"go to war to undo them*! And such war, though a Holy War, must once again tear open the wounds of a suffering people."[49] This was the moral dilemma of peace—two alternatives neither of which was savory. But one was lethal poison and instant death. Such counsel smacks of the Homeric warning in which even a justifiable argument can be carried too far. In this case "too far" meant nuclear annihilation, which was to be avoided at all costs.

Such counsel in the 1950s was a lightning rod for accusations of disloyalty to the American Way.[50] Hocking obviously was sensitive to the charge. He recalled that it was not traitorous to the democratic faith to join hands with imperial or dictatorial powers in a world war against the threat to international order—an elegant way of saying "they may be SOB's, but they are our SOB's." Why not, then, engage in competition with the Soviet Union not to control the world but to build a better social order? And, there was nothing to keep the United States and the USSR from co-operation in the same region. In Egypt the United States could build the roads and the USSR the Aswan Dam. It was not even a bad idea for the United States to help in the dam project.

To those rigidly against overlooking some of the evils of the USSR in achieving détente, Hocking also reminded that the United States had not been pure in the past with its bad record with Mexico and the cultural if not total physical genocide of the Native American. Implying that the United States had grown morally over the years, a questionable assumption, the same could be expected of the Soviet Union, given wise diplomacy on the part of the Americans. In any case, on a very practical level there was a distinct need for competition between the United States and the Soviets. Destruction of either would destroy competition to the detriment of both superpowers and the world. "Each is ready," he said, "without treason to its own faith, to tolerate the existence of the other in an honest rivalry for achieving the highest material and moral good for mankind." If the Cold War were to be transformed into peaceful competition, "purpose must take precedence of agreement on definitions of right & wrong in particular policies."[51]

Fascinating it is to see the present world condition devoid of the competition Hocking spoke of. He was more right than perhaps he ever knew about the value of diversity in unity, peaceful competition to the benefit of all, and yes, even the value of the strong hand on behalf of order that suppresses a greater evil—that of ethnic cleansing.

To facilitate peaceful competition between the two great powers, the role of the United Nations as the umpire among the pluralism of nations was crucial. The task at hand of "achieving the highest material and moral good for mankind" was no "empire's burden, no white man's burden, no capitalist burden, no communist's burden—it is a world concern. And by rights, the *existing* world union (UN) should assume it and guide its administration."[52] Only the UN could rightly administer lifting of backward regions to self-supporting status, preserving their right of neutrality or choice of affiliation. Again, Hocking's egalitarian nationalism is apparent. The selfish egoistic nationalisms of dominant nation-states must allow the flowering of the backward regions of the world encouraging their cultural and economic development. Such regions could thus fulfill not only their own aspirations but enrich world civilization with their unique contributions.

However, Hocking's conviction that each national identity should be preserved did not mean that just any revolutionary group or dependent people demanding independence and recognition as a nation-state in the family of nations should be recognized. The established family of nations had the right and responsibility to judge the worthiness of such demands based upon universal standards.

This assumption of having the wisdom to affirm or deny the legitimacy of a revolution and subsequent national legitimacy therefrom is one characteristic of nationalistic expression. It assumes a superiority in development, governmental skills, values, and morals that legitimates the rendering of judgment.

While the assumption of this power smacks of arrogance, Hocking's insistence on the existence of this right and responsibility was significantly qualified. No decision, either by a political dependency claiming national self-determination or by a controlling nation-state wishing to deny the claim was to be made unilaterally. No nation could sufficiently judge its own right to independence. The nation not ready for independence generally did not know it was not ready. The claim of being abused by a colonial power did not of itself mean that the abused people were ready for nationhood. It may rather indicate the need for a different guardian.

By the same token "no one state [was] competent to determine the right of any nation, whether outside its borders or within them to independence."[53] If the Philippines were not competent to judge their readiness for complete independence, the United States was not competent on that issue either. Rather, the right and responsibility of judging the claim of any nation to independence rested with all other independent states existing at that time. All independent states had a stake in the settlement of a war or revolution.

Standards in determining readiness for real nationhood and self-determination were considered universal, such as: Was there a significant experiment in living represented in the people seeking self-determination? Was the nation thinking and reflecting to affect the problems of its culture? Were ideas coming out of it? Has it besides its editors, politicians, pamphleteers, orators, also its poets, philosophers, prophets? Is it sound in energy and likely to be pregnant with something of general human value? These questions needed an affirmative response since every state "ought to be an *experiment in living*."[54]

While the standards were deemed universal, they were also deemed by the Harvard professor, hard to apply. It was not an easy task to sort out the natural nations from the construed ones. His observation in the 1950s calling the Balkans "a quarreling nest" with rampant nationalism "mangling the outlook for international economic balance"[55] has an acrid taste for the 1990s. Self-determination for peoples of the Balkans? Who has the wisdom to know how this should play out, he laments. Exacerbating the problem was the United States and the Soviet Union trying to force a remaking of the map without considering the natural aspirations of a people toward nationhood. Motivated by pan-Slavism and competition with the West, Soviets in the Balkans subordinated the dubious spirit of chauvinistic nationalism by imposing their will. The United States sanctioned the demolition of ex-Ottoman Asia into mandates and the later breakup of Palestine, shunting local national aspirations. The problem was to identify the entity which could rightly claim power in the area under question. Failing that—not that good faith efforts were always made—it was easy to succumb to the temptation to smother nationhood under an economic, political formula favorable to dominant parties.

While conceding frustration in such complex issues, Hocking still asserted universal standards to judge the legitimacy of nations aspiring to self-determination. Nations, like individuals, should be subject to a moral code either in determining the legitimacy of self-determination or as in guarding a dependency not yet ready for independent status. Judgments needed to be made in humility. Hocking, the idealist, probably knew as clearly as his critics the difficulty of implementing his idealism.

Hocking relied on similar values in evaluating the world's great religions. Even though he acknowledged the unique contributions of each (advocating that Christians in their missionary fervor not proclaim the truth but seek the truth alongside exponents of the world's great religions), he also believed that judgments on the degree of soundness in a religion were fair game. Distinctions needed to be made between religion of the people and religion of holy men, scholars, reformers, and intelligent laity.[56] Measure of soundness in religion was more the piety of the common people and less the theologies. Also, a less pleasing picture emerged in temples and priests, commercialism, ignorance, and routine performance of ritual. While superstition was not peculiar to any religion, to what extent had enlightenment, the scientific habit of mind in treatment of disease, agriculture, personal and political fortune, permeated the religion and society? By these standards a religion was to be judged. And on these issues Hocking clearly implied a positive influence of Christianity and the West on the other great religions of the world. Western economics and science drove out superstition.

In Hocking's egalitarian nationalistic style, all cultures, religions, nations had their contributions and unique features. All had something to contribute, all had something to learn, all had more in common than not in terms of aspirations, but not all were equal in enlightenment under the eye of God—just almost. Distinctions needed to be made, likenesses and differences observed, and judgments rendered on the basis of universal standards.

Hocking's assertions of universal standards (acknowledging relativism in implementation) between men and nations are apparent in his consistently applying these standards, whether addressing mandates from the League of Nations in the 1930s, the proper role of Christian missions in foreign countries, the relationship of Christianity among the world's great religions, or the desirable role of the United States in the Cold War era of the 1950s. His consistency in addressing these somewhat diverse but related situations is remarkable when one considers his life experience of World War I, the 1920s, the Depression 1930s, World War II, and the post–World War II and McCarthy era.

What is more remarkable than his consistency per se is what he championed in the face of continuous opposition. His positions never paralleled the spirit of the times. His survival pays tribute to the academic freedom in America which allowed him to deliver an unpopular message. The response to the inquiry *Re-Thinking Missions* was disappointing. Board secretaries, while friendly to the report, were killing it with silence. The YMCA, YWCA, and the Student Volunteer Movement dropped the original plan to study the report in the colleges. Charles J. Ewald, the secretary for the National Committee for the Presentation of the Laymen's Foreign Missions Inquiry, wrote to Hocking that they could not expect much if churches were going to be responsible for studying the report.[57] And only since engaging in a study of William Ernest Hocking over the past couple of years did I realize with some fascination that the report *Re-Thinking Missions* was not required reading in my missions classes at a liberal—for that day—divinity school in the mid-1950s. I understand why in part. The slogan at the time was "The sun never sets—on a Berkeley grad" said by an Aussie who was the president of the divinity school; and he would know. The Laymen's Inquiry enraged some, worried others, puzzled many, was applauded by an elite, and would probably have been used by most, had they read it, as a convenient rationale to cease supporting missions. To counsel missionaries to seek the truth with exponents of other religions rather than tell them the truth did not square with what they had been taught since being read to as children out of Edgermaier's Bible Stories. And it did not quite confirm the ringing chorus "and the darkness shall turn to the dawning and the dawning to noonday bright." The reaction of radical voices was totally predictable. "The antithesis between being lost and saved is lacking in the Report," thundered A. Z. Conrad, a Billy Sunday–type speaker. "It is an unspeakable blessing that some of the mission boards find their treasuries empty, because they can't send any more modern mission- aries to undermine missions." Even more explicit was Dr. Otto Bartholow, Methodist pastor from Mt. Vernon, described as a huge man with great white hair flowing out behind a massive dome. The report has "used weasel words," said he, "biting like a weasel. . . . Modernism is the same squat toad it has always been and the Report merely unmasks it."[58]

Hocking's advocacy in the 1920s and 1930s of self-determination for budding nation-states that had something unique to offer the world cut against the grain of world politics—a nice idea, but one that fell to the economic and political demands of dominant nation-states. His faith that people are more alike than different, that the general popu- lace of a country could moderate their recalcitrant leaders, that these same leaders had enough at stake to avoid nuclear destruction which made an American push to break the cycle of fear and suspicion worth taking—was as far removed from the climate of opinion in the 1950s as possible.

As for comparing Hocking with other personalities in the larger study, his egalitarian nationalism is nearly unsullied by any other form of nationalistic fervor. His approach clearly differed from Reinhold Niebuhr's. Niebuhr assumed that all human collectives were evil and that the best to hope for in a world full of such collectives was for one less evil to moderate the behavior and damage done to humanity by a more evil one. Hocking, on the other hand, rejected that the state was inherently evil, preferring to emphasize the natural and practical necessities that would draw adversaries together. These changes would come about slowly, "the mills of the gods grind slow," but the process of history figured heavily in his scheme. This made avoidance of war and especially nuclear confrontation essential to allow the natural and practical necessities time to heal.

The position most antithetical to Hocking's represented in this broad study was that of J. Gresham Machen, who was beside himself in frustration over the Laymen's Report. Machen and Hocking represent not only a clinic in opposites but also the most consistency in their oppositeness. This certainly illustrates the total lack of consensus among two Protestant leaders on central issues affecting the American people, their identity as a people, and their proper role and mission in the world. Between these two extremes ranged a plethora of Protestant opinions concerning American identity.

However, Hocking's writings on international politics, received much praise in many scholarly journals of his time. The Middle East press especially appreciated his advocacy of self-determination for national cultures in which unique values were realized. However, many of the United States journals in the 1930s in praising Hocking's nobility of mind were couched, as in one review which wondered if "It is perhaps too much to hope that the descriptive and the theoretical can be completely unified."[59] In other words, could Hocking's idealism be applied effectively to world realism? While acknowledging Hocking's awareness of the "ugly facts" of international hardball, on balance the Harvard philosopher's approach was called an "international Kantianism" dependent upon the best of the Western world in dealings with its dependencies.

The relevance of Hocking's idealism for the 1950s was also questioned, and most effectively by Charles H. Malik, a former student of Hocking's who presided over the General Assembly of the United Nations in 1959. Hocking, then eighty-eight years old, had requested his former student to respond to four propositions, the gist of which were included in *The Strength of Men and Nations* published in 1959. The extensive response by letter began and ended with the expression of "an eternal bond between a student and his master" and my thoughts "are hardly worth a penny." In between, the student graciously qualified the propositions if not totally dismantled them.[60] Citing Malik's response to one of Hocking's propositions illustrates the cleavage between the theoretical and the descriptive in the Cold War 1950s context. His response was devoid of any ideology and placed before his former teacher some very brutal, scary, human realities that I think Niebuhr would have endorsed in his system of Christian Realism.

To paraphrase the proposition: Because the United States and the USSR are coming together in ideology and economics, "pure hostility is out of order for men of intelligence. . . . Competitive coexistence becomes the rational basis of policy." And, no longer can any great power seriously profess world conquest as its goal. The USSR does not intend to administer the United States any more than vice versa.

Presuming to interpret Hocking's meaning of "pure hostility," Malik suggested the phrase could mean either extermination of the enemy by nuclear war if necessary, or it could mean hostility aiming at the extermination of the enemy by every means short of nuclear war. The first possibility was admittedly rationally improbable, but from a Communist viewpoint the second possibility was an absolute necessity, proudly claimed "a million times." And, while the first possibility was rationally improbable, three chilling qualifiers made it possible as well. Men were often not rational, and even if they were, they sometimes miscalculate. Finally, in a technologically revolutionary age it was possible to neutralize the enemy, tempting it to strike. Given the harsh realities of both ideological permanence and stated goals of world domination, the Communist call for peaceful coexistence meant coexistence only on terms that would ensure ultimate Communist victory. So ran the Malik response.

While the stakes were considerably fewer, the ground rules desired by fundamentalists and even by some liberal Protestants were similar in kind if not degree to those of Communist strategy cited by Malik. For example, while J. Gresham Machen advocated free competition between public and private Christian education, he advocated the preclusion of the same curriculum in both systems by limiting public education to the industrial arts. Such limits would automatically tilt the field in favor of private Christian schools. But with the kind of ideological conviction cited by Malik embraced by both Communists and fundamentalists the strategy of tilting the field was essential since both claimed absolute truth and predicted ultimate and inevitable victory.

It is apparent that Malik's perception of the descriptive was somewhat removed from his former teacher's theory. Hocking was aware of this criticism long before receiving Malik's letter. However, while steadfastly maintaining that his idealism was realistic, he also knew the cruel reality that the Cold War could blow up into nuclear holocaust, rendering all his writings literally immaterial. In a letter to Eugene Exman, editor of Harper & Brothers, the publishers of his forthcoming *Strength of Men and Nations*, Hocking wrote, "if friend Dulles gets us into war over the Quemoy-Taiwan situation, the present document [*Strength* . . .] loses its point."[61]

But still he was indefatigable to the end with his vision of the proper American role in a dangerous world. At age eighty-eight he was offering his services to John J. McCloy, United States representative on disarmament, willing to travel to Washington, D.C. if needed. In letters from April to September 1961, he offered suggestions of strategy to the State Department, using the expertise of Pearl Buck on how to get Chiang and Mao to agree without loss of honor to either. And, his numerous articles on Middle East policy got the attention of dozens of senators and representatives, such as Christian Herter, Warren Magnuson, Leverett Saltenstall, Henry Cabot Lodge, Jr., Owen Brewster, Hubert Humphrey, and Brooks Hays.

In whatever decade he wrote, his emphasis was consistent. He championed the rights of dependencies to become independent when certain "universal" standards were met. He urged preserving unique cultures in the world, warning the dominant powers not to obliterate these cultures in the name of "progress." He always urged, whether addressing domestic religious, economic, or political issues or international relations, that the distinction be made between diversity in unity, and rampant, individualistic, selfish, divisive pluralism. He, more than all other faces of nationalistic expression observed in this broader study, advocated a genuinely level playing field among adversaries. While others expressed the rhetoric of peaceful and fair competition, Hocking not only believed and lived this but also taught there was much to learn from diversity and much to give to it from one's own worldview. This was the epitome of his egalitarian nationalism.

CHAPTER 6

Nationalism and the *Sword*

And the three companies blew the trumpets and broke the jars, holding in their left hands the torches, and in their right hands the trumpets to blow; and they cried, "A Sword for the Lord and for Gideon!" . . . When they blew the three hundred trumpets, the Lord set every man's sword against his fellow and against the army.

—Judges 7:20–23.

This scripture passage was the basis for creation of the periodical *The Sword of the Lord* in September of 1934, by a colorful, fire-eating, hellfire and damnation fundamentalist preacher and evangelist, John R. Rice, who was the founder and editor for forty-six years until his death in 1980, dominating and overshadowing all contributors to the periodical. The statement of purpose heading each issue of the *Sword* reads, "An Independent Christian Bi-Weekly standing for the Verbal Inspiration of the Bible, the Deity of Christ, His Blood Atonement, Salvation by Faith, New Testament Soul Winning, and the Premillennial Return of Christ. Opposes Modernism, Worldliness, and Formalism."

Rice was Southern Baptist trained for the ministry but early on left the Southern Baptist Convention because, as his biographer Fred Barlow put it, "he could not serve Christ and denominational bosses— and he would not!"[1] Such parting was not surprising since throughout his career he was outspoken, spectacular, sensational, and fiercely independent. His periodical was independent of any institutional support, relying on subscriptions and underwritten by contributions from fundamentalist churches and individuals. Some of his sermon topics give an indication of his style, which made even the Southern Baptist Convention leadership nervous. A sampling of his homiletical renditions include: "The Man Who Went to Heaven Without Baptism, Without Joining a Church, Without a Mourner's Bench, Without Even Living a Good Life"; "Wild Oats in Dallas—How Dallas People Sow

109

Them and How They Reaped"; "The Dance-Child of the Brothel, Sister of Gambling and Drunkenness, Mother of Lust—Road to Hell!"; "Coming for Supper—And Not a Rite in the House"; "Filling Stations on the Highway to Hell."[2]

A list of writing contributors to the *Sword* is a Who's Who in extreme fundamentalism, including Dr. Bob Jones, Sr., Dr Bob Jones, Jr., founder and president of Bob Jones University, respectively, Dr. Curtis Huston, who succeeded Rice as editor of the *Sword* in 1980, Dr. Carl McIntire, founder of the fundamentalist American Council of Christian Churches, and the Reverend Jerry Falwell, a leader of the Moral Majority. For a time Dr. Billy Graham served on the *Sword of the Lord* Cooperating Board, and Dr. Rice on the Board of Trustees of Northwest Schools, of which Dr. Graham was president. Graham's revival messages were printed in the *Sword* along with the revival statistics of the Graham evangelistic campaigns. However, when Graham endorsed the Revised Standard Version of the Bible the relationship cooled, with Rice asking his subscribers to pray for Billy. When Billy actually cooperated in revival ventures with affiliated churches to the National Council of Churches, and refused to accept a New York City crusade under sponsorship of only evangelical, fundamentalist churches, "and refused to be classified as a fundamentalist—opting for the terminology 'Conservative-Liberal' or 'Constructionist' John Rice took his stand against his brother he loved in the Lord so that he himself might walk in the way of 'thus saith the Lord.'"[3]

In sum, the periodical title, the litany of sermon topics, along with the list of writing contributors to the *Sword*, suggest that Rice and his periodical represented the epitome of zealous nationalistic expression among Protestant publications and leaders. Further analysis revealed no surprises. There is in his message the driving force to redeem the world by destroying the wicked, viewing the world in manichaean terms. There is the unequivocal biblical literalism that is used to spell out in detail what America and the world should be, and advocating a separation from all who disagree.

Without the sense of anxiety in a Jerry Falwell or the finesse of a J. Gresham Machen, Rice led with the chin, shrill, unsophisticated, and uncomplicated. All the characteristics of a zealous nationalism are revealed as in a gaudy neon sign emblazoned across a black sky. Rice would probably have approved of such an image to convey his message. The world is black with sin with the neon message of God's redemption and judgement plain for all to see through the Bible. Every issue covered by the Sword revealed at all times an unambiguous position. "Right was Right and Wrong was nobodies' Right." The editors of the *Sword* knew that they expressed the truth of God as revealed in the Bible. The publication did not have the slightest tendency to agonize over controversial issues in a pluralistic American society.

Employing a selective biblical literalism that sanctioned classic zealous religious nationalism, Rice often spoke of Old Testament wars on behalf of God to justify modern-day and potential wars at the perceived behest of God. The God who thundered the call to slay the human-sacrificing Canaanites was the same God thundering for the annihilation of human-sacrificing Communists.[4] Moreover, on a near equal to Scripture for Rice was D. L. Moody, who "was not a pacifist either."[5] Not even the emergence of atomic power could change the position of the *Sword* in the slightest. Right was right after all, with situational ethics out of the question.

This kind of biblicism applied to American foreign policy called for and justified a belligerent course of action for the United States government in its foreign policy. Armed with Scripture, the *Sword* called the Iranian seizure of the American embassy "America's most degrading, devastating disaster" in which "a pygmy holds a prince hostage."[6] Abram of old rescued his brother Lot from Dan, smote his captors and returned safely with his brother, all their goods and women.[7] The Israelis in 1976 made a successful raid in Entebbe, Uganda, and brought their citizens triumphantly home. The West Germans successfully raided Mogadishu, Somalia in 1977, freeing their hostages. But, "America had no David to face the giant of the godless Philistine host,"[8] irrespective of President Jimmy Carter's confidence that the mission would be successful. What went wrong? The Bible supplied a ready answer for the fiery independent Baptist. "For which of you intending to build a tower, sitteth not down first and counteth the cost, whether he has sufficient to finish it?"[9] The answer was simple. President Carter had scaled down the operation for humanitarian reasons. But humanitarianism does not convince the Ayatollah Khomeini, reasoned the *Sword*. The failure of the mission rested in the fact that the president was "unwilling to use force in the conduct of foreign affairs."[10] In this lesson was the call for a strong military to smite the heathen.

Other reasons for America's failure was its turning its back on such friends as Taiwan, "our only friend in the Far East," and instead directing its love and loyalty to the socialist republic of China. The United States allegedly had done what God judged Israel for doing long ago. America was "as a wife that committed adultery, which taketh strangers instead of her husband. . . . Thou givest to all thy lovers, and hirest them, that they may come unto thee on every side for thy whoredom."[11] America had prostituted herself in her foreign policy by hiring her lovers.[12]

The most curious use of biblical literalism to judge American foreign policy was the *Sword*'s attitude toward the Panama Canal treaties of 1979. With the Eighth Commandment, "Thou shalt not steal," the *Sword*'s basis for rejecting the treaties, one is hard pressed not to remember the boast of President Teddy Roosevelt, "I took Panama" and marvel at the wondrous use of God's Word for direction in specific present-day issues. Without debating who pilfered what, the *Sword* identified the thieves as the Panamanians and the United States Senate, the latter which "by 68 to 32 . . . voted to give away the canal and associated property" in spite of many public opinion polls which showed the great majority of the U.S. public strongly against doing so. Speaking for the *Sword*, Captain G. Russel Evans USCG (Ret) declared: "This is stealing. The Canal and Zone belong to the people of the U.S.—paid for and developed with U.S. tax dollars."[13] As for Panamanians, they were "not satisfied with just stealing the canal." They demanded the buildings and facilities adjacent to the canal, restored and in useable condition, with all moveable equipment thereon becoming the property of Panama. Moreover, they demanded retroactive jurisdiction over businesses and individuals in the zone since 1971 for tax purposes. "Unfortunately the U.S. State Department has not challenged these claims. . . . The treaties are immoral."[14]

The *Sword* also applied biblical literalism to glorify American capitalism in general, often condemning the New Deal as a threat to capitalism in particular. According to Rice, the Bible clearly taught that the profit motive was good. While not overlooking the centuries of church history during which a social, cultural, and economic climate of opinion rejected the profit motive, Rice simply treated them as the dark ages of the church when God's Word was not followed. The biblical justification of American capitalism was the Ten Commandments, which Rice believed taught a free economic order declaring a man's right to own property. The Eighth Commandment, "Thou shalt not steal" meant that a man had the right to use his property as he saw fit to make a profit. The "profit motive is not a sin."[15] Moreover, it was the profit motive that made America great. In praising the profit motive, Rice was tireless in excoriating the New Deal as the antithesis of the profit motive with its "soak the rich" schemes that denied the fruits of labor to the productive members of society.

More than a justification for the profit motive, or direction in foreign policy, the Bible, according to the *Sword*, was the source of all knowledge for all of present-day living, complete with specific instructions. Since the subject of abortion was a present-day issue, there had to be relevant biblical instruction on that issue however implicit it might be. Knowing what needed to be found, John B. Ashbrook, a fundamentalist minister writing for the *Sword*, drew out Jeremiah 1:5 for the situation. "Before I formed thee in the belly I knew thee; and before thou camest out of the womb I sanctified thee, and I ordained thee a prophet unto the nations." Ashbrook then expounded: "Do you get the point? God considered Jeremiah a person and ordained him a prophet while he was still what we would medically call a fetus. Is the fetus a person? You just read the answer from the Bible. Add to this," continued Ashbrook, "the Sixth Commandment, Exodus 20:13 'Thou shalt not kill,' and you have the biblical answer on the abortion issue."[16]

The application of this alleged biblically based position was a condemnation of the National Council of Churches, and especially the General Conference of United Methodists and the United Presbyterian General Assembly, all of whom supported a move to take abortion procedures out of the criminal code by placing them in the medical practices regulations. "In other words," declared Ashbrook, "these clergyman recommend that abortions be considered like tonsillectomies and appendectomies."[17]

To accomplish its vision of a godly nation, the *Sword* did not wish to rely only on its declarations concerning moral issues, but advocated the use of government power to make the United States truly a nation under God. While on the one hand opposed to big government, on the other hand it advocated government legislation of morality. Government, it argued, must keep its hands off the churches, and it should not display any semblance of planning the economy or of implementing social reforms. It should not tax big cars since that would "hurt our missionaries [who] do God's Work," nor force school busing for integration since that wastes gas. But government should clamp down on television profanity, smash pornography, harass homosexuals, abolish abortion, outlaw smoking in restaurants and airplanes, close shopping areas on Sunday ("to save gas"), and keep possession of marijuana in the criminal category.[18] Government involvement in these and other similar moral issues should be on all levels, local, county, state, and federal. The *Sword* even called on all of its readers to write to President Carter requesting his support in these moral issues.[19] There was no question about the *Sword*'s unambiguous position on the right and the wrong, even if it was not consistent on the appropriateness of big government in American society. It was all to make America as God meant it to be.

A key institution, along with government, needed to make America great was the public schools. However, the *Sword* reserved some of its harshest criticism against this institution. While much of the nation wrestled with the status of its public schools, the areas of strength, its ills, the regional differences, and the various proposed solutions for a better educational system, no such agonizing occurred with Rice and the *Sword* since the issue was considered quite simple. To Dr. Don Boys, an educator writing for the *Sword*, the public schools of America were "poisoned pots" and the poison was humanism. School boards needed only to get rid of humanistic teachers, humanistic textbooks, and humanistic administrators, and then, putting God and discipline in the classroom, the problem would be solved. Even identifying the poison was simple since humanism was seen as a creed without variation. Moreover, it was taught by all public schools, from Alaska to Florida, Maine to California, Texas to North Dakota. To demonstrate such a sweeping generalization let the *Sword* through Boys speak for itself: "The humanist has made it clear where he stands. He says in his statement of belief: 'I believe in no God and in no hereafter. It is immoral to indoctrinate children with such beliefs. Schools have no right to do so, nor indeed have parents. I believe that religious education and prayers in schools should be eliminated. I believe that denominational schools should be abolished. I believe that children should be taught religion as a matter of historical interest, but should be taught about all religions including humanism, Marxism, Maoism, Communism, and other attitudes of life. They must also be taught the objections to religions. I believe in a nonreligious, social morality. Unborn babies are not people. I am yet unsure whether the grossly handicapped are people in the real sense. I believe that there is no such thing as sin to be forgiven and no life beyond the grave with everlasting death.' That is the heart of humanism. . . . This is the heresy that students are getting in *all* [emphasis mine] public schools and in some Christian schools."[20]

An example of humanism in English textbooks, representative presumably of all English textbooks used by all public school departments of English in the United States, was a text entitled *Mixed Bag*. Said Boys, "In *Mixed Bag*, a high school English text, some examples of poetry are offered. 'Roses are red, violets are black, you'd look better with a knife in your back!' That seems to encourage violence. Well how about the following cultural offering for high-level thinking? 'Boys are made of greasy, grimy gopher guts, marinated monkey meat, French fried parakeet, all that vomit rolling down a country street. Wish I had a spoon.' Such humanism is degrading our schools and destroying our society. The religion of secular humanism is being taught in all the public schools, even though it is unconstitutional to teach

religion in tax-supported schools and the United States Supreme Court
has ruled on two occasions in 1964 and 1969 that humanism is religion."[21] In a more magnanimous mood, Boys declared that present texts
"in most public schools are riddled with sex, vulgarity, and violence.
They are anti-American, anti–free enterprise, and anti-parents."[22] The
reader who takes the *Sword* seriously is left with no doubt about the
nature of humanism, and its place in American public schools.

The complex was made simple yet again by the *Sword* in its consideration of the relationship between socialism and communism.
Ambiguity was not in the *Sword*'s vocabulary on this subject because
it saw no real difference between the two to begin with. Franklin D.
Roosevelt, while not a Communist, gave communism an entree by
creating the socialist New Deal.[23] Socialism, according to Rice, was
defined as a democratically controlled economy that went by such
various names or phrases as: "economic democracy," "a more Christian economic order," "social justice," "economic brotherhood," or
the "social gospel."[24] Since Russia claimed to have all of the above
features in her society, they were obviously Communistic features,
and therefore inappropriate in American society. If the *Daily Worker*
were to take any position on an issue, one was duty bound to take the
opposite view or one was considered soft on Communism. When the
World Council of Churches condemned the use of atomic power and
encouraged disarmament, the *Sword* condemned the WCC because
they were "naive do-gooders, who are un-American, unpatriotic, short
sighted and irresponsible, following the line of the *Daily Worker*, a
Red paper."[25] Again, nothing was ambiguous, and issues and people
could be easily identified as either good, bad, or deluded.

Armed with biblical literalism, which spelled out in detail what
America should be, it followed that those who perceived such absolutes (the saved) should separate themselves from the unsaved.[26] The
periodical insisted on the practice which was nearly elevated to a doctrine. According to Rice, there were only two plans for salvation. The
first was salvation by human works believed and practiced by Catholics, liberal Protestants, Hindus, and Mohammedans. "It is all one
thing" with these religions. The second plan was salvation by the
blood of Christ subscribed to by all Bible-believing fundamentalists.
According to the *Sword*, "you are not to have those two kinds of seeds
in the same field."[27] One qualification to this precept was that it
referred only to "hitching [believers with nonbelievers] up for the
Lord's business." That was forbidden. But the practice of separation
did not apply to riding on the same bus with the unsaved, trading at
the same supermarket with them, unless the market sold beer, riding

in a train with a conductor who was not a Christian, or working in a company in which some employees were unsaved. "The ox and the donkey may be in the same pasture, they may even walk together."[28] But they must not join together to do the Lord's work.

What appeared to be a contradiction to this rigid call for separation was not only the *Sword*'s immersion in political issues, using literal interpretations of scripture to justify their political affinity, but also its support of politicians whose religious affiliations represented communions historically and bitterly anathematized by Protestant fundamentalists in general and the *Sword of the Lord* in particular.

One such religion historically hated by the *Sword* was Roman Catholicism. Typical of the *Sword*'s traditional view of this major communion was an editorial in which the *Sword* graphically described the dangers of the Roman Catholic system to the safety of the United States. "Romanists Still Claim the Right to Burn Heretics" declared the editorial title. Quoting a Father Gallagher, chaplain of St. Anthony's Boys Home in Albuquerque, New Mexico, the editorial continued: "If one of its members [the Roman Catholic Church] goes wrong it has the right to cut him off, to excommunicate him, and if need be *burn him at the stake*. . . . The Church has the innate and proper right independent of human authority to punish her guilty subjects with both spiritual and temporal penalties."[29] The editorial went on to warn that New Mexico was not only the state where Roman Catholics were behind senatorial vote frauds, but also the state where the "Romanists" were plotting to extract special privileges at the expense of the Protestant majority. Worse still, it was the state that to prevent nuns from teaching in the public schools had to take court action. In other editorials and articles throughout its fifty years, the *Sword* has accused the Roman Catholic Church of being idolatrous, blasphemous, hostile to the Bible, full of shame, bigotry, and intolerance.[30] The alleged goal in such Romanist activity was to take over the governments of the state and the nation through Catholic officials.[31]

However, fear of the Roman Catholic Church miraculously vanished with the rise of Roman Catholic senator Joseph McCarthy and his anticommunism crusade of the 1950s. Editor Rice wrote in 1954: "We are for the work Senator McCarthy is doing in exposing Communists infiltrating our government. We agree with the commendation of Mr. J. Edgar Hoover, so long head of the FBI. He says: 'I've come to know Senator McCarthy well, officially and personally. I view him as a friend and I believe he so views me. Certainly he is a controversial man. He is earnest and he is honest. He has enemies. Whenever you attack subversives of any kind . . . you are going to be the victim of the most extremely vicious criticism that can be made, I know. But sometimes a knock is a boost."[32]

The danger of popery suddenly emerged in traditional fashion with the potential presidential election of John F. Kennedy. In this case "Politics is not the issue," declared Walter Hanford, assistant editor of the *Sword*. Rather, "The issue is a religious one. . . . What is actually at stake in this current campaign is our whole basic idea of liberty and freedom of worship. We believe it is impossible for a man to be thorough going Roman Catholic and to follow the dictates of his religious leaders, as good Catholics are expected to do, and still be faithful to the obligations of the president of the United States."[33]

Curiously, however, religious liberty and freedom of worship was not an issue in the 1964 election since the *Sword* supported Senator Barry Goldwater and his Roman Catholic running mate William Miller. Lest one conclude that Miller's Roman Catholicism was not an issue since he was only a vice-presidential candidate, one need only recall the *Sword's* rejecting the Johnson-Humphrey ticket of 1968. John R. Rice opposed Hubert Humphrey for vice-president because "a man who is elected Vice president has a thirty percent chance of becoming President according to past records." The thirty percent chance that Miller would have had of becoming president did not seem to bother Rice.[34] Whereas if Humphrey, with his alleged Socialist persuasion were president, a litany of disaster would ensue. Humphrey's election would include a turning loose of the liberals, "the friends of Russia, the friends of Red China, those who want to make peace with Castro, those who want to disarm America, who want to give the United Nations power over our country, who want to increase federal power over the states, increase public spending and public debt. Humphrey is a dangerous left wing liberal."[35]

A left-wing liberal was perceived to be more dangerous than a right-wing Roman Catholic. The *Sword* was always consistent on the dangers of the political left if not consistent on the dangers of Roman Catholicism. Adlai Stevenson was "Unitarian, Socialist and pro-Truman, and hence should be rejected in favor of Eisenhower." In fact, "Christians everywhere ought to vote for the Republican nominee, ought to send Republicans to Congress and so free American from the hateful, immoral, unchristian New Deal administration which threatens to throttle private enterprise."[36] The *Sword*, in a typical display of invective, asserted that the New Deal administration gave East Germany to Russia, welcomed the Communists to Japan and "sold the Christian president Chiang Kai-shek down the river and insisted that he allow Communists to come in and take a controlling part in his government. Roosevelt, Truman and Acheson, with the help of Democratic leaders, turned China over to the Communists, did it willingly and gladly. They suppressed the facts from the American people because they were personally favorable to Socialism which is the guiding principle of the Communists. Christians should remember that the New Deal administration kept Alger Hiss high in the federal government when he was a traitor. . . . Remember that it was Senator Nixon, the present Republican vice-presidential nominee, who led in exposing Hiss, though he was endorsed by Truman, by Dean Acheson, and Adlai Stevenson. . . . Remember how Truman fired America's greatest general, MacArthur, even as he now derides General Eisenhower."[37]

Hence, the *Sword* was not only immersed in the politics of the nation in spite of its attitude of separation, but the religious affiliation of public officials, even though they be Roman Catholic, clearly took a secondary importance to their political philosophy. But consistency in itself was not an issue of concern to the *Sword*, especially if such inconsistencies were to be cited by the heathen. What mattered to the *Sword* was whether or not the Lord's will, as the periodical perceived it, was being accomplished through the efforts of the faithful. Hence, inconsistencies in political and social philosophy, in separatism, in attitudes towards the dangers of Roman Catholics to American life, or in the practice of biblical literalism, were all merely examples of the Lord's anointed doing battle with the "wisdom of this world." "For the wisdom of this world is folly with God."[38] If the God of Israel could make the sun stand still or part the waters of the Red Sea, it was certainly no startling or incongruous feat for God to use an anathematized Roman Catholic or two for His purposes in the twentieth century. Hence, the *Sword* was impervious to the views of all, both in and out of the Christian tradition, who did not share in its view of what God was saying to His people through His Word.

Whatever one may say about this zealous nationalistic face represented in Rice and the *Sword* the influence of this perception of America was considerable. Rice's writing and editing was not limited to publishing the *Sword*, but by the time of his death included over 200 different titles of books and pamphlets with a combined circulation exceeding sixty million copies. Added to this prolific record was the circulation of the *Sword's* 150,000 subscriptions, including readers in every state in the union, 100 foreign countries, and forty thousand preachers, evangelists, and missionaries. The influence of Rice and the *Sword* was obviously formidable.

The *Sword* must be viewed as a major leading publication for zealous religious nationalism, and it was comparable to the voice of the American Council of Christian Churches and Carl McIntire, the *Christian Beacon*. Both publications featured articles from each other. Rice was published in *Christian Beacon* and McIntire in the *Sword*. Moreover, both treated not only the same political and social issues of the day, but posited similar conclusions as well. They were both far to the right of the New Evangelicals in the sense of rejecting any cooperation with moderate or liberal churches or denominations, and in the sense of steadfastly adhering to a premillennial theology.

Together they constituted a very influential force not only among the thousands of independent evangelical fundamentalist churches across America, but within denominational churches as well. Within this latter quarter, the *Sword* is subscribed to by thousands of church members who belong to mainline churches, and who, through the influence of the *Sword*, sometimes represent what might be described as a fundamentalist fifth column within churches and denominations. This kind of influence affected not only monetary contributions to denominational churches adversely, but was undoubtedly influential in pushing those churches that happened to have a substantial number of members under the influence of the *Sword*, to a more conservative theological, social, political, and economic stance.

CHAPTER 7

Nationalism and Realism

One must understand the "brutal character of the behavior of all human collectives, and the power of self-interest and collective egoism in all inter-group relations."[1] The above statement represents the consistent base out of which Niebuhr's inconsistent conclusions concerning the nation-state as a human collective and the international mission of the United States unfold throughout his incredibly productive life. His conviction of the inherent limitation of human nature, imagination and intelligence, and the tendency toward prejudice, egoism, misuse of power, social conflict, and passion devoid of reason was unchanging. The human condition, thought Niebuhr, "lacks the humility to accept the fact that the whole drama of history is enacted in the frame of meaning too large for human comprehension and management."[2]

Not that the human species should be annihilated for such depravity. Individuals could rise above the herd and moderate the "brutal character" of collectives. With excruciating effort, individuals could reconcile with individuals in a group. But reconciliation between groups is virtually impossible. This is why such relations "must always be predominantly political rather that ethical" the determinant of success being related, to the proportion of power possessed by groups in question.[3] To moderate these potentially exploitive situations, some enlightened few would occasionally see through a glass darkly that power "cannot be wielded without guilt since it is never transcendent over interest even when it has the best intentions of supporting universal standards."[4]

Niebuhr rejected out of hand a liberal faith in the evolutionary process to bring about positive change in the collectives of the world. His censure of the optimistic, automatically progressive mentality of early-twentieth-century Social Gospelers is well documented. He rejected, too, the idea that man could control his destiny; both bourgeois and communist cultures shared these illusions, but their conquest of nature through science, which was supposed to save humankind, threatened to be a "cure" of annihilation, worse than the "disease" of human misery. Saving humanity by destroying it became a real possibility.

Among the human collectives, the nation-state is foremost in brutality. It is held together more by force and emotion than by mind. Even national disavowal of selfish economic aims does not preclude cultural imperialism bleeding through the white gauze of high idealism. The unwary individual, too, is swept along in the process. Paradoxically, patriotism "transmits" individual unselfishness into national selfishness as the individual projects his egoism through state policy. "A combination of unselfishness and vicarious selfishness in the individual . . . gives a tremendous force to national egoism."[5]

The nation-state employs hypocrisy for self-deception and for outside consumption by the international community. Self-deception is essential if the state is to claim the loyalty and devotion of the individual "as his own special and unique community, one which embodies universal values and ideals."[6] For its deception of the international community, the nation-state enjoys only a temporary advantage until its hypocracy is unveiled unleashing outrage in the world at large. This hypocrisy affects the simple and the cultured citizen alike. For the simple citizen it works as though he were a part of a mindless herd. Men of culture swallow the line, though less consciously, "because their own inner necessities demand the deceptions even more than do the simple citizens."[7] Since they cannot give themselves to merely national aspirations, they must cloak the machinations of the state in the surplice of universal values. Though the state's values are relative, they are seen as universal. Such rationalization makes these men of culture even more dangerous than the simple citizen. The most graphic example of this hypocrisy, according to Niebuhr, was the hypocrisy and sentimentality justifying the Spanish-American War—the hypocrisy of government, and the self-deception of the intellectuals. Along with claiming to protect universal values, the nation-state asserts its uniqueness in defending civilization and culture. The nation-state sees itself as endowed with the aura of the sacred, the messianic, and religions, which claim universality, are easily appropriated by national sentiment and "melded into the whole for legitimation."[8]

With its messianic view of itself, the nation-state, according to Niebuhr, unlike some individuals, places survival and power above nobility. "All nations . . . lack the capacity to prefer a noble death to a morally ambiguous survival."[9] It is nearly impossible for the nation-state to give up national interests for the good of the international community.[10] Because its will to power constitutes the nature of man, it is all-pervasive and cannot be eliminated. It is "sin in its quintessential form."[11] Claiming rational ends, it lives on emotion. Asserting universal ideals, it has relative values. Declaring a unique and messianic mission, it intends common self-interest. Feigning peaceful altruism, it craves power. Though being the dominant religion for modern man, it is the most irreligious. And God, seeing the irony, laughs. "He that sitteth in the heavens shall laugh. . . . He laughs because 'the people imagine a vain thing.'" God's laugh is "'derisive' having the sting of judgment upon our vanities in it."[12]

But the nation-state must not be dismissed as a total wash, even though it is the worst of human collectives. While its egoism is to be expected due to human nature, such egoism is not to be accepted as normative since it is possible for the nation-state to discover enlightened self-interest. In fact, "a narrowly conceived pursuit of national interest is poor politics . . . as well as immoral."[13] It would appear that for Niebuhr positive results can accrue from selfish motives if a nation-state is smart enough to know the difference between wise and unwise selfishness. Society can and should be meaningfully improved. Niebuhr does not demand the impossible, that a nation sacrifice its own interests. Rather, "the highest morality possible for nations . . . [is] a prudent self-interest, which knows how to find the point of concurrence between its interests and the more universal interest."[14] National self-interest "must be harmonized with the interests of others to be moral"[15] and to be in the best interests of the nation-state. An element of state moderation is possible, but never more.

As for world government (another human collective that must deal with the nation-state), the hope of such a collective creating a new world order of peace among nations or shaping human destiny, is likewise vain. Rather, hope lies in the ultimate triumph of God outside of history. Put in political terms, Niebuhr stated: "The fallacy of world government can be stated in two simple propositions. The first is that governments are not created by fiat (though sometimes they can be imposed by a tyranny). The second is that governments have only limited efficacy in integrating a community."[16] Put in evangelical terms, he declared, "We are saved not by what we can do, but by the hope that the Lord of history will bring this mysterious drama to a conclusion, that the suffering Christ will in the end be the triumphant Lord."[17]

On the other hand, while recognizing that world government in general and the United Nations in particular were inherently imperfect because of the human condition, Niebuhr promoted all possible international cooperation, warning against utopian versions of world government "that overlook the complicated task of securing the precarious order and justice that was available within the existing system."[18] Encouraging a world community, he knew that forces of particularism, such as ideology, culture, and nationalism were stronger than forces of unity, brotherhood, and peace.

Evangelical moderate Barney Grey Barnhouse, editor of *Eternity*, echoed much the same position. Writing in 1957 on the heels of the McCarthy era, he stated: "Even though on Biblical grounds we know that the U.N. is doomed to ultimate failure, we must, of course, do everything in our power to follow paths of righteousness and desire a peace that will be something more than temporary even though human peace is never just or durable."[19] And, again, "it is our duty as Christians to use every possible instrument to ward off the approach of war and take our stand as believers must, on the side of national righteousness as well as individual righteousness."[20] His statement that "our only hope of peace is the Second Coming of the Lord Jesus Christ" had a distinctive evangelical flavor, although even here the statement is compatible with Niebuhr's frequent remark that history will be fulfilled outside of history.

A pattern thus emerges regarding Niebuhr's view of the nation-state and its role in world affairs. Human problems will never be solved in the history of the human race. There will always be wars and rumors of wars due to the inherent "brutal character of the behavior of all human collectives, and the power of self-interest and collective egoism in all inter-group relations." And yet instead of being written off as ineffective entities doomed to inevitable failure, these same collectives (nation-states, the UN, etc.) could moderate the brutality of human collectives. Put another way, the nation-state, seen as a power-hungry, egoistic monster, was needed to check other nation-states even more power-hungry. This would be like hiring the wolf to protect the henhouse from the fox.

Niebuhr applied this perception of human collectives to his analysis of governments. He was not optimistic about democracy. Rather, it appeared to him to be a system less objectionable than other forms of government. Politics was a mixture of good and evil, like the human condition. Applying this perception of the human condition to the United States role in world affairs, he was aware of the conundrum of trusting either the wolf or the fox, warning of the need to discriminate between degrees of evil in British and Nazi imperialism where neither could be justified by any standard, moral or otherwise. But the threat of Nazi tyranny was more evil than participation in a war to stop it.[21] A similar choice was necessary concerning United States–Soviet relations during the Cold War. Matching the two Cold War superpowers (each ironically the self-righteous wolf defending the henhouse from the deceitful fox), one face of Niebuhr's nationalism revealed itself as clearly identifying the nation holding higher moral ground. Both claimants to virtue were certainly not disinterested parties in their drive to redeem the world, a behavior to be expected given the nature of human collectives. But Niebuhr's list of virtues detailing American superiority was a long one, coupled with explanations of why the Soviet Union and China were found wanting.

The United States, without seeking it, had become the most powerful nation in history. Its "moral advantage lies in the fact that [it] does not have a strong lust for power which always accompanies its possession."[22] It had learned from history reasonably well. It exercises common sense rather than depending on abstract theories that create unrealistic models sure to lead to tragic conclusions.[23] In the democratic tradition, it is wise enough not to invest its elite with a monopoly of power. It has heeded the warning, "let not the wise man glory in his wisdom, let not the mighty man glory in his strength."[24] Given the nature of man, the American democratic system is the best. Since the greatest danger is unchecked power, the American system is especially well conceived to curb this will to power with its checks and balances, elections, and separation of powers.[25] The system was not created to be efficient but rather to preclude arbitrary power. The American system of democracy emphasizes the innocence and perfectibility of the individual. The nation has a "common people" with the wisdom to reject the hysterical nationalism revealed by the right wing of the Republican Party after World War II.[26] It has achieved a degree of justice which has prevented the injection of Marxism into its system. It has not been as abusive as Communism. Clearly, the American system is a milder form of evil.

Confronting American superiority after World War II was the "absurd religio-political creed" of Soviet Communism.[27] America was forced to deal with this vast movement, "which generates more extravagant forms of political injustice and cruelty out of the pretensions of innocency than we have ever known in human history."[28] Its power base is "in the hands of a cynical group of tyrannical oligarchs operating from the base of a powerful nation and seeking to bring the nations of the world under its domination by their fear of its power and their confidence in its virtuous intentions."[29]

Such a withering word-lashing not only described the adversary confronting America and the West but declared none too subtly

American moral superiority to a monstrous system that threatened civilization. Communist tactics, too, were clever in wooing the Third World. Using a built-in advantage, Communists tell the Third World that America is imperialistic by definition since it is the most bourgeois and most powerful nation against the Communist East. They fuel "resentment against feudal injustice [easily prompting] the youth of decaying feudal societies to espouse the cause of a new collectivist culture."[30] They exploit the spiritual as well as material poverty of the Third World. In words typical of the 1950s, but which caused my students in the 1990s to draw in their breath, Niebuhr declared: "There is no spiritual basis in the Orient for what we know as the 'dignity of the individual.' This is one reason why there is little prospect in China for heroic resistance to totalitarianism. . . . [China's] lack of historical dynamism makes it an easy prey to Communism. . . . [China] cannot be expected to feel the loss of liberty with the same sense of grievous deprivation as in the West."[31] For Niebuhr, China's past was understandable though regrettable. Her centuries-long tradition precluded her from tasting for herself Western enlightenment.

Niebuhr further theorized that a lack of technical development in the Third World, too, made Communism a surface attraction and added evidence of United States superiority. One should expect the underprivileged world to naturally resent "the centers of technical power"—resentments both justified and unjustified.[32] Such resentment was certainly not due to "Commies" under the bed. Nor was it to be explained as another act in the cosmic tragedy of "tyranny versus liberty." That breast-beating slogan only articulated utopian illusions among sentimental, supernationalistic Americans. Rather, the conflict with the Communist world would be understood in large part on the basis of their inferior cultural background. In coping with this volatile, uneven mix—bad chemistry—Niebuhr advised a waiting game while taking "such measures as are necessary to combat the more immediate perils."[33]

Examples from the past he cited to support this advice included the rise and fall of Stalinism and the rise of Islam, its challenge to Western civilization, and its decline. In both situations waning occurred, not because of foes but because of internal corruption. Again, explanations for the conflicts and advice for coping, contain the language of American superiority. Were Niebuhr alive today, the recent collapse of the Soviet Union would serve as the ultimate example of the wisdom of a waiting game. I suspect he would advise the same policy toward the current resurgence of Islam. America need only wait it out and engage in a holding action when necessary.

From American superiority came a clear sense of a God-ordained mission of American world leadership to head off international anarchy.[34] The use, or potential use, of American power was a necessary, though not exclusive, means of fulfilling the American mission. Moreover, the United States must find a way to use its power wisely. The world problem could not be solved if the United States did not accept its full share of responsibility.

As early as World War I, Niebuhr saw the American role in world affairs in these terms. While revolted by clerical tub-thumpers who saw the war as a holy war, he was also uncomfortable with pacifists. His position, therefore, supported the war. Germany threatened American interests, the concept of a League of Nations was sound, and he was impressed with Wilson's Fourteen Points. He saw the war as a crusade to establish a new world order.[35] Disillusioned when Wilsonian idealism melted away, he reverted to a pre–World War I sympathy for pacifism.

With World War II, Niebuhr's sense of the need for American world leadership intensified. And he thought God had chosen Britain and the United States to play key roles in the postwar world. God chose various nations for special missions in history. The British and United States were to relieve Europe after the war.[36] Franklin D. Roosevelt's foreign policy of world responsibility earned Niebuhr's admiration. Such a policy marked a new level of maturity in American foreign policy.[37]

As the United States moved more deeply into the Cold War, Niebuhr's sense of American mission and the place of power in it, became even more urgent. In 1948 he wrote: "The future of the world literally depends, not on the display of our power (though the use of it is necessary and inevitable), but upon the acquisition of virtues which can develop only in humility."[38] In the following year, reflecting his view of the nature of the state and international tensions, he wrote: "No political order whether national or international is ever a pure incarnation of brotherhood or the fruit of pure unselfishness. Order and justice cannot be maintained by coercion alone; but they cannot be maintained without it."[39] Politics, international or national, must assume that humanity is selfish.

It would appear, however, that at times Niebuhr applied his concept of mission with American and Western interests in mind advocating the use of force in fulfilling these interests. American superiority must be evident wherever and whenever American interests were at stake. Since Niebuhr did not think Egyptians could competently operate the Suez Canal, the United States should use its power to protect its interests there. For him, there was good imperialism and bad imperialism, and American intervention on behalf of Western interests at Suez in 1956 would have been good imperialism. With great power was to come the great responsibility to use force "when necessary to secure the interests of their Allies and themselves."[40] For Niebuhr, the Dulles policy represented a new legalism when it condemned France and Britain in the name of the United Nations charter and of the neglect of national interests. He said, "The U.S. treated the U.N. as if it were a true vehicle to act authoritatively for the community of nations. Rather than being a channel for international diplomacy, as it should be, the U.N. was acting as a world government. The U.S. substituted legalistic platitudes for diplomacy."[41] These mistakes of the Dulles-Eisenhower policy on the Middle East were alleged as typical of "the liberal democratic theory of reliance upon collective security."[42] "Peace, anti-colonialism and the United Nations," said Niebuhr, "currently are invested with absolute ethical value."[43] For Niebuhr this policy misused America's greatness and its power to head-off international anarchy fomented by an incompetent Third World leader.

But even though in retrospect one may criticize Niebuhr's concept of the American mission, his articulation of American superiority and mission was always tempered with caution due to the impossibility of human innocence. In a more theoretical and reflective vein, he reminded the reader during the dark days of World War II of the real meaning of being called to mission: "We [U.S.] have not been chosen for our particular task in order that our own life may be aggrandized." Nor was the nation called to receive some special advantage from the mission. Rather, with special mission came special peril, "a precarious moral and historical position." And woe to the nation if it didn't produce. Therefore, says the Lord, "You only have I chosen, therefore will I visit you with your iniquities."[44] In that sense God had chosen America.

Being chosen to fulfill a mission did not depend upon being good enough to deserve leadership. Rather, the honor was to be seen as a gift of grace perhaps revealed in the "geography and climate of history and fate which lead to eminence despite the weaknesses and sinfulness of the beneficiary of such eminence."[45] If the United States were to view its power as merited, such power would "turn into a curse."[46] Approaching a condition of excessive pride, the United States, in Niebuhr's view, was in danger of "sinking into a mood of self-congratulation which must be, as indeed it is, a trial to all of our friends no matter how grateful they may be that our strength is dedicated to the cause of freedom."[47] American pride embarrassed the democratic world. And the more Americans indulged in "uncritical reverence for the supposed wisdom of our American way of life, the more odious" it was in the eyes of the world, and the more its moral authority was diminished with concurrent impotence of economic and military power.[48]

For Niebuhr, this tendency toward self-congratulation was ironic since the view of human nature reflected in the Constitution was pessimistic, yet Americans declare that they are "innocent," "God's American Israel," "the chosen." Both the Puritan New England and Virginia deistic traditions proclaimed such, involving "us in ironic incongruity between our illusions and the realities we experience."[49] Puritans saw America as the culmination of the Reformation's purifying of the church, a new perfect society. Jeffersonians thought a form of Christianity ran through the Enlightenment—the power of "nature's God" over history. Both portrayed "a new beginning in a corrupt world." For Niebuhr, Americans did better as a nation when they did not take "the early dreams of [their] peculiar innocency too seriously."[50]

Feeding these dangerous deceptive dreams, the president (Nixon), perverted religion by bringing ministers in as court chaplains to conduct White House services—a practice that encouraged preachers to become priests, promoting complacency and pride. They not only legitimated the administration's policy, but its pretense of virtue.[51] Excoriating such displays of piety, Niebuhr quoted the prophet, "I hate, I despise your feasts, and I take no delight in your solemn assemblies. . . . Take away from me the noise of your songs; to the melody of your harps I will not listen. But let justice roll down like waters, and righteousness like an everflowing stream."[52]

Also, successes such as the resolution of the Cuban missile crisis tempted Americans "to play the role of omnipotence."[53] American pride, self-righteousness, and over-confidence led the country into the tragic situation of Vietnam. "Ironically," he said, "our strength had led us into a burden too heavy to bear which had taken on the proportions of tragedy."[54] The United States needed to discover the limits of its power, acknowledging that Communism could not be stopped everywhere in the world. Engagement in Vietnam forced the administration to create a series of "obvious fictions or myths calculated to obscure the hiatus between our idealism and our hegemonical responsibilities. . . . Unfortunately, these myths and pretensions of our foreign policy are not sufficiently credible to obscure our real hegemonical purposes."[55] In exposing American hypocrisy and pride and the illusions and incongruities of American history, Niebuhr hoped to free the United States to exercise responsibility and creative leadership in world politics. He wrote the *Irony of American History* to "free his country from illusions which hindered its wise conduct of foreign policy."[56]

When he expressed both American superiority with mission and the danger of vainglorious pride, Niebuhr revealed a form of egalitarian nationalism with the brakes on. He was disturbed at the American unwillingness or inability to appreciate the plight of the poor nations of the earth. The reason for this lack of appreciation was not hard to discern—the unique and favored circumstances of unlimited resources and space afforded by a whole continent to a fraction of the world's population. But still, the disparity between American abundance and the poverty of the Third World contributed to "very stubborn forms of 'aggressiveness' intensified because of spiritual, historical, social, and cultural forces, which cannot be measured by our computations taken from biology." America was in danger, therefore, "of facing the international class struggle with an uncompromising fury or complete dismay."[57]

Niebuhr revealed a realism here—not a boasting of American superiority but a realistic recognition of a nationalism of the poor nations of the world. While not ascribing equality to cultures before God in the Herderian sense, he understood, respected, and appreciated the inherent differences between cultures, warning of the inadvisability of imposing American democracy on Eastern cultures. He often warned that the values of a democratic society most highly prized in the West were neither understood nor desired outside Western society. In fact, for Niebuhr, democracy, even without defects, was not immediately relevant to the East or to Africa "as was generally supposed."[58] Rather, each country had individual needs, thus precluding a single political, social, or cultural system. This reality made it unnecessary, indeed inappropriate, for the United States to promote a particular social-political system. The American responsibility was to encourage and defend each open society to make its own choice.[59] In any case, Americans could not have their own way even when they believed their way was best for mankind. American destiny was interwoven with the destiny of many people. Other wills contrasted with the American will. And the success of America in world politics depended upon its ability to establish community with many nations despite the hazards created by pride of power on the one hand, and the envy of the weak on the other.[60] American success in the world was seen as depending on disgorging the pretentious elements of its original dream and recognizing the validity of differing practices and institutions of other nations.

Niebuhr "particularly feared any policies which would give the United States military power to equal its economic power. He thought the wedding of the two would blind the U.S. to rightful claims of other nations."[61] The world required a wider degree of community. If this community were to be genuine it could not be superimposed by American or any other people. Said Niebuhr, "All peoples and nations must find their rightful place in the fellowship." And he stressed with growing vigor the contributions of other religious traditions in the world, even declaring in the 1950s that "the church should not attempt to convert Jews to the Christian faith."[62] Such were Niebuhr's sentiments, revealing an egalitarian nationalism.

But, then, not so fast. While displaying a broad-minded recognition and respect for differences, Niebuhr used Western individualism as the lodestar with which to judge other cultures. In describing the cultures of the world, he would end with phrases that there is no "emancipation of the individual" in non-Western cultures, or "the individual is locked into the group." The "earthbound humanism of Confucianism still does not offer the individual a more significant place in the scheme of things" because of its orientation to the family. Pantheistic religions of Buddhism or Hinduism had no significance for the individual since the purpose of religious redemption was the annulment of individual existence.[63]

In spite of Niebuhr's statements that democracy was not appropriate for all cultures, he could not liberate himself from the assumption that democracy may be ideal in any culture as the best check on irresponsible power. Only the lack of preconditions for democracy in these cultures could inhibit democratic development. Should adequate preconditions be achieved, democracy of varying degrees could take root regardless of culture. There would need to be a degree of ethnic and linguistic uniformity sufficient to serve as a community base for a free society. A degree of literacy and technical development sufficient to provide the intellectual maturity and social flexibility necessary for a system of self-rule would need to be in place.[64] A nation would need to be sufficiently unified to withstand "sub-national group interests."[65] Humanism of individual rights and values would need to be present. And, there would need to be a balance of power within a system to allow for the development of tolerable levels of social justice.[66]

The central issue for Niebuhr was not whether to accept differences in cultures that precluded democracy as a good thing in and of itself. Rather, it was a matter of calculating how much to interfere in the internal affairs of a country in order to create economic and social conditions which would make democracy viable.[67] Niebuhr usually urged Americans to appreciate and accept cultural differences around the world in the context of encouraging American behavior that would not exacerbate relations with potential converts to the democratic way. Citing the centuries over which Western democracy evolved reminded Americans that changes toward democracy in the Third World would take time—a change desired and nurtured by the West. Important, too, was recognizing and supporting the rise of nationalism among Third World countries. But this was applauded in the context of these nationalisms resisting Communism.

And so, we have gone back and forth and back again. On the one hand, we have Niebuhr's broad-mindedness recognizing and accepting differences in cultures, and his statements that democracy, even without defects, is not immediately relevant to other cultures. He appeared close to declaring the equality of all cultures. On the other hand, he cited differences in cultures to explain why some fell prey to Communism, implying that America was superior in having avoided such a disaster. The mere assumption of American superiority with all of its defects meant that all other cultures were inferior with even more defects. Furthermore, these cultures lacked the preconditions for democracy, and American policy should assist, perhaps even intervene internally, to bring democracy to birth. But, then, American success in this depended on recognizing inherent cultural differences and remembering how many years its own set of values had taken to develop.

To observe this in Niebuhr is to observe his pragmatism, which is very American. Any analysis of American nationalism which includes consideration of American values, and solutions to American problems, must consider pragmatism, which has been called the American philosophy. If that is the case, and I believe it to be, William James was its creator, and Reinhold Niebuhr was its apostle. Niebuhr's pragmatism was an expression of his nationalism. But here, too, as with his belief in American superiority, American mission, and his egalitarian nationalistic face, his pragmatism was restrained. His pragmatism could be said to account for the appearance of inconsistency and moral relativity of his various nationalistic views. This is not to make him appear amoral. His pragmatism with the brakes on prevented that. For him, moral influences were valid in the sense that issues of right and wrong were "ultimately potent."[68]

When Niebuhr analyzed United States–Middle East relations in the late 1950s, he was using pragmatism to attack an alleged simplistic moralism in American foreign policy. A key flaw in the policy was that "In every case power political realities are being obscured by moralism."[69] In explaining why the UN was effective in getting France and Great Britain out of Egypt in 1956, but not in getting the Soviets out of Hungary, Niebuhr interpreted Eisenhower as saying it was because our Allies are moral nations and the Russians are not. In this statement, said Niebuhr, Eisenhower obscured the flaw in the UN Charter, and was guilty of a simplistic moralism which is always "pathetic." Niebuhr's "aim was to discover a way to make moral claims relevant to international politics," avoiding the "errors of either overly consistent realism or idealism,"[70] rather than being forced into an insipid face-saving rhetoric defending a simplistic and inadequate morality in the real world. He admitted that his relativism could lead to cynicism but argued that such ambiguity would maintain a healthy "tension between the ideal and the realizable relative good."[71]

In applying a hard-nosed morality shorn of "overly consistent realism or idealism," Niebuhr crafted a goal-oriented pragmatism consistent with his perception of the transcendent Christian values. Western culture and international order must be protected. Institutions should be evaluated not in the light of ideology but rather according to their usefulness to human life consistent with Christian values. He liked Franklin D. Roosevelt's pragmatism. The president was not a systematic thinker but rather, like a quarterback, chose the next play in part from the results of the previous one. He liked the fruits of FDR's pragmatism—"By their fruits ye shall know them," a genuine American sentiment.

The Americans for Democratic Action also was accorded his praise. He was not only proud to be among the founders of the ADA but was gratified to see it effectively opposing Marxism on the international front and McCarthyism on the home front, while avoiding the errors of idealism, the cardinal sin of the Social Gospel. Niebuhr's respect for liberalism grew after World War II due to his realizing that liberalism need not be wedded to idealism and optimism and his perception that it produced a greater amount of justice. The results— the usefulness of liberalism shorn of optimism—seemed to fit his view of the brutish human condition. It was the best that could be afforded given the realities of this temporal world.

Niebuhr's pragmatism also imbued through his encouragement of Third World nationalism. In preserving the values and institutions of Western civilization from Communism, he saw non-European nationalism and modernization as chief bulwarks so long as movements in these directions occurred without upsetting international order and the loyalties of European allies.[72] This qualifier that justified Third World nationalistic revolutions was a pragmatic, nationalistic American understanding of the relationship between itself and the rest of the world. Third World nationalism could be useful in thwarting Communism. Americans should evaluate wisely which "nationalisms" to support in this struggle against Communism and which ones to reject.

Having determined this, America should support good nationalisms and resist those which could easily develop in a dangerous direction.

Using this pragmatic approach, Niebuhr advocated a flexible policy that evaluated each situation as it related to United States interests. Since the Suez crisis of 1956 was seen as critical to the interests of the United States and of Western powers, he was critical of the Dulles-Eisenhower sellout to a Third World dictator who exemplified a nationalism that developed in a dangerous direction. In his view, the United States had a decisive responsibility in directing Third World matters.

On the other hand, American intervention in Vietnam bothered Niebuhr, the difference being that he did not perceive Vietnam as a primary threat to United States interests. Yet, while doubting the wisdom of supporting the Diem regime, he also recognized that occasionally the United States must support questionable leaders for strategic reasons.[73] He would quote FDR concerning undesirable allies: "They may be bastards, but they are at least our bastards."[74] In any case, it was impossible to stop Communism everywhere in the world. Rather, there needed to be a common sense understanding of the limits of power.

The issue of power often engaged his concern. American power exceeded "that of the storied empires," yet, how and when to use this power? America was anti-imperialistic "in political creed" in a world in which anti-imperialism and self-determination had become universal political dogmas despite the vast disproportion of power and responsibility between the two supernations and the emergent new nations.[75] Again, a recognition of the "brutal character of the behavior of all human collectives" governed Niebuhr's formula. Avoid moral absolutes in international politics. Reject the escape from the international power politics attempted in the 1920s and 1930s. Distrust concepts of human perfectibility and moral progress. Studying and using history, empirical evidence, and personal experience, will lead to an explicit and realistic concept of man as prerequisite to sound political thought. Such was the pragmatism of Reinhold Niebuhr.[76]

What, then, is one to make of Niebuhr's nationalism? In knowing him as the exponent of Christian Realism, we perhaps can better understand the various faces of his nationalism. Half of the puzzle is his practical, pragmatic, genuinely American side—what works. It is the realism side, a side that Americans can relate to. Strip away the fuzzes that are inconsistent with the real world. Attractive, too, is his urging that national interests guide behavior in this real world of international hardball. And thus what Americans feel like doing naturally in that world is apparently legitimated by one of America's foremost theologians of social ethics.

A clue to the other half of the puzzle of Niebuhr's nationalism is what appears to be his ambiguous side. The practical, pragmatic side is shrouded with ambiguity. It is defined to mean the practical, pragmatic way to achieve the highest form of justice on this earth consistent with transcendent values of the Christian faith. But this appears to be tied to national interests as the guiding principle for behavior in the real world, which is also a matter of definition. He did distinguish between enlightened national interest that recognized and supported the legitimate needs and aspirations of other nation-states as over against a national interest that ignored broader universal interests. But his identifying legitimate American national interests consistent with broader universal needs was not always apparent, and those who would applaud his stance in the 1956 Suez crisis would no doubt be puzzled, if not outraged, over his Vietnam position, and vice versa. Ambiguous, too, were his expressions of American superiority in power and morality in the world with concomitant mission and his warnings of hubris leading to nemesis.

In reading these mixed signals, one is likely to plead: Will the real Reinhold Niebuhr please stand. One critic of Niebuhr's thinking put it: "If we are neither cynics nor utopians, neither absolutists nor relativists, neither liberals nor conservatives, what precisely are we?"[77] The critic goes on, "The simultaneous `possibility impossibility' dichotomy strikes us as unnecessarily ambivalent."[78] Without careful analysis the words of Niebuhr can be used to justify intervention anywhere in the world where Western and American interests, as defined at the moment, are threatened. Niebuhr was apparently concerned about this, "grieving at rightist applications of his thoughts."[79] Other of his words, of a more egalitarian nationalistic bent, can be taken as maxims to live and let live in the world. Of course, neither generalization does justice to the man. Niebuhr at least needs to be read in context.

But, even granting that, there is a problem. Not only are Americans disinclined to take time to consider context, this "peculiar people"—this "almost chosen nation"—has been identified as ideologically conservative yet functionally liberal. Scholars have written about the "divided mind" (Conn), the "bifurcated mind" (Mead), the "two-party system of American religion" (Miller-Schmit, Marty), and I will add "warts and beauty marks." We should be so lucky to experience simple polarization—liberal versus conservative. What has impressed and surprised me is the extent to which, within single individuals, Niebuhr included, is the divided mind, the bifurcated mind, the two-party system of American religion, and, yes, warts and beauty marks—the holding of two antithetical propositions simultaneously. Hence, Niebuhr's "contradictions"—differing nuances and relativity actually reflect the American identity confusion. Niebuhr's relativism, to some extent, contributes to reflecting the confusion about who we are, what we are about, and how we are about it as an American people. At best, the careful reader of Reinhold Niebuhr, can only conclude that the real world is immensely complex, defying simple, worldly, universal solutions. And complexity frustrates Americans.

Still, having said this, on balance one is left with the impression that in Niebuhr's view, America with all its warts was the best hope for the world in existence. The world was a little less harsh with the presence of American power, ideals, and morality than it might otherwise have been.

CHAPTER 8

The Nationalism of Moderation

Beginning with confidence in proclaiming biblical absolutes to an American society in crisis and to a world locked in a game of nuclear chicken, the editors of the evangelical *Christianity Today* (*CT*),[1] got an education over two decades in unforeseen lessons, in the inadvertent results of seemingly sound national policy, and in the frustration of divided opinions among the faithful. Prodded by this ambiguity in their world, *CT* editorial themes evolved from a simplistic 1950s McCarthy-style zealous nationalism of easy answers on complex issues to a moderating and more sophisticated understanding of national and world problems in the Cold War era and of America's proper role in it. Such thoughtful, subtle changes prompted Ed Dobson, spokesman for Jerry Falwell, to chide that the tendency of

> Evangelicals is to be concerned. If you want to be an Evangelical you have to be concerned. But it must be a conditional concern. [The Evangelical will say] "I'm concerned about abortion. But I'm also concerned in light of abortion about A, B, C, and D." [Or] "I'm concerned about pornography. But we must also take seriously the First Amendment and how that may encroach on people's freedoms." And once you begin adding all the "buts" essentially what you're saying is you really don't believe in it to begin with. . . . The Evangelical pastor will tell you the books he's read. The Fundamentalist pastor will tell you how many he got baptized. The Evangelical is interested in thinking. . . . The Fundamentalist is not interested in the intellectual community. . . . They don't care what intellectuals are writing. They don't read them to begin with.[2]

In other words, evangelicals in general and the editors of *CT* in particular were guilty of "conditional concern," of indulging in a moderating and more sophisticated understanding of national and world problems because they actually read and studied issues and engaged in the writing process. Hence, they were less cocksure about what God was saying to America in regard to *specific* political, social, and economic issues.

Not that *CT* caved into, or even inched toward, the liberal agenda for America and its role in world affairs as articulated by a William Ernest Hocking. Far from that! Nor did *CT* display the near frantic vacillation of a Jerry Falwell whereby one moment America was about to buy the farm, and the next moment such a catastrophe was impossible since God was ready to blow up the Soviet missiles aimed at America in their silos. Rather, *CT* editors, led by Carl F. H. Henry, maintained a steady conviction that a normative God exists above and outside of history but works in and through history. And every aspect of human behavior stands under the judgment of God through His revealed Word. The liberal, on the other hand, was seen as an ethical relativist obedient to the climate of opinion.

While holding to such an absolutist position, evangelicals were ultimately forced to acknowledge that God did not reveal all the precise details of implementing His absolute Word in regard to issues such as Vietnam. Human fallibility accounted for misreading the Absolute, a misreading that could lead to public embarrassment as seen in Billy Graham's close association with President Nixon before Watergate. But never did *CT* question the existence of the divine normative for human life.

A second constant, at least declared so, was the separation of church and state as to divinely ordained roles and functions of each. The church's task was clearly to win souls to Christ with the belief that if enough souls were won, the problems of society would be resolved. With this major premise, it followed for evangelicals that the institutional church should not get involved in programs for social or political change that they saw occurring by the National Council of Churches[3] and advocated by the liberal journal *Christian Century*. As for the divine role of the state, its primary function was to exercise negative power, to keep order in the society, to ensure fair play for equal opportunity—not necessarily for equal results—and to refrain from intruding on the sacred role of the church.

But determining when the civil intrudes on the sacred, or when the church oversteps its mission and intrudes on the role and function of the state is always a matter of definition, and *CT*, while advocating functional separation of church and state, ironically eased away from separation to justification of Christian institutional social responsibility. As a voice of evangelicalism, *CT* consciously addressed the same social, political and economic issues of the republic as did the more liberal *Christian Century*. The difference lay in the remedy; the patient was the same. And even the remedy sounded more consistent with *Christian Century* as time wore into the late 1970s and 1980s. *CT* walked a very fine line. On the one hand, while advocating that social problems could be healed when enough conversions occurred, the editors made it quite clear that conversion entailed Christian social responsibility. And, while it was perceived to be improper for the institutional church to get involved in programs for social and political change, *CT* itself was a Christian institution, a surrogate of sorts for evangelical churches, making a case for Christian social responsibility and defining its implementation.

In exercising this Christian social responsibility, *CT* editors, clearly picturing what America ought to be, agonized over what they perceived to be moral deterioration of American society. The litany of societal evils was so comprehensive in the 1950s and 1960s editorials as to cause one to wonder if a regenerate society were possible. No segment of society escaped condemnation for abandoning the values of the past. Through the electoral process, Americans allegedly had voted for government paternalism, socialism, centralization, and bureaucracy.[4] The will to greatness was being stifled by the demands for "security of a sort which will be bought at a price of national solvency and personal freedom."[5] Americans were in danger of thinking that progress could be maintained, not through hard work but through leisure; not through personal and corporate initiative but by government guarantees. The bureaucrats held out to people, "whoring after false gods of ease and security,"[6] the "mirage of ease, pleasure and security."[7]

The loss of industry and thrift, unpunished labor racketeering, unchecked crime rates, and inflationary spending, added up "to further disintegration of Puritan character in America."[8] The twenty-fifth anniversary of the repeal of prohibition brought "tremendous increase in drinking and liquor propaganda." Tobacco and drug consumption soared. In the same breath CT lamented the millions of dollars in free publicity for the Roman Catholic Church upon the death of the old pope and the election of the new. "We must not be lulled by any innocuous promises from any candidate who is a Roman Catholic," warned the *CT* editors.[9] America was in a corner, threatened not only by Moscow and Rome but by secularism at home.

Even the apparent all-time high percentage of people in church each Sunday in the 1950s was shallow, misguided religiosity. Political speeches, business ads, labor programs all wanted the "province of piety." Christianity had been leveled to a "flabby and flat" religious neutrality. The annual presidential prayer breakfast "reflects something of this religious ambiguity in American life" with its tendency to applaud religious sentiments rather than to appropriate them. There were no sweeping evidences of repentance and faith in American life. Indicative of the spiritual malaise was Conrad Hilton's proposal to host non-Christians—Buddhists, Shintoists, Mohammadans, and Hindus— at the president's prayer breakfast. Such a proposal was anathema to *CT* editors. Hilton simply did not understand "the uniqueness of the Hebrew, Christian revealed religion." The Apostles did not have contact with Buddhists and Hindus, "but they did with Jews and left no doubt where they stood!"[10]

The most tragic evidence of American moral and spiritual deterioration for *CT* editors rested with reports that thirty-three percent of American prisoners of war in Korea collaborated with the enemy.[11] Such a deplorable situation was alleged to be due to the American soldiers' lacking spiritual and moral conviction, having no understanding and appreciation of the American heritage, no discipline in the sense of basic right and wrong, and no understanding of Communism. Further, these moral and spiritual inadequacies stemmed from too many broken homes and no Sunday school. American soldiers had not been properly indoctrinated in the American tradition.

And, why should the American soldier not be undependable and morally and spiritually bankrupt, having been raised in an utterly rotten society? The same "monster" communes that swallowed up the homes in China were "gulping them down in this country." There was "smoldering social dynamite in the slums—the dark-skinned teenager out of school out of work. . . . There are more female barmaids (not country barflies) than college coeds. These poor girls will not make very good mothers." The campus was "not snow white" either. "The most impressive classrooms and field houses include cheating. . . . At night the golf course can be a brothel."[12] There was a cheap and artificial sense of values and thought. The popular was right. The "god of conformity snares individuals into group thinking." There was a detachment from civic responsibility.[13]

The deterioration of American society impacted America's ability to defend itself against the communist military threat. Scientists as well as religionists were doom conscious due to Soviet superiority in satellite technology and her ability to reach the United States in less than fifteen minutes with her intercontinental ballistic missiles. The United States seemed vulnerable, if not totally helpless, because of her loss of scientific world leadership, the soaring cost of her government, runaway inflation, and punitive taxation. America was a second rate republic on a "collectivistic toboggan slide" ruled by a creeping secret totalitarianism. America, like Rome, may have crossed its Rubicon, lamented an editorial. "Conditions in the old Roman Empire were not far different from ours."[14]

While the liberal churches of America were at fault for allowing such social deterioration, the favorite whipping boy was John Dewey, who had injected naturalistic, evolutionary thought into education, denying the supernatural, rejecting changeless truths and moral standards, teaching that whatever worked was "true," and spurning the relevance of historic Christian theism.[15]

The *CT* prescription to restore America to its true self was as absolute as its diagnosis of societal illness, although it confessed that evangelicals, to say nothing of the church as a whole, had been guilty of ambiguity, uncertain voice, vagueness, and vacillation. The church's mixed message on one end of the spectrum revealed a supernaturalism and special revelation that mandated pietistic withdrawal from the world, clearly inadequate for *CT*'s editor Carl Henry. At the other end of the Christian spectrum were the Social Gospelers who wanted to bring the Kingdom of God to earth but who neglected the personal gospel of Jesus Christ's substitutionary atonement and supernatural revelation, seeking to graft Christian ideals on unregenerate human nature. That, too, was just as inadequate for Henry.

Rejecting the Social Gospel message were those independent churches, premillennial dispensationalists, and social pessimists who suspected even spiritual renewal in a society as phony since conditions were expected to deteriorate in society in the dispensational scheme, not get better, also a position totally unacceptable to Henry. Rather, a consistent voice could come from contemporary evangelicals trying to fuse the two, the social concern and personal religion. This, for Henry, was the absolute, unitary message America needed to hear.

Evangelicals, having a mission to restore America to its past glory, were running out of time. A *CT* editorial implied that even creation in the form of earthquake, wind, and pestilence seemed to be connected to sin in society. "If we could see our country once more," wrote an editor, "not on our own or at the whim of Communism, but as a servant of God, creation would stop shaking and begin again to make sense. . . . Panic would be inconceivable among a people who knew first hand that they could trust their King."[16]

Another *CT* editorial, referring to the novel *On The Beach*, which ends with only two people surviving an atomic holocaust (with a touch of a Falwell vacillation "it can't happen, it could happen"), assured readers that "no Christian expects that the human race will end up 'on the beach'; our faith teaches otherwise. . . . But unless we heed the warning of [General Douglas] McArthur and bring back God's law and bring people back to God, unless spiritual fiber of character is restored, the future of our great nation is in peril."[17]

While *CT* affirmed saving America involved fusing social concern with personal religion, the emphasis was clearly on the latter as the prerequisite for national healing. For Carl Henry and the *CT* editors, "social sin" was the sin of individuals that affected social life.[18] Social disorders were a commentary on the disorders of private life. When government failed to achieve justice, it did so because the individuals running the government were sinners. Therefore, work for the conversion of the individuals running the government and the mandate will be fulfilled.[19] Individual regeneration was the chief and indispensable means of social reform.

The same solution was implied regarding American foreign policy. The problem with American foreign policy, according to Henry, was that it harbored optimistic liberal assumptions about human nature and history. Foreign policymakers had bought into liberal Protestantism's social concern by supporting specific modern enterprises and goals such as the League of Nations, the United Nations, labor unions, and integration.[20] The solution to American foreign policy for Henry was to assume human sinful nature, knowing that peace could never come until the human spirit was regenerated through Christ—an unlikely prospect in one's lifetime, if ever.

However, such a pessimistic outlook was modified by Henry in a series of articles on Christian social action. In contrast to Niebuhrian pessimism that all human collectives, Christian or otherwise, were evil—some simply more evil than others—Henry and *CT* editors asserted that a distinctive social morality was as possible for the community of evangelical faith as it was for the sanctified regenerate individual. Even as the individual could be regenerated through conversion, so it was possible for a regenerated human collective to be created through the conversions of its individual members. Furthermore, these evangelical leaders held hope for the same dynamic to work in the society. To disparage the possibility of "the ideal Christian culture [as simply one competing sinful human collective among many competing collectives] failed to do full justice to the power of the Holy Spirit in the life of the redeemed community."[21]

However, in asserting this possibility, Henry and *CT* editors linked this process of social redemption by advocating a free enterprise economic system they claimed to be biblical. Contrasted to this was "the socialistic and totalitarian assault on free enterprise, private property and the profit motive, as well as other principles approved by the biblical doctrine of human rights and responsibilities."[22] Therefore, to assail national strongholds of evil in quest of a righteous nation, to challenge institutional sin as a way of widening Christian influence over human society, were essential to the Christian conscience. Affirming both the Lordship of Christ and the imperative of the Great Commission provided impetus to seek the renewal of society.[23]

The purpose of the church in all of this was to exhibit to the society what could be done to transcend social injustice in a spiritual society of redeemed persons. Social justice was a divine requirement for the whole human race, not for the church alone. Implied also was that individual regeneration would affirm capitalism, private property, and the profit motive, and that regenerated individuals and the regenerated community should press the system for these values. This was how Henry and *CT* editors saw the relationship between conversion and social responsibility.

Restoring the true America also entailed returning to the American values of the past. Repeatedly *CT* editors implored Americans to turn to the founders for more faith and light.[24] Why did we leave England in the first place?, asked the editors. What did our fathers die for? What heritage is ours "to have and to hold that our young political playmates down at the UN don't know about?" What makes a nation great?[25]

CT was a clinic in the selective use of the past. While acknowledging the deism of Jefferson and the Calvinism of Puritanism as two chief sources of American values, *CT* clearly wished to emphasize the latter while distorting somewhat the former. American deism was acknowledged to be influenced by the French Enlightenment and John Locke, and dropped at that, while Calvinism clearly had the high ground with its emphasis on the sovereignty of God and its correlate of man responsible to God "with a dignity upon which others may not trespass."[26] When the words of Jefferson were employed, they were such statements as "I have sworn upon the altar of God eternal hostility against every form of tyranny over the mind of man.[27] No attempt in this instance was made to explain the kind of God Jefferson was talking about. It certainly was not the God of *CT*. Yet the Jeffersonian statement was used to give the impression that this great author of the Declaration of Independence was some early republican theist.

Most of the signers of the Declaration of Independence, too, were alleged by *CT* to be "evangelical believers theologically at home in the doctrines of the Bible." And these founders had been careful "to separate neither the individual nor the state from an obligation to God." Furthermore, their concept of God was not nebulous or left to private interpretation as is the "current tendency." By "God" the founders meant a personal supernatural being, "the Creator (a distinctly theistic and biblical conception)" who endowed the human race with "inalienable dignity and with inalienable rights."[28] Not only did *CT* editors make the founders larger than life, unable to accept them as "earthen vessels" with normal human flaws, but they also advocated a conformity to their perception of traditional American values and customs. Being advocates of strict construction of the Constitution, *CT* engaged in a loose construction interpretation of the preamble of the Constitution that would have made Alexander Hamilton blush. The preamble declares the purpose of the Constitution to be "promoting the general welfare." According to *CT*, general welfare "means moral welfare too." A stand against gambling would work for the "general welfare" since gambling interests invaded the government and corrupted the people. A stand against *Lolita* and all obscene literature would protect the children of the land and hence would work for the general welfare. *Roe v. Wade* was evidence that the nation was deteriorating morally, and resisting abortion would be working for the general welfare.[29] Demanding the removal of textbooks that were "debunking" and "insulting" in their portrayal of American life would be working for the general welfare of the country.[30] Instead, a fresh approach to American history was needed in order

> to recreate a sense of American purpose. . . . Every lecturer before making a speech, every author before writing a book or article, every movie or television producer before shooting a script, might well take a personal oath along some line as this: "I will not degrade the country I love. I will be fair but I will not exploit the weakness of her citizenry for my own financial profit. I will not traffic in violence, slaughter or immorality, or glamorize those who commit such things. I will not expose the culture of America to scorn and ridicule of her enemies. I will uphold the honor of the United States. . . ." Christians believe that allegiance to God is the only foundation of national loyalty that he himself will honor.[31]

All these examples represented a deterioration of former American values which placed the nation at risk. Restoring these values was prerequisite to restoring national moral health.

To convey such values necessitated a reform of American education. Deterioration of American education allegedly occurred after World War I when nonrationality "overpowered the general social consciousness" of education in America. Anti-intellectualism and speculative philosophy revolted against reason. Protestant schools of liberal theology taught the irrational and "betrayed the theology of revelation by excluding any objective metaphysical knowledge of God."[32]

Because of this drift in modern thought, and because of the nature of the Christian religion, evangelical theologians, said Henry, "have good cause to resist the growing revolt against reason [since] Christianity seeks to conform human reason and all its achievements to Jesus Christ, the Creator, Redeemer and Judge."[33] Hence, there was need for reform in education that would affirm the unity of all knowledge in Christ. Fact and faith were one. "Science and scholarship must unite with spirituality and service to God. [We] must live, move, and have our modern being in both Christianity and culture at one and the same time. . . . Christ *alone* is able to blend and bind culture and conscience, civilization and Christianity, society and spirit. . . . Whatever ignores him, therefore, is part-truth and part-lie, or actually, not the truth at all. . . . Christian integration of all thought and life is still the great and transcendent priority for coordinated social effort."[34] Such was the educational philosophy of Carl Henry, implementation of which was essential to restore America.

To implement this philosophy of Christian education, Henry and *CT* editors advocated a national Christian university, a concept enthusiastically endorsed by Billy Graham. The time for such an enterprise seemed ripe, given the anti-intellectual tide in American thought and life. Such a university would challenge pagan and secular theories of reality and history. It would train Christian leadership in all professions to deal with issues in the context of the Bible. It would teach the history of thought "in systematic orientation to Jesus Christ as the revealed center of history, nature, conscience and redemption," bringing ancient, medieval, modern, and contemporary minds under the judgment of divine revelation. It would integrate the totality of life's experiences within the perspective of the "Christian world-life views," delineate the political, social, and economic implications of Christianity, and provide "consistent criticism of and alternative to collectivistic revisions of the social order."[35] Such a university would have high academic standards and moral purity, with faculty engaging in corporate conversation, research, and writing to produce textbooks challenging the monopoly held by secular scholars.

Public education no less than higher education was indispensable in helping to restore the true America of the past. While there were anemic calls in the late 1950s for teaching about religion in public school curriculum, Carl Henry insisted that even this was not a sufficient infusion of religion into the public curricular mix. He agreed that schools should teach "the historic role of religion in American life and culture."[36] But more than this he insisted that schools must teach about "transcendent reality."[37] This meant instruction in a Protestant Christian[38] worldview, including creation science and the saviorhood and Lordship of Christ.

Thus far in the inquiry we have cited the absolutes and the constants articulated by Carl Henry and other editors of *CT*. There was the conviction of a divine Judeo-Christian normative for human life under which every individual human action and every institution stood judged. Consistent also was *CT*'s affirmation of church/state separation and its articulation of the divinely ordained roles of each in carrying out the divine will for American society. Other constants were *CT*'s perception of traditional American values which obeyed the divine normative and its agony over the deterioration of American society in relation to these norms. And, finally, we have cited *CT*'s remedy to restore America to its former greatness.

Within these overarching absolutes, however, was agony over practical implementation in a very complex, scary world. *CT* demonstrated what to some would be applauded as intellectual and spiritual growth in the process of wrestling with complex issues, altering, modifying, even reversing its positions with humility and some embarrassment. To others the wrestling would be seen as a serious waffling and compromise with evil. To that agonizing process revealed in *CT*, we now turn. Between the 1950s and 1970s *CT* went from expressions of a zealous to a moderate nationalism; from a near rabid "better dead than Red" condemnation of the "Evil Empire" to a pro-détente stance with the Soviet Union and recognition of Red China; from support of American involvement in Vietnam to questioning that involvement.

Early editions of *CT* reveal silly, absurd zealous nationalistic drivel announcing that even should the atomic holocaust occur "the atomic dust will reveal Christ standing in the shadows, keeping watch above his own."[39] Should the fallout shelter fail, the true Christian does not consider the end of earthly existence the ultimate catastrophe. True Christians would never pay any price to perpetuate the race. Rather, they have "no choice but to fight always on God's side [by bringing] holy judgments of God to bear against the present fear, appeasement and confusion which threaten to destroy Western unity and open the gates to atheistic communism."[40]

To counter appeasement of the "Evil Empire," *CT* supported all possible expenditures for nuclear deterrence, opposing suspension of nuclear weapons testing. The "great tragedy of the twentieth century," said one editor, "would be if, in the effort to conserve the creative power of the atom for Jesus Christ, the atom bomb should unwittingly have been given to the destructive service of Karl Marx."[41] Therefore, the World Council of Churches' urging that the United States unilaterally suspend testing of weapons "climaxes a Communist drive . . . to deter the development of new atomic devices in the West thus to alter the balance of power between the Communist and non-Communist worlds."[42] But if in spite of such precautions of nuclear deterrence, the nuclear holocaust should happen—"Kill them all, God will know his own."[43] The rhetoric of *CT* in the 1950s and early 1960s was as blatantly the rhetoric of the "jihad" as ever uttered in any era by any religion.

This call for headlong abandonment of the human race in a nuclear holocaust for Christ was predicated on the assumption that God could in no way use Communism in any positive way for the human race.[44] Implicit also was the suggestion that God could not speak through his church in Marxist, Communist lands.[45] "Only a fool" said one editor, "would close his eyes to the fact that the free world and the slave world are at war, that there is no coexistence peaceably, and that any hope of a lessening of this competition is wishful thinking."[46] *CT* editors denied that any variations existed within the Communist world. One editorial criticized John C. Bennett's assertion that "Polish Red" was different from "Chinese red." Whenever Communism prevailed no true freedom existed, asserted the editor. The Christian faith inherently brought freedom, but Communism could "lead only to the loss of freedoms."[47] There was no possible way to work with Communists.

In asserting that the total depravity of the Communist system precluded any possibility of coexistence, *CT* was equally asserting a manichaean declaration of American superiority and cosmic significance in spite of its lengthy litany of societal evils. The struggle was between the kingdom of good and the kingdom of evil; and between flesh and spirit; Bancroftian cosmic struggle of freedom and oppression; Communism and the Christian faith. Europe and America had "most reflected the basic postulates of the Christian philosophy of life in their basic laws and mores." American society was advanced in art, science, industry, and social betterment. The whole world had felt this influence to its betterment. The United States was the bulwark of world freedom and along with the Western allies was the "world's surest earthly hope of political and social well-being." Ninety-six percent of Americans professed religious devotion, and the majority of government personnel were Christians, even if nominal. And United States representatives to foreign lands and the United Nations were mostly Christian. This meant that government officials and people as a whole were "somehow wedded to . . . Christian traditions and have a respect for God and His Word as basic to the American way of life."[48]

The cosmic significance of American genius was "the experiment in liberty [producing] the free American society and its free government had never been attempted by any people anywhere."[49] The ancient Greek experiment in democracy was disqualified because it was based on slavery. Apparently *CT* editors had never heard of the three-fifths compromise that wrote slavery into the American Constitution, a compromise which enabled that document to see the light of day in 1789 outside the confines of the convention hall.

The New England town meeting, grassroots origin of American democracy, was the standard by which one *CT* editor judged the proceedings of the United Nations, again crafting the issue in manichaean terms. Instead of discussion and debate, as took place in the New England town meeting, the UN was bombarded with Soviet propaganda. Instead of courtesy and common decency as in "any town meeting" in the United States, debate at the UN "has been marked by vituperation . . . as crude and coarse as could be found among the most debased elements of society." Instead of the honor, honesty, and integrity "intrinsic in the New England town meeting," proceedings of the United Nations Organization were frequently dishonest, double-dealing, and "outright deceitful." In contrast to enlightened dynamic development within the New England town meeting, "the course of United Nations action has been dominated by the stubborn, unyielding, strict-constructionist position of the Soviet Union." Worst of all, there was no moral basis for the United Nations, which was accused of unwillingness to hear evidence of Communist atrocities involving prisoners of war and civilians.[50]

In its editorials of the 1950s and 1960s, *CT* unabashedly asserted American superiority, linking the Christian faith to democracy, to capitalism, and to American culture and values. Christianity allegedly made democracy in America possible. "Without Christianity," said one editor, "the grand, historic American experiment in democracy would not have been possible. The continuance of democracy in America depends on the degree to which Christianity flourishes in our land. . . . Christianity has made and must continue to make its profound contribution to free society."[51] Ironically, like the liberal Walter Rauschenbusch's depiction of Jesus as a "democrat," *CT* called Jesus the "great democrat." Carl Henry and *CT* editors went a step further with biblical justification for capitalism. Democracy was biblical, Protestant, Calvinistic, and capitalistic.[52]

Beyond the editorials that depicted communism versus capitalism as a religious cold war, the *CT* staff marshaled the influence of J. Edgar

Hoover, Billy Graham, J. Howard Pew, Fred C. Schwarz of the famed Christian Communism Crusade, David V. Benson, president of Russia for Christ, and a host of others writing on the same theme—that spiritual warfare was at hand; that evangelical Christians must become the chief resistance to communism; that there must be Christian renewal in America or ruin at the hands of atheistic communism. Editorials and guest articles on anticommunism dominated the space in *CT* during the fifties, sixties, and early seventies in which communism was "a dedicated servant of the anti Christ,"[53] and when Soviet leaders appeared to be somewhat malleable in detente, they were discredited since "Even the Devil Wears a Smile."[54]

In a less shrill but still manichaean mode, *CT* was critical of the Voice of America which "blurred" the distinctions between the Hebrew-Christian heritage and other world religions. The *Voice of America Bulletin* in its October-November 1956 edition had observed Mohammed's birth with a quote from Dr. Elton Trueblood, famed Quaker leader and pacifist. In his recognition statement on the Prophet's birth, Dr. Trueblood gave special praise to the Prophet's insistence on the unity of God and his rejection of all forms of idolatry. Because of these teachings, said Trueblood, "we glorify him and send congratulation to all the Moslems of the world."[55] *CT* was not only disappointed in Dr. Trueblood's "handling of Christianity and Islam," but also was galled at the use of tax monies for the publication of the statement by Voice of America. The American government seemed "at times to go out of its way to flatter the pagan religions, and indirectly to undercut America's vital spiritual mission to the world."[56]

Similar criticism was leveled at the World Council of Churches, which in *CT*'s view failed to emphasize the gap between Christian and non-Christian religions. "Alongside ecumenical inclusivism," said the editor, "an incipient universalism rather commonly embraced all mankind in final redemption."[57] Anything short of declaring Christianity as redemptive, revealed religion versus non Christian religions as nonredemptive, speculative religions was inadequate. And the issue for *CT* was increasingly critical "in view of the failure of pagan faiths to provide adequate moral dynamic and spiritual vitality to cope firmly with the Communist threat."[58]

CT even took the issue a step further by rejecting diversity in unity within the Christian community. The diversity was too great since Orthodox sacramentarianism and ritualistic emphasis were antithetical to the character of Anglo-Saxon Protestantism. Furthermore, rather than viewing Eastern Orthodoxy as part of the body of Christ, evangelicals saw subjects for conversion. Given such a view, it was inconsistent to talk of ecumenicity and cooperation. To even think of including Eastern Orthodoxy from behind the Iron Curtain was beyond the evangelical ability to discuss. The thought that anything could be learned from one another through such diversity was out of the question for *CT* editors.[59] As with the attitude that nothing could be learned from the Communist/Marxist world, so nothing could be learned from diversity within the Christian world.

In studying both the *CT* response and that of William Ernest Hocking to the issue of diversity in unity, one is struck by the antithetical approaches to the question. Not only were there opposite views on the value of diversity in unity (Hocking's conviction that one is enriched by diversity in contrast to *CT*'s manichaean rejection of real diversity), but there was no agreement in identifying the gravest problem facing the nation and world. Whereas Hocking recognized a growing secularism as more dangerous than Communism—a danger from which he saw resistance to secularism by linkage of Christian and non-Christian religions—*CT* emphasized Communism as the gravest problem. And, CT did not see the non-Christian religions as helpful in the anti-Communist struggle. On the contrary, non-Christian religions according to *CT* provided fertile soil for Communism. *CT* feared that the Far East would take the West's heritage of technology, science, and democracy and ignore the spiritual underpinnings that had made the West great.

But *CT*'s icy rigidity began to melt in the mid to late 1970s. No longer did it picture the conflict between capitalism and Communism in cataclysmic terms. Rather, *CT* assumed that the war between the United States and the Soviets would be fought with political, economic, and social weapons, and not bombs.[60] And *CT* hinted that perhaps the West could do business with Russia under certain conditions. When Russia had a bad harvest and needed grain from the United States, *CT* recommended that the United States provide grain on the condition that the Soviets grant the right of Jews to emigrate to Israel, grant real religious freedom, allow the free flow of literature including Bibles, and intervene on behalf of missionaries detained in South Vietnam.[61]

More dramatic still, *CT* got "burned" when their investment in and identification of the Christian faith with the conservative political agenda turned sour with Watergate and the revelations of government deception regarding Vietnam. Billy Graham in particular and *CT* in general had "egg on the face" with such turns of events. An editorial confessed that the nation could "no longer point the finger at other nations that transgress against moral principles until it first acknowledges its own transgressions."[62]

Moderation of *CT*'s opinions was also observed in its attitude toward Red China. Originally critical of the NCC for endorsing Red China entrance into the UN,[63] *CT* a dozen years later was intrigued with President Nixon opening-up visits to the People's Republic of China. The editor even conceded that as much as "we may dislike the communism of the People's Republic of China . . . it is a well-entrenched government controlling more than 700 million people, and it has as much right to recognition by the world as the Soviet Union."[64] Entering into the reality of world politics, *CT* suggested that the United States might even be able to use Red China as a counter-point to the USSR in the worldwide struggle for hegemony. And the United States had always been pure in its dealings with China, never wanting any of her territory, never demanding a sphere of influence. Who knows, exulted the editor, this may ultimately lead to the time when the door will be wide open for the Gospel in China![65] A mere fifteen years before this editorial, *CT* declared that Red China was not a member of the family of nations and condemned those advocating UN entry for this massive nation as guilty of political expediency and moral bankruptcy.[66]

On the issue of the Arab-Israeli conflict, *CT* moderated its views over time. Expressing wholehearted support for Israel in the 1950s and 1960s on grounds similar to those articulated in Jerry Falwell's premil-lennial theology,[67] by the 1970s *CT* was not as sure of itself, beginning to question Israeli behavior. Considering Israeli domination of the Arabs, an editorial declared the need to view the "Palestinian issue in human terms instead of in terms of the maps in the backs of their Bibles."[68]

Continuing to move toward moderation, *CT* applauded President Reagan's "dismissal of his 'evil empire' comment from several years ago."[69] While still acknowledging the danger existing between the two superpowers, the editorial reminded the readers that each side was human and conceded that the United States must not pretend that it has always been truthful in its dealings with the USSR and other nations. Remarkably, *CT* went on to admit that the Bible did not advo-cate either modern democracy or Marxism: "Rather, it offers much more basic rule of thumb by which to measure the effectiveness of political systems."[70] Under the basic rule of thumb, which was Romans 13, wherein Paul asserted that good government keeps the peace and promotes the common good, democracy was still "vastly superior over all the garden varieties of Marxist-Leninism."[71] Nevertheless, *CT* sensed that significant changes were coming about and maintained the hope that doors would open for a host of cooperative ventures.

During the late 1970s and early 1980s, *CT* also moved away, gradually, from the blatant assertion of the biblical roots of capitalism with the acknowledgment that there were Christians in Marxist countries who "will not automatically espouse American-style capitalism; that, in fact, they may find ways to be both good Christians and good citizens of their systems."[72] Another editorial acknowledged that evangelicals must be sensitive to the need to "distinguish the gospel from the political and economic practices of their homelands."[73]

Clearly, *CT* conveyed a more moderate tone. The journal wanted to be an agent for social change, and it condemned "uncritical patriotism" which the church had been guilty of whereby it "welcomed into the evangelical church [the official line] before the church [was] aware of its true nature."[74] This more mature shift from uncritical patriotism to critical analysis of national social issues brought *CT* closer to the more liberal *Christian Century*. The two journals were concerned about more of the same social issues with more similarities of opinion than earlier. Issues of environment, nuclear arms, the Third World, and U.S.-U.S.S.R. Middle East relations filled the pages of both journals.

On the question of the place of religion in public schools, *CT* revealed an ambiguity which showed sensitivity to this complex issue. On the one hand, they acknowledged that church-state separation precluded sectarian education. On the other hand, they showed confusion in defining "sectarian." Blaming Dewey for the installation of a public school god which was "the product of the cult of professional educators [and was] . . . as much sectarian as the God of Roman Catholicism, of Judaism, of Protestantism," the editors proceeded to declare that since the personal, biblical God of the Judeo-Christian revelation was the God of the foundations of early American education, and the foundation of the republic itself, there must be a return to the dominance of that God in national life.[75] This was sectarian as well, given how the word was applied to Dewey's public school god.

Possibly sensing the inconsistency, the editors declared that by the First Amendment "The Christian teacher is entitled to no more right to press for a particular religious identification in the course of professional duties than the secular teacher or any other teacher who speaks of spiritual values only, or of deity in some abstract and speculative sense."[76] This statement urged that Christian teachers be given at least equal opportunity to convey Christian convictions with those who favored the multisectarianism of modern education. Implied was advocacy of an equal time solution since a total return to a Judeo-Christian God was not likely.

But this concession was not a comfortable one for CT either since the conflict was "between specific sectarianism and a multi-sectarianism wherein the student acquires almost as many concepts of God and religion as he has instructors," with the danger that "men will worship and do only that which is right in their own eyes."[77] Lamentably, the American republic and public education no longer held a unitary spiritual outlook, as though it ever had one. The personal biblical God of the early republic was "being displaced by an abstract god manufactured by a combustible society that desperately needs Christian virtues but denies their supernatural origin and support."[78] And, in becoming detached from the Judeo-Christian revealed religion, public education became "attached to moral and spiritual values as a sort of humanistic embroidery on the fabric of evolutionary naturalism. Contemporary public education was constantly seeking a synthetic deity—a god-in-general assumed to be acceptable to all religious traditions because it is *not any god-in-particular*."[79] Affirming that there should not be sectarianism in public education, *CT* yearned for Judeo-Christian sectarianism.

The *CT* editorial wrestling with the 1960s Supreme Court ban on prayer and Bible reading for worship focused on the dilemma faced by evangelicals. On the one hand, the Court was accused of exchanging freedom of religion for freedom from religion. The journal anticipated that momentarily the Court would remove "In God We Trust" from coins, "One Nation Under God" from the Pledge of Allegiance, and chaplains and opening prayers in Congress and state legislatures.[80]

On the other hand, *CT* was apprehensive about implications of state-sanctioned prayer and Bible reading in the schools. To reinstate prayer and Bible reading would open the door to reading the Book of Mormon, reciting Hail Marys, and other kinds of non-Protestant and non-Christian exercises. *CT* was not comfortable with being on the same side as the Roman Catholic Church in opposing the ban since Roman Catholic motives included their traditional preference for church-state union. In thinking it over, the editors of *CT* were comfortable that the Court's decision was not anti-Christian since the New York Regent's prayer, which was challenged in court as an official state-sponsored prayer, was so generic, and the prayer so innocuous that no harm was done banning it. And the decision was seen as compatible with a proper Christian attitude toward government stipulation of religious exercises. It did not preclude any one from praying or groups from praying but only excluded government sanctioning of prayers.[81]

While *CT* did not advocate return of prayer and Bible reading for worship in the schools, it did advocate using the Bible for more than a mere study of literature as the Schempp case encouraged. Rather, *CT* wanted the Bible used as an objective guide for transcendent justice and morality.[82] Also, it supported moments of silence in the schools and favored "released time."[83] It called for the Supreme Court to establish guiding principles "That will prevent both anti-religious government and sectarian government."[84] CT was searching for any legal means by which America could be returned to its values. It supported the Court decision more because it found the alternatives unsavory. It lamented the need for the Court decisions because Protestantism had lost its de facto establishment status. Likewise, CT was having second thoughts on the insistence of teaching "creation science" in the classroom. In a "halfway-covenant" like statement, an editorial implied that perhaps creation science's geological timetable may be inaccurate after all. But still the editorial advocated that "Bible-believing creationists" be allowed to teach the position alongside evolution in science classes,[85] a strategic retreat at best designed to mollify conservatives and at the same time gain a modicum of intellectual respect.

One of the more dramatic shifts revealed by CT over the twenty-year period from the 1960s on was in the issue of Vietnam. Typical of its zealous nationalistic style of the late 1950s, CT threw its whole weight of influence behind American intervention. As the "greatest bastion of freedom," the United States had no choice but to intervene.[86] The conflict was pictured as being directly related to preserving American freedom,[87] and CT was distressed that American allies did not see a similar implication for their security, hence leaving the burden of defense to the United States. "Even the Vietnamese themselves apparently manifest some measure of indifference," lamented an editorial, since South Vietnam Foreign Minister Phan Huy Quat had to be told that the battle for Vietnam would be the last battle in Asia, if it were lost to Communists, with India and Japan being next on the Red agenda. Especially galling to CT were the 105 clergy in District of Columbia who petitioned President Johnson to negotiate a peace as best as possible and get out of Vietnam. The clergy, said CT, would "do best to put their hands to their mouths" on issues on which they are not informed.[88]

It is instructive to reiterate that CT was selective in asserting when it was appropriate for the church and clergy to speak out on public issues and when to take a pietistic stance. In its earlier years when CT agreed with government policy, it cloaked itself in pious expression that the church's role was to save souls. It was obliged to speak out on public policy when it was not in agreement.

Some of CT's harshest criticism during the Vietnam War was leveled at students in protest of the war. These students left campus, "ten to fifteen thousand of them, to tell President Johnson what to do about Vietnam. One wonders how undergraduates get so smart so soon," sneered an editor.[89] "The best protest," continued the editorial, "comes from the person who knows what he is talking about."[90] Obviously students who went to college did not qualify since "Abraham Lincoln, whose campus was only a hearth was sufficiently enlightened to remark that 'there is no grievance that is a fit object of redress by mob rule.'"[91] This was a typical *CT* attempt to appeal to the past, put down students and education, and offer a patronizing compliment to those enlightened students who spent their energies on the Mississippi levee helping stem a flood. On the other hand, protests of many students seemed to *CT* as less than conscientious, definitely lawless, and Communist-inspired. "Burning Selective Service cards," said one editor, "is certainly a far cry from 'panty raids' in the springtime. What these students did is perilously close to treason."[92] Such students should be expelled at once and "no expelled student should be allowed to enroll in another school unless willing to post a $10,000 good conduct bond."[93] *CT* highly praised President Johnson for resisting the pressure to withdraw from Vietnam exerted by international community, press, pulpit, and students in the face of Communist aggression. The United States was pure in its motives, wanting no territory and willing to help development and growth in Southeast Asia. Hanoi, Peking, and Moscow, on the other hand, were evil in intent.[94]

Uncritical support for the war, however, began to wane during the late 1960s. While America was pictured by CT as humane, meting measured destruction in contrast to the Viet Cong who were practicing tribal savagery based on religion, the war was stalemated and could cost ten billion in 1966 alone and last for ten to twenty years. In spite of American nobility in the cause of freedom, "such a diversion of the resources of the richest and most powerful nation on earth [was] sad to contemplate" for CT.[95] Editors were as frustrated as the nation. Caught in the predicament, all CT could say was "God help us. . . . It may be that the strongest and finest nation on the face of the earth will be taught in a small and weak country . . . that it is not by might, nor by power, but by God's Spirit that kings reign and nations prosper."[96]

Increasingly, from this point on, *CT* editors displayed a much more thoughtful and sophisticated approach to the Vietnam dilemma. On the one hand, the journal cautioned that just because a half million American soldiers were in Vietnam did not mean that administrative policy was right. On the other hand, the editors were concerned that the growing questions about the wisdom of the war not destroy the morale of the soldier.[97] However, when *CT* discovered that government testimony concerning the Ho Chi Minh Trail was misleading and that Americans could not trust government information in the event of nuclear attack, that instead of radio stations going off the air in case of nuclear attack as people were told, the stations were told "to broadcast reassuring messages that the air force was devastating the enemy in retaliation," *CT* was much more explicit in its criticism of administration policy. Perhaps "we need to legislate 'truth-in-testimony' for the executive branch," sneered an editor.[98] The sneer turned to deep concern with the revelation of the Pentagon Papers. *CT* was noticeably shaken. On the one hand, the journal was disturbed at government deception; on the other hand, it worried about how the *New York Times* got the information—a violation of the secrecy of classified information. *CT* was grappling with the conflict between the people's right to know and abuse of classified information to prevent political embarrassment.[99] The Calley issue heaped on even more damaging evidence that not only led to further questioning of the wisdom of the war but also revealed the level of barbarism formerly attributed only to the Viet Cong now engaged in by American soldiers.[100]

With these turns of events and revelations of government deception, *CT* softened its position on antiwar student protests, approving peaceful demonstrations. Never did the journal approve shutting down the government, and it always maintained that there were "hard-bitten Maoists and Trotskyites [in these protests] concerned about Vietnam not because of loss of life but because they [saw] there an episode in the historic struggle between communism and capitalism."[101]

By late 1971 *CT* explicitly called on President Nixon to "end our involvement at the earliest possible date consistent with the safety of our men and a chance for South Vietnam to remain viable."[102] By 1973 *CT* was questioning whether the United States should have gotten into Vietnam to begin with, either for moral or pragmatic purposes. *CT* took a particular slap at President Johnson who proceeded to do what he had promised not to do, that is, when he defeated Barry Goldwater in the 1964 presidential election, engage in a military solution. Nixon, on the other hand, had the sympathy of the journal as an inheritor of the war who did the best he could under the circumstances. His resumption of the bombing probably brought Hanoi to the table. The result was an agreement the United States could live with as it searched for issues of guilt and the role of a great power in a divided world.[103]

As the real impact of American withdrawal sank in, *CT* in a final note of resignation lamented that if Americans had known in the beginning what it knew now it would probably not have committed troops to Vietnam or even supplied military aid. But it did commit, and it withdrew, and worse yet, withdrew aid at the very time China and the USSR increased aid to Hanoi. The result was a bloodbath with Hanoi taking it all. Most seriously, *CT* saw the credibility of the United States damaged because of its inconsistency.[104]

And yet recovering from its morose analysis, *CT* recounted that the United States' commitment cost 56,000 Americans dead, 303,000 wounded and $150 billion in treasure—not a negligible commitment. Only an attack on Hawaii would have motivated a greater effort. So the United States was all right after all. The lesson was that if the United States had invested in evangelizing Vietnam "just 1% of what the Pentagon spent in fighting the war the conflict might have never occurred."[105] The connection of religion to national identity and policy would never go away for this evangelical journal. More than that, American Christians now had "the opportunity to seize the *cultural initiative in a new way*" by extending love to refugees with a "fresh implementation of biblical mandates . . . and unparalleled spiritual opportunity."[106] Try as it may, *CT* could never separate American culture from Christianity. It could only state the separation as an ideal.

Within a few short years, then, *CT* reflected with crisp, sharp clarity the American dilemma of trying to apply in a meaningful way the ideals which were believed to have made America great. In this process of trying to apply transcendent norms to American society, *CT* evolved from a display of zealous nationalism of the 1950s and 1960s to a more reflective sophisticated wrestling with the complex issues facing the republic at home and abroad.

In so doing it earned the chiding from separatist fundamentalism that accused it of waffling. Extreme liberals on the other end of the spectrum could never separate evangelicals from fundamentalists, thinking that conservative is conservative, given their insistence that there was a transcendent norm for society. Liberals of a more moderate centrist stripe were encouraged that a cadre of evangelical scholars not only produced excellent academic scholarship on religion and American society but also expressed a genuine social consciousness that described the American identity, role, and mission in much the same terms as found in the more liberal *Christian Century*. *CT* in the process over some thirty years had developed a nationalism of moderation.

CHAPTER 9

The Nationalism of Survival

And a great portent appeared in heaven, a woman clothed with the sun, with the moon under her feet, and on her head a crown of twelve stars; she was with child and she cried out in her pangs of birth, in anguish for delivery. And another portent appeared in heaven; behold a great red dragon, with seven heads and ten horns, and seven diadems upon his heads. His tail swept down a third of the stars of heaven, and cast them to earth. And the dragon stood before the woman who was about to bear a child, that he might devour her child when she brought it forth; she brought forth a male child, one who is to rule the nations with a rod of iron, but her child was caught up to God and to his throne, and the woman fled into the wilderness, where she has a place prepared by God, in which to be nourished for one thousand two hundred and sixty days. . . .

And the great dragon was thrown down . . . who is called the Devil and Satan, the deceiver of the whole world—he was thrown down to the earth, and his angels were thrown down with him. . . .

And when the dragon saw that he had been thrown down to the earth, he pursued the woman who had borne the male child. But the woman was given two wings of the great eagle that she might fly from the serpent into the wilderness, to the place where she is to be nourished for a time, and times, and half a time. . . . Then the dragon was angry with the woman, and went off to make war on the rest of her offspring, on those who keep the commandments of God and bear testimony to Jesus.

Revelation 12:1–6; 9:13–14; 17.

This passage was the culminating statement of a numerological determinism used to articulate an extreme American zealous religious nationalism. Through the employment of biblical prophecy Clyde Edminster, a retired cement contractor in the Pacific Northwest, believed that America was born as a nation under God, being His New Israel destined to rule the world. But before this could happen there were internal and external conspiracies afoot to corrupt this new nation under God which had to be destroyed, all as part of the Divine plan. America had to first perish in its own internal corruption so that a new America could arise as the Kingdom of God on earth. The external Communist conspiracy against America also had to be crushed in the cleansing process of this nation of Divine destiny. The wicked would be slain, both the Communist invaders as well as the corrupt in America. In the holocaust a remnant would be saved from the "modern Egypt (World Plan System)" to become the "modern children of Israel (the United States)."

This theme of American chosenness by the Divine with the extermination of its foes was developed in a monthly pamphlet, *Christ is the Answer*. The pamphlet expresses the views of Kingdom Identity, a survivalist group founded in the 1960s by Clyde Edminster, who, with his family, edits the publication at the family's forested enclave of some half-dozen houses situated a few miles east of the hamlet of Rainier, Washington. When I arrived at the headquarters of Kingdom Identity, a wiry, sweaty, bare-chested man with a mustache appeared, his face and body spattered with paint from the use of an air gun. He introduced himself as Clyde Edminster and invited me to sit on a patio overlooking the Deschutes River, whereupon he quickly edged his freshly poured concrete. After completing his task, on that summer afternoon in 1982, this smiling, self-confident man shared with me the message that has been printed since 1967 in *Christ is the Answer*.

The dominant theme of *Christ is the Answer* is that the United States is the New Israel, its experience paralleling that of ancient Israel so closely that the records and prophesies of both testaments of the Bible constitute a record of the American past and the program of its inevitable future. This parallelism, called "type and shadow," reveals how God will deliver the modern children of Israel (the United States) from the modern Egypt (any World Plan System) across a modern Red Sea (Communism) to the Kingdom of God on earth.

To establish that the United States is the New Israel, Edminster cited the passage above, which allegedly prophesies the birth of a great nation (the man child) which shall become the nucleus of the Kingdom of God on earth, and the destroyer of this present "Satanic world order."[1] "Heaven" in the passage, according to Edminster, means where the physical seed of Israel resides; namely, in the British Isles and Western Europe. The woman is National Israel and she is "none other than the divorcee, Mrs. National Israel, for the clothing of the sun, moon and the stars unmistakably identify her."[2]

Mrs. National Israel could not stay true to her husband, Yahvah, after the marriage at Sinai, whereupon Yahvah made preparation for the divorce by dividing the House of Israel into two: the ten northern tribes and Judah. Since this division did not cause Mrs. National Israel (ten northern tribes) to repent or change her ways, Yahvah was forced to take strong action against her, saying, "I will chastise you seven times for your sins."³ Since a "time" is 360 years, seven times is 2,520 years that Mrs. National Israel was to be punished for her rebellious and adulterous nature.⁴ To administer the punishment, Yahvah sent Assyria, which carried her away to the Caucasian Mountains, from which she was to retain the name "Caucasian" to describe her racial origin.

However, Mrs. National Israel was given two wings (God's Word and Spirit) so that she could fly (emigrate) into the wilderness (Isles of the Sea, meaning Britain and Western Europe) into her place where she would be nourished "for a time, and times, and half a time from the face of the serpent."⁵ In other words, this was accomplished in a span of three and a half times or 1,260 years, and since Mrs. National Israel went into Assyrian captivity beginning in 744 B.C., 1260 years added to this date would bring us to A.D. 516. This year was purported to be the beginning appearance of Mrs. National Israel in the British Isles of the Sea and Western Europe via the migration of the "galls [sic], Celts, Goths, Picts, Angli, Vikings, Saxons, Cymri, Normans, and the Danen, etc."⁶

Long before Yahvah divorced her, He had made certain promises to Jacob. The promises were that "I am God Almighty: be fruitful and multiply; A NATION AND A COMPANY OF NATIONS shall be of thee, and kings shall come of thy loins."⁷ During the time of chastisement, Mrs. National Israel was impregnated by the Word of God. "And as a woman pains to deliver, so [Mrs.] National Israel pained desperately to be delivered. She was certainly getting big as most pregnant persons do because she was complaining in Isaiah 49:19–20 about her place as being 'too narrow' and 'the place is too straight for me: give place to me that I may dwell.'"⁸ Mrs. National Israel grew crowded in the Isles of the Sea and Western Europe and so it was time for Yahvah to reveal to her the vast new world and continent that had been reserved to bring forth His first born nation under God. Quite naturally, since Mrs. National Israel was a nation, she would not only bring forth a nation, but a nation that bore a striking resemblance to its mother, namely the thirteen colonies that became the United States corresponding to Israel's thirteen tribes. Both constitutions and format were patterned after the Word of God.

This great event, this birth of a nation, occurred at the end of the seven times chastisement of Mrs. National Israel. It occurred with the successful birth, after a time span of 2,520 years beginning in the year 744 B.C., of the new nation in 1776!; God's New Israel revealed before our very eyes, and "destined to rule all nations with a rod of iron."[9]

Edminster interpreted the history of the United States as a reenactment of the story of the Children of Ancient Israel in Egypt. A few examples will demonstrate both his method and his message. Even as Jacob and his offspring went to Egypt for food and grain during the great drought,[10] so the Pilgrim Fathers, starving spiritually under the European state-church system, went to the new world to seek a place where spiritual bread could be eaten. This fulfilled the promise of Yahvah in II Samuel 7:10 and I Chronicles 17:9. Between 1620 and 1776 several million Anglo-Saxon, Scandinavian, Germanic, "and other Israelites" emigrated to America, and on 4 July 1776, America was born as a nation under God. America was in fact Joseph's land, the land of Goshen, the most fertile land in the world.[11] The Kingdom of God on earth was at hand. This new nation was complying with the laws of God and hence Yahvah was blessing America. In the same way, God had prospered Egypt, because under the seventy-one-year reign of Joseph, Egypt honored Yahvah. Joseph's reign in Egypt corresponded to the "golden years of our great republic . . . an era of harmony and good feeling under a truly constitutional form of government."[12]

But the new nation early on began its slide into apostasy due to the great Red conspiracy beginning with the Papacy and the Holy Roman Empire, and was brought on by the dragon, or Satan and his serpent race. Revelation 12:3 states that the Great Red Dragon with seven heads and ten horns and seven crowns awaits to devour the new child of Mrs. National Israel. Not only was this description identified as the Holy Roman Empire but it was to reign from 606 to 1866, or for 1,260 years. Furthermore, even as Joseph died and was replaced by the evil pharaoh Magron, who had an evil, violent, and corrupt government, so in 1847 "righteousness ceased to reign in the fullest sense in the U.S. and corruption and manipulation began to be manifested in our government with the advent of political parties which began to influence the policies of our land."[13] The Democratic and Whig parties began to flex their muscles until the advent of the Republican party in 1854. Additionally, international money interests and big business directed the United States. From 1847 to 1888 (forty-one years, paralleling the reign of Magron in Egypt) "America began to experience a departure from our divinely inspired Republican Constitutional form of government which honored Yahvah God of Israel and his national laws to a new form of government called Democracy."[14] The Red Dragon, working through World Zionism, allegedly enjoyed, and continues to enjoy, the surrogate services of socialism, communism, Nazism, Fascism, Marxism, Fabianism, and Judaism—all of which are one and the same World Zionism.[15] Such an overwhelming Satanic force had begun to infiltrate God's New Israel and it was from this that the new nation was to be delivered.

Through infiltration and conspiracy, the great Red Dragon, that is, Zionism, the Soviet Union and a long list of dupes and surrogates who were either the willing or unintended servants of Evil, foisted a long succession of abuses on the New Israel. For example, Lincoln successfully, though temporarily, thwarted infiltration of the Rothschild agents, a select group of Jewish moneylenders in his cabinet, whose intention it was to "infiltrate, undermine, seduce, propagandize, capture and destroy Christianity and the white race of people in their bid to establish and dominate a super-red, one-world socialistic kingdom."[16] Lincoln saw through the scheme, thwarted it, and paid for it by getting assassinated by John Wilkes Booth, "a member of one of their secret societies."[17]

The continuing litany of evil included Jewish money for the captains of industry, the Aldrich-Vreeland Bill, the Federal Reserve Act, the 16th and 17th Amendments, tax-free foundations, the creation of an international foreign policy, the Anti-Defamation League, and universal military training. The Aldrich-Vreeland Bill was passed allegedly due to infiltration of Congress and control of Woodrow Wilson by the Illuminati. All the rest were due to "that infamous day of December 23, 1913, when most of our loyal patriot statesmen had gone home for Christmas, at which time the international bankers strapped the American people into an international straight jacket by railroading into law" all of the above-mentioned bills and amendments.[18] For *Christ Is The Answer*, all of these events had their direct counterpart in the life and experience of ancient Israel in Egypt. While Egyptians of old used taskmasters to whip ancient Israel into obedience, "our modern Babylonian-Egyptian masters are using the I.R.S., the F.B.I., the C.I.A., and especially the A.D.L. (Anti-Defamation League), to defame, vilify or coerce anyone who opposes their Zionist program in our nation. Their favorite war cry is Anti-Semitism."[19]

In spite of the hardships and whippings imposed on the ancient Israelites they still multiplied and increased in number, whereupon the pharaoh Melot devised through his planners a means to destroy the children of Israel more quickly by instructing midwives to kill the baby boys.[20] And so today birth control allegedly serves as the means to liquidate the modern-day children of Israel, the white race.

However, the sons of Isaac were "genetically programmed to call on God as their final recourse."[21] The great and terrible day of the Lord was coming. Because there was a parallel between the children of Israel in Egypt, and the history of the people of the United States, the date of the deliverance could be known. Since Israel's experience in Egypt lasted 210 years,[22] 210 years of American experience put deliverance in 1986. Edminster stated: "So the more I studied into this possibility, the more I was convinced that Israel's sojourn in Egypt was the pre-written history of the United States of America."[23] Edminster interpreted biblical stories allegorically and "deciphers" coded messages of the Bible to reveal the "wonderful plan of redemption, deliverance and restoration." It was all "crystal clear" to him. Therefore, even as Ancient Egypt suffered through the great plagues before the children of Israel were released, so America was suffering through the plagues in preparation for Armageddon and its deliverance. The Egyptian plagues were a "type and shadow" of the plagues suffered today. A few examples will suffice. The sixth plague to hit Egypt was that of boils. The modern counterparts included cancer, tumors, sickness, and heart trouble. The seventh plague (hail) had its analogy in the bombing raids since 1940 on England, Germany, Italy, Japan, and Vietnam.

Because of these plagues, conditions were to worsen until 1986 when the world situation would be characterized by lawlessness, anarchy, and starvation, all kept in control by a huge military police and the firing squad. World planners would realize they were wrong to think they could control human nature through electronic computer devices. In America religion would be compulsory under government control. The real Christians would be underground, finding it impossible to live under the One World anti-Christ economic system without taking the "mark of the Beast." Interracial marriages would be compulsory under the threat of a genocide treaty. The white Israel race would become completely homogenized with alien races of color.

In response to the people's cries deploring these conditions, Yahvah would decide in 1986 to consummate this age and put an end to Satan's reign over the kingdom of this world. Yahvah, therefore, would put His hooks into the jaws of Gog and Magog[24]—Gog being Red Russia and her satellites, and Magog being Red China and her satellites. They would begin a gigantic invasion of America, the site of Armageddon.[25]

There would be several preliminaries to the invasion, however. A neutron bomb would be exploded[26] followed by the command by Yahweh—in preparation of the final plague of the destroying angel, International Communism—to apply "The blood of Christ over the doorposts and lentals of your hearts and homes even as of old the Israelites are told to use the blood of a slain animal on doorposts as a sign of faithfulness so that the angel of death would pass over that home and not destroy the first born."[27]

As the mist of radioactivity clears, the huge invasion would begin, consisting of 200,000,000 Communist armed forces, whose task would be to mop up all pockets of people who escaped bombardment. The remnants of Israel would see the power of the blood as they were spared from the mop-up operations. They would be sheltered in "the secret place of the most high God."[28] Edminster saw his forested enclave as one of those secret places where his survival capability of location, beauty, productive ability, and storage would bear good fruit. Moreover, as people saw the protection afforded those who applied the blood to their lives, many would repent.[29] "And I will remove far off from you the northern army, (200,000,000 Communist troops) and will drive him into a land barren and desolate, with his face toward the east sea (Atlantic Ocean) and his hidden part toward the utmost sea (Pacific Ocean) and his stink shall come up and his ill savour shall come up because he hath done great things."[30]

Once the purge was complete, that is, once all the chaff or the unfaithful in America were destroyed either by the bomb, or the mop-up operations, Yahvah next would destroy the Communist invaders. This would occur at the valley of judgement which is the valley of Harmongog near the Mississippi River valley.[31] Here Yahvah would stir up a scourge among the millions of these Communist invaders "according to the slaughter of Midian at the rock of Oreb."[32] This refers to the incident where Gideon and his 300 hand-picked troops went against thousands of Midianites and Amalekites and slew them, a "type and shadow" of Jesus and his "Delivering Company" of over-comers who would completely destroy the millions of Communist troops by their spiritual anointing. Communists would kill one another, "lifting forever the yoke of Satan's Serpent Race of people, the Amalekite-Canaanite-Zionist world conspiracy, from off the neck of Jacob-Israel. It will take seven months to bury the dead,"[33] said Edmin-ster, "after which we can look forward to Israel-America's deliverance in the year 1986 when we will have completed our 210 years of Egyptian bondage. America would do well to profit by the light given in the spirit of prophecy."[34]

This newly cleansed "man-child nation" would be much more than a nation "under God." It would be a nation "born of God and His word"; every inhabitant alive would be in "the Spirit of God" and part of God's great theocratic government of love and righteousness.

In listening to Clyde Edminster and in reading his material one would conclude him and his movement to be blatantly racist in general and antisemitic in particular, holding to a conspiratorial explanation of events, characteristics, all, of a zealous religious nationalism in the extreme. Even the freeze damage of Florida oranges which in turn "raised the price of your orange juice" was caused by Soviet manipulation of the United States' climate beginning in 1977 and 1978.[35] However, such an indictment leaves much unsaid. While Edminster would be classified as antisemitic by any definition he could hardly have been accused of hating Jews. In fact, he took sharp exception to being called antisemitic. Rather, his approach to the issue was to emphasize that God had set up his system in a proper order. Therefore Jews or blacks were not to be hated. They were simply being used by God negatively, much as material forces had created capitalism in order to destroy feudalism. There was nothing that could be done about this. It was the natural order in action in much the same manner that the ancients perceived slavery as a natural part of the social and economic structure of society. Additionally, in this God ordained system the whites were the inventors while other humans were copiers. Also, "natural" was the fact that Jews came from Esau, were impure, anti-Christ, Red, and, in an inversion of modern history, found their spiritual home in the Soviet Union. Israel, on the other hand, stemmed from Jacob, was pure, white, and was embodied by the United States. The problem of the "natural," according to Edminster, was that it was being polluted by the unnatural. The United States was pure until it allowed the immigration of Orientals and integration with blacks. Moreover, "adultery" to Edminster meant "racial mixture." Since the United States had strayed by encouraging an unnatural mix of races, God would have to remove the impurity. Edminster and his followers were merely in the grandstands waiting to watch the purification process occur, and they thought they know when it would happen.

While Edminster and the Kingdom Identity are survivalists, they are not of the variety that would gun down those who might need their aid in time of crisis. Moreover, his survivalism was expressed in a concern over the massive pollution of nature caused by greedy entrepreneurs in American society. On this issue Edminster definitely parted company with the traditional right-wing position. He chastised American society for allowing the dumping of wastes in streams, burial of wastes, radioactive fallout, pollution of air, and nuclear power plants. He lamented that the Environmental Protection Agency was understaffed and limited in its power and authority to bring large industrial plants and businesses into conformity to its codes.[36] The reason for this was that "America doesn't have many people with love in their hearts." Rather, people had become carnal, selfish, and rebellious. The solution was for America to perish in its own corruption (2 Peter 2:12) so that a new America could arise as the Kingdom of God on earth.[37] In a word, Edminster was a survivalist not merely to prepare for the future Armageddon, but to protect himself and his followers from the present pestilence of physical and moral pollution.

This unexpected position on the environment demonstrated that Edminster was very much his own man and that he and the movement were not tied to any set institutional structure, or to the fundamentalist movement. While there were theological similarities to fundamentalism's historic five-point creed there were differences as well. An outline of the theological position of *Christ Is The Answer* would include the following:

> Belief in:
> Jesus Christ, the only begotten Son of God, and His atoning sacrifice at Calvary.
> "The virgin birth, resurrection and ascension, and second coming to judge this world in righteousness."
> "The bodily return of Jesus Christ who will take the throne of David and reign as King of Kings for a thousand years."
> "His people Israel, consisting of twelve tribes, the descendants of the twelve sons of Jacob, were set apart by God to be His chosen servants through whom all nations are to be blessed."
> Belief that:
> "The present Zionist state of Israel in Palestine is an atheistic, counterfeit version of the Messianic one and will be destroyed by God."
> "The modern Israel nation must and will, under God, lead the world out of the chaos and misery that now affects mankind. And after much chastisement for their sins, the favor of God will again be upon them for the blessing of the world."[38]

Edminster and his colleagues also claimed that their constituency consisted of people from all religious backgrounds. Edminster and Kingdom Identity had no connection to any other religious persuasion, but they displayed great sympathy for those groups which practiced glossolalia. Such groups allegedly had the spirit of God if not a totally accurate interpretation of Scripture.

A similar analysis would be appropriate concerning Edminster's political stance. On the one hand, he and the movement were intensely nationalistic, hence supportive of the political system. On the other hand, in Edminster's view the system had been almost totally subverted standing in need of total cleansing. Any voting that would take place was seen as one's individual responsibility as an American, but the general outcome would conform to prophecy.

The United Nations Organization was simply another place for the Red Jewish menace to have its worldwide platform in order to subvert true governments of Israel. It was part of the reason for subversion in America. It was in part the reason for "adultery" in America. This was a prime example of the world planners and world government in action. But this development in human history, too, was merely a sign of the impending end. Although a conspiracy was responsible for American woes, it was a conspiracy used by God to warn those who do wrong to repent. In other words, God was in control of events in spite of the apparent chaos, with Edminster and company in the grandstands watching. This differed only in degree from John Calvin. Ironically, however, in being so close to Calvinism on the above question, Edminster was antithetical to Calvin on the issue of knowing God's plan. This was perhaps the single most characteristic feature of Edminster and his publication: Knowing God's Plan. "Ambiguity" was not in his vocabulary.[39]

In the Western world, the need for certainty runs deep. Ambiguity, speculation, contemplation, and insecurity disturb the Western mentality. On the other hand, the kind of certainty and knowing exuded by Kingdom Identity was simply an extreme and contorted rendition of a common yearning in American society. Everything about the movement, its leader, the location and its beauty and seclusion spelled SECURITY. The world may be topsy-turvy. People may be fraught with uncertainty, fear, and frustration. The news may be filled with violence, duplicity, immorality, and tragedy. Even nature may writhe with violence through wind, earthquake, and flood. No matter, it was all in the plan made plain to those who studied God's word correctly. "He that dwells in the secret place of the Most High shall abide under the shadow of the Almighty."

CHAPTER 10

The Nationalism of Anxiety

In a paper delivered to a conference at Calvin College, Grand Rapids, on the political activity of evangelicals in the 1980s, Ed Dobson, spokesman for Jerry Falwell, quipped: "I'm sure you know the difference between a Liberal, an Evangelical, and a Fundamentalist. You can tell the difference if you ask the simple question: Are there literal flames in Hell? The Liberal will say 'hell, no.' Very simple, very easy answer. The Evangelical will respond with a thirty-minute recitation on the implicit goodness of God in light of His eternal retribution, and at the end of the thirty minutes you'll not really be sure whether he actually believes there are literal flames in Hell. You ask a Fundamentalist this question and he'll respond, 'yes sir, and hot ones, too!'"[1]

From this candid admission of the place of sheer terror in Falwell's theology—the belief that those dying outside of Christ face literal flames for eternity—it seems appropriate to resurrect insights from Eric Fromm's model of a theology of anxiety for our inquiry into the possible motivating forces behind the nationalistic face of Jerry Falwell.[2] It is a model that is perhaps appropriate not only for those like Falwell and his fundamentalist followers but also for those who experience the anxiety of a society gone awry, fear dire consequences in the future, and in turn engage in a strategy of zealous nationalism[3] that gives the comfort of action rather than the frustration of helplessness.

I hasten to add two disclaimers. This discourse does not analyze Falwell's followers and does not plea for epicurean elimination of fear as motivation for action. Fear has been experienced by all and often motivates action, much of it positive. Rather, the focus is on Jerry Falwell and the extent to which Fromm's observations of behavior emanating from a theology of anxiety (fear out of control) apply to this Baptist minister and the nationalism of anxiety which I believe he clearly expresses.

To employ the Fromm model, one would cite his observation that from Calvinism comes emphasis on the absolute sovereignty of a God who is all-powerful and all-knowing, having foreknowledge of all He has created. While through His Scriptures, this God tells humans how they should live, His ways are past finding out. One can partially detect through signs what God's will is, but to know God's will fully is to claim to know what God knows, which is blasphemous. Given this belief, a fatalistic attitude might seem an appropriate response to theological determinism. But ironically the claim to not know God's will fully was responsible for an activism in Calvinism that on the surface seemed very illogical. In practice, these Calvinists, who believed in the human inability to change what God had ordained, were among the most ardent workers toward bringing about change. Why?

For Fromm, some psychological considerations explained the activism of Calvinists. A state of anxiety—feeling powerless and insignificant in a topsy-turvy world—"represents a state of mind which is practically unbearable for anybody." One possible way to escape this uncertainty and paralyzing feeling of powerlessness is to engage in frantic activity, striving to do something, a distinguishing trait of Calvinism.

Illustrating from the natural anxiety of a patient in the hospital awaiting diagnosis of an illness that can mean life or death, Fromm suggests that the patient may count the windows of an adjacent building. If the number is odd, a bad sign, if even, a good sign and all will be well. A childhood ritual of picking off the petals of a flower is similar: "She loves me, she loves me not," and with the last petal comes the sign that announces the result. Not sure of one's future—it is in God's hands—one must try to relax. But still the urge is irresistible and fervent activism may be a sign of election, even as the number of windows may signify health, or "she loves me" in the last petal be evidence of glory and joy in the future! The irrationality of the effort in any case is not to create a desired end or to change fate since the end has already been determined. Rather, effort serves to announce or forecast a predetermined fate. It gives evidence of what had been determined beforehand, independent of one's own activity or control—namely, for Calvinists, election. At the same time, the frantic effort was reassurance against otherwise feeling powerlessness. It was the psychological result of feeling powerless.

The application of this thesis to Falwell appears useful in a number of ways. For one thing, Falwell's theology is a theology of signs and evidence—signs of the end of time. No one knows the hour, but there are signs that the end is near and evidence that legitimates that. On a most visible level the evidence and genuineness of one's faith and piety is seen in how active a person is.[4] The literature of Falwell and the

Moral Majority is full of the call to action: "Now is the time to begin calling America back to God, back to the Bible, back to morality."[5] "We the American people have to make a choice today. Will it be revival or ruin? There can be no other way."[6] The fundamentalist mentality is not what one thinks about the American condition, but what one is going to do about it. "You are judged by what you do,"[7] said Dobson. Fundamentalism has "simple answers to complex problems. Jerry Falwell doesn't appeal to the intellectual."[8]

Action as evidence of one's faith and piety is even seen on the football field and basketball court of Liberty Baptist College, now Liberty University, founded by Falwell. Sports are very important and winning is seen as part of being Christian. "We have to show people that Christianity is not some sissy religion," said Falwell to the team. "Jesus was a he-man." Be "champions for Christ."[9] Ironically, the rhetoric is comparable to the Soviet emphasis which placed excellence in sports as testimony of their superior system.

But the importance of signs and evidence goes much deeper. Signs uphold meaning for existence itself. Falwell could not state the crisis of knowing more clearly. Says he, "People are not willing to live endlessly with ambiguity. There is something within us that is violated by feeling that we are adrift."[10] Fromm could not have described the problem any better either. Most obvious in the search for certainty for Falwell is obsessively detecting signs in biblical prophecies that are to be taken literally, looking to current events for signs of the end and the Second Coming. According to an interpretation of Daniel and Revelation, the drama was to begin when the Jews returned to Israel. The creation of the State of Israel in 1948, the Jewish return, fit this prophecy. Now humanity could look forward to the time when the Beast and Antichrist would unleash the "great tribulation" in which Jews would suffer persecution again. The Bolshevik Revolution of 1917 confirmed for dispensational fundamentalists (Falwell is a dispensationalist) a prophecy that the Beast will come from Russia, and the tribulation will begin with a Russian attack on Jerusalem—the City on a Hill. Only true Christians will be saved from the tribulation through the Rapture as they meet Christ in the air. Christ will then come with an army of Saints to defeat the forces of the Beast and Antichrist and begin the millennial reign on earth with peace and justice. The United States will supply the army of Saints. It had been worked out in precise detail. Now all that remained was to look for signs of the unfolding drama.

But, then, not so fast. Dispensational certainty was laced with vacillation almost as obvious as counting even/odd-numbered windows, or intoning "she loves me, she loves me not." This was clear in Falwell's statements concerning the potential for America's destruction/survival in the Cold War and the prediction/nonprediction of an imminent rapture and Second Coming of Christ. "God gave this nation her freedom and her liberty," said Falwell, "not for our enjoyment, but rather that out from here we might have a launching pad for world evangelization." Continuing the challenge, he reminded his listeners that there were "four thousand million souls in the world, all for whom Christ died, all important to the Lord, and if we lose our liberties as Americans, the cause of world evangelization, as I see it, will be down the drain."[11] Yet Falwell elsewhere confidently stated, "There is a hedge around America, a high fence. God will breathe fire on Russia. God will cause their missiles to blow up on the pad" because America has the largest number of Christians per capita than any nation on earth.[12] Further, the United States "is the greatest nation on the face of God's earth"[13] but, on the other hand, it was in danger of losing its chosenness due to moral corruption, straying far from the intent of the founding fathers two hundred years ago.[14] But then God would never allow that because He needed America to save the unsaved of the world. And, "there is power in the name of Jesus Christ, and it is the only power that can turn back godless Communism. If God is on our side, and he will be if we will turn back to Him as individuals and as a nation, no matter how militarily superior the Soviet Union is, they could never touch us." God would miraculously protect American power.[15] But it would seem that if America were to get better and better by turning from her wicked ways, the premillennial scheme would be subverted, which would postpone the Second Coming. Falwell addressed that sweet/sour note with the assertion that American doom loomed, that the apocalypse was near. "The twilight of our nation could well be at hand" perhaps by 1985, he said.[16] The Soviets in an attack would kill 135 to 160 million of our people and we'd kill only three to five percent of theirs.[17]

However, with "Imminent Doom: Meanwhile Boom."[18] Though America was at the point of financial and moral collapse, which would usher in the Rapture, Falwell was very busy being an American—that is, very active building apartments for retired people and recreation areas; preparing books and tapes on how to keep a marriage together; supporting the efforts of the PTA and AMA against immorality and violence on television; working with Anita Bryant in the crusade against gays; and developing a socially active program at the Thomas Road Baptist Church, which included a sports center, a home for alcoholics, a ministry for unwed mothers arranging for adoptions, taking in girls from other towns so as to save them from local embarrassment, and "Treasure Island," a resort for underprivileged children. Only fervent activity could turn America around, which, if accomplished in effect would fly in the face of evidence that the end was near. If America did not turn around she would lose her "chosenness," which meant that either America was not really chosen to begin with, or God changed His mind, which was not possible since that would mean that man thwarts the Almighty. America may get blown up by the Soviets if it does not build up its arsenal, but even if the Soviets were ahead of the United States 10 to 1, God would never let that happen anyway because the United States was chosen for a mission. Yet the Middle East situation was evidence of imminent destruction. Jesus was coming soon so we should be prepared. Things could hardly get worse. Society was totally immoral, including "'amoral' movies and literature, Sonny and Cher, Johnny Carson and 'Baretta,' acid rock music, homosexuals, sex education, welfare cheaters, the New Deal and the New Frontier, Andrew Young and the metric system." Barring a miracle, the financial system of America would collapse in a couple of years.

But "I'm not a prophet of doom," said Falwell.[19] On the brighter side, neither the Soviet Union nor one hundred million Arabs could prevent the people of Israel from possessing their inheritance. But on the other hand, "Islamic Fundamentalism is one of the most dangerous movements on the face of the earth. . . . I feel that the spread of Fundamentalist Islamic religion must be looked on as a very dangerous phenomenon in the 1980s."[20] But "when all looks lost there'll be the sound of the trumpet and we'll go up to be with God."[21] "She loves me she loves me not, she loves me she loves me not. . . ."

Other manifestations of vacillating faces were apparent. The issue of authority versus freedom appeared to be a particularly pestiferous problem for Falwell. Confusion was apparent on the level of academic freedom versus doctrinal correctness, and the relationship of the authority of the state to that of God. On the issue of academic freedom, Liberty University believed itself to be progressive. Their claim to this was based on inclusion of both evolutionism and creationism in their science courses. "We present evolution as a theory to our students, not as a fact," said A. Pierre Guillermin, president of Liberty. "We [also] present the biblical account of creation as a belief."[22] Falwell was more direct. "Here at LBC [Liberty Baptist College] we teach every ideology, but we also teach what's wrong." Further, at this institution of "academic freedom" faculty must be fundamentalist. "It's important to have a Christian faculty," said Guillermin, "because that is the primary value we want to communicate to our students. We provide knowledge—we don't exclude anything—but in a Christian context."[23]

The undergraduate catalogue of LBC struck the colors of the institution clearly. Included was a list of doctrinal tenets the student had to sign on to before acceptance in the school. In doing so the student affirmed the verbal inerrancy, inspiration, and authority of the Bible; Man's fallen nature; belief in the Trinity; salvation by faith alone; the imminent Second Coming of Christ; and "everlasting conscious blessedness of the saved and the everlasting conscious punishment of the lost."[24] Said Ed Dobson, the dean of LBC, "if you preach a Bible full of error, about a Christ who wasn't God, didn't die, and isn't coming back, then you have nothing to convert people to."[25] The authority side of the ledger clearly won out on the dress code and student behavior issue as well. "The student who is interested in doing his own thing will not be happy in the atmosphere of Liberty Baptist College."[26] The dress code mandates the men in dress slacks, shirt, tie, forbidding hair over the ears and down to the collar. Women are to wear dresses and skirts no shorter than two inches from the middle of the knee. Clearly the image that Liberty wished to strike was one of valuing academic freedom, yet displaying a firm commitment to theological correctness. It appealed to the academic reputation of Harvard with an approving quote from its catalogue—its seventeenth century catalogue: "Everyone shall consider the main end of life and studies to know God and Jesus Christ which is eternal life."[27]

An even greater confusion existed in sorting out the authority of the state from that of God. On the one hand, Falwell declared politicians to be crooked and deceitful, "engaged in a deliberate effort to disguise the true situation."[28] On the other hand, "the powers that be" were "ordained by God" and "whether [our leaders] are aware of the fact or not" are in their position "by divine ordination."[29] The confusion continued in a sermon in which the listener was told that "To love God we honor and respect Caesar but we love the Lord. Is it ever right to break Caesar's laws? Only when they violate God's laws. . . . [When] we can't go to church, we can't pray, we can't read the Bible, we can't win souls. Then Caesar's law be hanged. We revert to a higher authority and that is God's authority."[30] But then in the same sermon he declared that every king, government, parliament, congress "is established and set up of God. . . . These men are ministers of God— ministers of God, which doesn't mean they're all saved. It means they are servants, or ministers of God, whether they know it or not." Furthermore, a proud feature of his students at Liberty was that "They never rebel against authority."[31]

On a folksy level Falwell declared his loyalty to the authority of the state—sort of. Complaining about the federal fifty-five mile per hour speed limit, he confided to his congregation that it is "too slow for me. But it's the law. And if I violate that, whether I like it or not, I pay the fare. Thank God, I haven't paid it for a long time. We've got the Assistant Chief of Police back here [in the congregation], that might have something to do with it, but I haven't paid it for a long time, because the powers that be are ordained by God."[32] In other words, apparently the authority of the state and its mandate to punish breakers of the law was sanctioned by God whether one was cozy with law enforcement or not. Enforcing or not enforcing the law in this case was equally sanctioned by God since the sheriff's office was of God.

A similar confusion reigned in Falwell over whether the United States was a Christian nation. In extolling the glories of the United States Constitution, Falwell cited the Ten Commandments as the cornerstone of this document. While conceding that it was not written under Divine inspiration like the Bible, it was "inspired." The men who wrote it, said Falwell, "were led of God as they prayed and sought His face." The principles of the Constitution are "the teachings of Christ as you find them in the Sermon on the Mount. It is unreal how they parallel. And there's no question about it, this nation was intended to be a Christian nation by our founding fathers."[33] On the other hand, Falwell declared explicitly elsewhere that "I think America is great, but not because it is a Christian nation; it is not a Christian nation; it has never been a Christian nation, it is never going to be a Christian nation."[34]

Falwell was also "a study in vulnerability" regarding evangelization of the Jew.[35] On the one hand, the Jew who converted to Christianity represented a "fulfillment" of Old Testament prophecy. On the other hand, "Christians are not to replace Jews," and the church had not come to replace Judaism. But Judaism was not an alternate path to Christianity either "in the sense that it might lead one to the same destination as Christianity" because "Jews or anyone else without Christ have a missing dimension in their lives." Yet this missing dimension did not make Judaism a degenerate path, unless a Christian were to convert to Judaism. In that case, converts engaged in an "act of abandonment," since after studying the evidence, they had concluded that Jesus Christ was not the Son of God, but was rather "a liar or a lunatic." But that aside, God was not yet finished with the Jews. Both Israel and the church were to maintain separate identities. Even with the Second Coming of Christ when the Jewish nation "will believe on the Messiah," Judaism will continue with a double identity as "Hebrew [and] Christian." God had outlined a vast and glorious future for Israel. Its present day role "is that of waiting."[36] The American role was to protect Israel. "Since America has been kind to the Jew, God has been kind to America. . . . The Christian must politically involve himself . . . to guarantee that America continues to be a friend of the Jew."[37]

Walter Capps summarized the incongruity of Falwell's assessment of the Jews by noting that Falwell's mediation between Christians and Jews was essential if he were to make good on his positive attitude toward Israel. Yet "an absolutist 'born-again' Christianity is not an accommodating basis for a working partnership."[38] And the incongruity extended well beyond Falwell and the Jews. In answer to the question whether Falwell wanted the whole world to become Christian (converting Hindus, Buddhists, Muslims, Jews) the answer, on the one hand, was the wish to convey openness and tolerance. On the other hand, democracy was intended for the whole world as the best form of government for mankind. Christianity and democracy were entirely compatible.[39]

If all of this is confusing, incongruous, and vacillating, it either "proves" that the wisdom of the world is foolishness to God, or it further manifests a nationalism of anxiety in which the search for identity appears confused at best, frantic at worst.

Falwell employed the manichaean rhetoric of black and white to convey his message. It perfectly conveyed a nationalism of anxiety by appealing to the psychological needs of exhortatory and mimetic audiences for safety, security, stability, protection, and strength.[40] At its worst it legitimated a zealous nationalism which encouraged the literal destruction of the "wicked" at home and abroad. At best it pictured the world in simplistic terms of evil versus good. Falwell did this by employing two rhetorical conventions: "fear appeals and emotive words." The fear appeals was accomplished by portraying America as "approaching the brink of disaster" at the hands of the "godless communists" who were dedicated to world conquest.[41] And, the United States was in danger of becoming "another Poland, Afghanistan, or modern-day Sodom and Gomorrah." Little children will be "assaulted and proselytized into the camp of the deviates." The cause of American "capitulation" will occur because "God is angry with this nation" and has pushed the "panic button."[42]

Falwell's words were emotionally charged "god-terms" and "devil-terms." God-terms included "wives," "mothers," "girls," "God-fearing Americans," "free enterprise system," "Christians," "majority," "morality," "heterosexuality," "moral Americans," "pregnancy," "child-

birth," "full-time housewives." Devil-terms would be, "feminists,"
"lesbians," "ERA," "Godless Humanists," "Communists," "socialism," "liberals," "minority," "darkness," "homosexuality," "pornographers," "idolaters," "abortion," "murder," "genetic manipulation,"
"creeping," "infesting," "bleeding heart liberals," "apostate," "witches,"
as in "What is NOW? . . . the national organization of witches? . . . Oh
excuse me, but I'm talking about the Betty Friedans, Gloria Steinams,
Eleanor 'Schneels' [not Smeal], Bella Abzugs, and all the other thugs."[43]

Buttressing his God-terms and Devil-terms was his appeal to the
authority of God, which legitimated his manichaean perception of the
gigantic struggle of good versus evil in the society. The weapons in the
battle included rhetorical devices to energize the faithful and convince
the skeptic. There was the name-calling device whereby Falwell
complained that he had been attacked by homosexuals, Nazis, liberal
clergy, abortionists, pornographers, politicians, bureaucrats, humanists
and Communists. Attacks against Falwell by the unsavory were
always the work of Satan.[44]

Falwell also used glittering generalities by which his audience was
reminded that members of the Moral Majority were not all fundamentalist Baptists but "Americans who believe in the family, in decency,
and all the things this country stands for." And, "Christians don't
believe in equal rights for women. Christians believe in superior rights
for women."[45] The "everybody is doing it" bandwagon device was a
generalization par excellence. "I've been so delighted," said Falwell,
"that in recent years everybody is quoting that verse (2 Chronicles
7:14) claiming it as a promise for America. Yes, even the President of
the United States believes that God can heal America. And that if we
meet His conditions, God's conditions, He will in fact heal America."[46]
Name-dropping and the testimonial were two related rhetorical devices
used to marshall support from notable personalities. "In a recent
meeting with President Reagan at the White House," said Falwell, "my
heart was warmed as I heard him say again that he believed abortion is
the taking of human life."[47] Also, Falwell played on the American
admiration of humble origins with "The Plain Folks Device" in which
he assured listeners that he was a regular guy who knew the pressures
experienced by common folk. He spoke of his "little radio studio" in
his basement that he could get to only by walking "through my wife's
laundry room to get here."[48]

Card-stacking, another rhetorical device, can be comforting when
facing a battle with the Devil. In speaking of the Equal Rights Amendment, Falwell assured his listeners that the ERA was supported by
"women, most of them failures, wanting to do their own thing."[49] As

for government-sponsored daycare and Head Start, Falwell declared that "They're advocating daycare units . . . for ages two and up with mandatory attendance so that they will capture the minds of the little ones and fill them with humanism and atheism and socialism and godlessness."[50] As for homosexuals they "come out of the closets and out of the cesspools." They come out to "magnify their immorality and glorify their perversion. And they found wicked and base politicians who said to these deviates: 'Do your own thing.' I believe in 'freedom of speech,' but that does not give you the right to pervert and attack and assault little children or to proselyte into the camps of the deviates, helpless young people who cannot protect themselves."[51]

Falwell's rhetoric of black and white was a call to action not just to inspire but also to instill an outrage that would lead to action on behalf of a way of life threatened by overwhelming evil forces in the society. His rhetoric did not lend itself to rational dialogue. It was rhetoric that could be used to easily justify firebombing abortion clinics and shooting doctors who "murder babies" even though Falwell has never advocated such violence. The power of rhetoric is dangerous because it can induce action well beyond the intention of the speaker or writer of such inflammatory rhetoric. Herder's imploring Germans to "spew out the Seine's ugly slime" was a rhetorical excess designed only to encourage Germans to speak German—to be themselves and not ape the French—rather than a call to physically pulverize the Gallican. C. C. Goen illustrated the power of church press rhetoric in the coming of the American Civil War.[52]

So Falwell's rhetoric of anxiety about a way of life that was slipping away spawned the rhetoric of a zealous nationalism that spoke of "A little bearded boy scout [who] takes over an island ninety miles from Miami called Cuba, shakes his fist in our face, and we do nothing about it." It was a rhetoric which expressed a yearning that "my President . . . say to those murderers and liars from the Kremlin. . . . Fellows, 'if you step over [this line] we will drop everything we have on you,' and mean it! . . . I do not for one moment subscribe to that Harvard philosophy, 'Better Red Than Dead.'"[53] It was a rhetoric that on the one hand excoriated America for its immorality and on the other hand declared, "I'm for loyalty . . . to this country. I told you last week, I won't even wear a pink shirt! . . . I'm against anything that is not loyal to America. Wherever you are, I'm to the right of you! And I'm not ashamed of it. I love this country, I love every square foot of this land."[54] Further, the rhetoric served notice to all the secular humanists and communists who criticized America that they needed to "think about what might happen if all emigration and immigration restrictions were suspended for thirty days. At the end of thirty days, the United States would be teeming with people—they'd be all over, in bus depots, on the highways, in the streets, everywhere. And, at the end of thirty days there'd be but two people in the Soviet Union, Mr. and Mrs. Gorbachev, and 'even Mrs. Gorbachev would be packing her bags.'"[55]

The rhetoric of zealous nationalism could spawn a "Christian" jihad if taken literally. "We teach patriotism . . . as being synonymous with Christianity," said Falwell. Furthermore, good Christians not only make good citizens but good citizens do not rebel. Speaking of students at Thomas Road Baptist church and Liberty Baptist College, Falwell declared that they do not desecrate the American flag nor burn draft cards nor march against Washington. "You will not find them in a place of rebellion." Rather you will find them praying, winning souls, reading Bibles, living and behaving like children of God, honoring those in places of authority "Because the Word of God says so."[56] All the components of a zealous nationalism were there: the call to eliminate the "Evil Empire," religious justification for doing so, and obedient citizens to the state who saw patriotism as synonymous with Christianity. All that would be needed would be those in authority ordering the action.

"The worship of a past that never was" is also often a part of a nationalism of anxiety. Memories, real or imagined, play a powerful role in the history of nationalisms, providing comfort amid confusing social change and a motivation to resurrect the past. Falwell's own television program, "The Old Time Gospel Hour" is an obvious throwback to a program that provided warm personal security, Charles B. Fuller's "The Old-Fashioned Revival Hour."[57]

More significantly, fundamentalists in general and Falwell in particular have been dismayed by "the deinstitutionalization of Christian morality"[58] in American society and have tended to draw on their perception of a more glorious past as comforting and as a model for a hoped-for encore in American society. It is the period of 1776 when the United States was founded "by men (underscore *men*, as in Founding Fathers) whose guiding principles were informed and supported by the authority of that same authentic Christianity [Falwell] is working diligently to reinstate."[59] He is passionately committed to the values purported to have existed in the past, including the traditional family, rugged individualism, self-reliance, honesty, God-fearing scripture-believing reverence, a peace-loving but always ready-for-war patriotism ("Don't tread on me"), discipline, faith in the ordinary man, prosperity, and a mission to the world to show the better way.

It does not matter much if that past ever existed. The rhetoric and vision were more important because they gave comfort and "certitude in the face of the ambiguities of modern life." And they provided the reason for existence, namely, taking up the unfinished challenge set before the nation by the founders.[60] The "God Bless America Survival Kit," distributed to thousands, appealed to the glorious past. The kit contains a copy of Francis Schaeffer, *A Christian Manifesto*, Falwell's *Listen America*, and a "framable certificate" which lists "Seven Principles That Made America Great."[61]

Falwell also took comfort and inspiration from previous fighters for Christian morality who vociferously opposed the Social Gospel and modernism, and who sounded the alarms against German rationalism, Bolshevism, Catholicism, Darwinism, socialism, evolution, immigration, and Kaiserism. Falwell's excoriation of San Francisco for its homosexuality and AIDS epidemic could have taken a page out of Billy Sunday's same condemnation of the sinful city by the Golden Gate.[62] "No wonder God shook that old town with an earthquake and swept their cussedness with fire," said Sunday. "There wasn't a rottener city on the American continent than San Francisco."[63] And Sunday's zealous nationalism could only inspire shouts and cheers, hats flung in the air, and a stirring model in his rip-snorting challenge that "Our little trouble with Spain was a coon hunt as compared with this scrap we have on hand with that bunch of pretzel-chewing, sauerkraut spawn of blood-thirsty Huns. . . . So dig down deep and let us fill Uncle Sam's bank vault high with our money and help send shivers down the crooked spine of the Hohenzollerins who are dancing on the thin, thin crust of Hell and thus help the guns of the army and navy to dig their graves, then the world can live in peace."[64] Those good old days of past revivals allegedly snatched the nation from the jaws of immorality, exuded patriotism and at the same time saved thousands of souls for eternity. It happened in the past; perhaps it could happen again.

Yet in spite of a rhetoric that repels the skeptic or vacillations that bemuse Christian and non-Christian alike, a dispensationalism of dire predictions at the hands of the "Evil Empire" that fizzled into a Soviet national meltdown, and "worshiping a past that never was," Falwell's nationalism of anxiety did articulate the societal malaise and a clear mission and strategy to address the sickness. Fear/anxiety can be used to motivate focused action which tries to address the reasons for fear. This was also part of Falwell's nationalism. One may or may not agree with Falwell's identification of the American societal problem or the solution. But this was a clear nationalistic response by this Baptist minister to a generally agreed upon fear/anxiety that something was very wrong with American society and that something needed to be done about it. Falwell insisted that God was not yet finished with America in spite of the litany of her evil. America had a special covenant with God to be the moral light to the world. Specifically, "God has raised up America for the cause of world evangelization and for the protection of his people, the Jews. I don't think America has any other right or reason for existence other than for those two purposes."[65] In fulfilling these tasks, the church and the state were to be partners, the church's primary task being world evangelization, the state's task exporting democracy and resisting Communism. While the church was primarily to meet the spiritual needs of its generation, it was also obligated to "be concerned about the world's physical and emotional needs as well."[66] In attempting this, Falwell and Dobson perceived themselves to be in line with nineteenth-century evangelicals who were in the "Social vanguard for national reforms, from abolition of slavery to child labor law reform and prohibition."[67] Dobson even admitted that fundamentalists should have been engaged in the Civil Rights movement of the 1960s and been concerned about sexism in American life.[68]

With the election of Reagan in 1980, Falwell was encouraged that moral reforms could once again take place in America, that a restoration of patriotism would make America the world's last hope against Communism. The American mission to export democracy had allegedly been thwarted by surrender in Vietnam due to "pressure from left-wing radicals in control of the American press and media that produced misplaced and illegitimate guilt on the collective American psyche."[69] This left-wing power allegedly eroded America's ability to maintain leadership as a world power at an especially dangerous moment in history, for such weakness placed at risk America's ability to protect God's people, Israel and to thwart Communism's objective of world conquest. The opportunity had arrived for church, state cooperation in fulfilling America's reason for existence.

The most visible attempt to marshall church-state cooperation in addressing society's ills was the Moral Majority founded in 1979. Disclaiming any intent to turn America into a theocracy, Ed Dobson, speaking for Falwell, insisted that fundamentalists long frustrated over societal deterioration realized that their voice was not taken seriously in the political process, "kicked in the [political] door," and said "we will be heard; we will be part of the political process."[70] Sensing that vast numbers of conservative Americans outside the pale of fundamentalism shared the same anxieties, and that fundamentalism alone

could not have a significant political impact, Falwell sought association with Jews, Mormons, and even Catholics in forming a nonreligious organization that would exercise significant influence in the
political process to bring about a moral reformation consistent with a
conservative agenda. Those with different agendas for America were
prone to accuse Falwell and the Moral Majority of engaging in inappropriate mixing of religion and politics. However, claiming belief in the
separation of church and state, Falwell said it was "a misconception to
call the Moral Majority a religious organization."[71]

While that statement was no doubt crafted to silence his critics on
issue of mixing politics and religion, Falwell also said he did not
believe the founding fathers intended the church to be separated from
government. Moreover, the Moral Majority was structured as nonreligious in order to attract conservatives of any religious faith. As a
result, it was a coalition of "religious people." In any case, church
people regardless of persuasion have generally considered political
involvement of the church as legitimate when moral issues were
involved. The sticking point was always, Which moral issues, and Are
the issues deemed as moral really moral? It just so happened that the
moral issues targeted by Falwell included homosexuality and abortion
on demand. For him, homosexuality was against God's Word, and
abortion was murder. On the other hand, to show his good-faith commitment to church-state separation, he expressed personal opposition
to giving back the Panama Canal but did not get politically involved
because in his view it was exclusively a political issue.[72] In Falwell's
view the state should not legislate moral issues, such as prohibition,
since such laws could not be enforced. The ideal for Falwell was a
harmony between law and morality balanced with enforceability,
since "good laws that were unenforceable and widely disobeyed casts
all the law into disrepute."[73] It was a matter of definition since such
issues as nuclear freeze and Salt II were considered moral issues by
liberals and hence eligible for political involvement by the church.

No matter how much Falwell attempted to facilitate church-state
cooperation on moral issues while disclaiming the Moral Majority as a
religious organization, both ends of the religio-political spectrum were
not buying his explanation. Liberals still saw Falwell as a man who, if
he had his way, would prefer at least a de facto fundamentalist, Protestant establishment that would turn America "back to God." Old-line
separatist fundamentalists were not buying his explanation either. To
them this self-proclaimed separatist fundamentalist was no more
separatist than Billy Graham. In Bob Jones' eyes, he was even worse
than Graham and hence "the most dangerous man in America" for
hobnobbing with Mormons, Jews, and Catholics in his Moral Majority.[74]

While expecting criticism from liberals, the salvos leveled at Falwell from ultrafundamentalist colleagues were cause for serious concern. Such internal sniping within separatist fundamentalism was allegedly due to Satan working overtime to discredit the movement. It was to Satan's advantage to create such internal mayhem. Satan enjoyed it when backstabbing among separatists occurred. Such public display of disunity posed a "great opportunity for unbelievers . . . to blame the gospel and excuse themselves for their own renunciation of the faith we embrace."[75] Therefore, it was time that "fundamentalists and separatists learned to be gentlemen." It was "time to allow others [within separatism] to think, preach and write whatever they please and love one another in spite of it."[76]

To those outside the fundamentalist separatist camp, Falwell's other face emerged. "It [was] right to go to war over Biblical truth [and] pleasing to the Lord for His children to stand firm for faith once delivered." Those who called themselves fundamentalists and separatists, but who were not, needed "to be exposed."[77] Christian leaders should stand openly against worldliness and modernism, to expose organizations that published "liberal and modernistic material for distribution among the people of God" and to be on guard lest apostasy creep "into our colleges, seminaries and churches."[78]

It was, then, a tightrope walk for Falwell. He was not only trying to unite fundamentalists, evangelicals, and charismatics—no small task by itself—for common moral goals for society but also trying to enlist Roman Catholics, Mormons, Southern Baptists, and Jews for the same purpose. He appeared on a Unification Church–sponsored platform and on the Phil Donahue show with Mose Durst, president of the American branch of Reverend Moon's church, all the while insisting that he was a separatist fundamentalist. Yet Falwell was not likely to invite Billy Graham to speak in his church because of Graham's crusades with churches affiliated with the National Council of Churches. To accomplish this remarkable balancing act, Falwell was able to separate his faith from his politics, although it was his faith which determined the political issues he considered appropriate for support or criticism from the Moral Majority.

Another very visible strategy Falwell employed to facilitate a societal turnaround with nationalistic overtones was his pride and joy, Liberty University. This educational enterprise developed a curriculum and program to nurture loyalty to God and country with a mission to the world. The name "Liberty University" was chosen by Falwell "because it symbolized his interpretation of the role America should take in leading the world in the cause of American-style democracy."

The university also had a religious vision for society and an educational strategy to implement it. The catalogue states that the school is "a training ground for Christian statesmen and governmental leaders of tomorrow."[79]

While the catalogue assures the would-be enrollee and benefactor that though the university curriculum is based on "sound theory and philosophy," it is also "action oriented."[80] This latter emphasis turned out to be primary, reflecting not only fundamentalism as "an action-oriented movement with little commitment to philosophy and reflection,"[81] but Falwell himself as a man of action. Students and faculty also were expected to actively express fundamentalist views in church and civic life and to enhance the democratic process and free enterprise system. The emphasis on sports, the use of military metaphors, the university sports team name the *Flames*, the title of the university newspaper *The Champion*, the university motto "Knowledge Aflame," and the university's mission statement to "train young champions for Christ" are all action images. Still the movement needed academic respectability, and Falwell called upon the memory of "Old Tom Jefferson [who] had the right idea. If you want to shape history you shape the minds of young people."[82] A university, which is supposed to be interested in philosophical discussion, among other things, was just the place for such a thing.

To enhance the image of the fundamentalist ideal for American life, Falwell was not interested in the school being a Bible institute or Bible college. Rather, his goal was a fundamentalist Notre Dame that would excel in athletics, academics, and morals. It would train a new kind of fundamentalist who could address the world on its own terms. "Liberty Baptist College became Liberty University because Falwell [believed] increasing Fundamentalism's social and academic legitimacy [was] necessary in order to compete on an equal basis with the secular world."[83]

The university curriculum further reflected fundamentalist priorities with its statement on its teacher education program as a promise to provide "a broad general education which will equip the student with knowledge, values, attitudes and ideas essential for the performance of responsibilities as an American citizen."[84] The university's heavy emphasis on its School of Business and Government and its Political Science Department further revealed the goals and strategy of the university relative to the society. The School of Business and Government catalogue states that it trains

the leaders of tomorrow in the worlds of business and government. America needs Christians in command posts and leadership in corporations, businesses, small and large, and government at every level. Aiming at more than technical competence, the School of Business and Government is producing men and women with the vision and values needed to restore the spirit of free enterprise and republican self-government, the twin pillars of a free society.[85]

The mission was clear, to train "leaders in all the disciplines who will go out there and shape society in general and make it possible for Americans to salvage the society."[86] "Imagine," said Falwell, "what ten or twelve thousand graduates each year could do for a sin-sick society."[87]

Such an army of the "saved" could not only support the right of school boards and parents to influence the books that children read in public schools but also would serve on such policymaking bodies. The issue was too important to leave to libraries and teachers exclusively. Quick to deny advocacy of removing any books from a library, Falwell urged that conservative Christian books be included on the shelves while at the same time insisting that porn publishers be put out of business. Christian school boards could also restore prayer and Bible reading since the end of such practices had been evidence that America was less and less a "nation under God."

Crucial in helping to build a nation under God was electing the right kind of president/commander-in-chief. This man, said Falwell, should be a president who says, "I am a Christian. More than that I believe this is a Christian nation. And though we welcome into all the luxuries of first-class citizenship every nonbeliever within our borders, for that is the American way, nonetheless, as long as I am President, I shall lead this country in the ways of Christ as set forth in this Book, God's Holy Word."[88]

And, as a host to a foreign head of state, the president should give "some orange juice or tomato juice, have a good minister come in and read a few verses of Scripture, and if he doesn't like that, put him on the next plane back home! I believe America needs a Christian leader who will take a stand against sin."[89] Furthermore, said Falwell, "I don't know why every one of our presidents thinks he has to wine and dine every drunk who comes over here from some other country and dance with his wife."[90] The president should come out against sin in any form. Convicted drug dealers should be given a mandatory death sentence. He should come out against premarital and extramarital sex. "And in case Madam President [Roseline Carter] got her tongue twisted, as has been known to happen, and said something that was quoted out of context, I would like for him to take her upstairs and have a little talk with her and send her right away back to that same microphone and this time say it so clearly even Walter Cronkite would get it: 'We are against premarital and extramarital sex.'"[91]

The kind of president the United States needed should also balance the budget by "ending unnecessary welfare spending at home and abroad." While Social Security was good in the mind of the Lynchburg pastor, welfare spending for the "shiftless" was out of hand. "I don't believe," said Falwell, "we ought to feed that lazy, trifling bunch lined up in unemployment offices who would not work in a pie shop eating holes out of donuts. My edict for them is, Let Them Starve."[92]

Falwell not only used graphic language to express his views on almost everything, but also he loved to spin homespun yarns about his personal life and family as examples of frugality for home and nation, minister's family, and the president's family. Setting the stage for a good one, he informed his readers of having one wife, three children, four dogs, two which were poodles, who live inside and are "hers," and two Irish setters that live outside and are "mine." Parenthetically he tells us that they are dog lovers, and "I don't care much for folks who are not." Now for the lesson in frugality. When the setters were purchased, he was told what kind and how much meat to give the dogs. Too much for the family budget. Falwell "went to another store . . . and bought a big bag of Purina and . . . gave them two heaping bowlsful. And, sure enough, those spoiled dogs would not eat a mouthful of it. But after four days they did! [Lesson] And if we let those bums get hungry enough, they will find a job and they will go to work and become productive citizens."[93] Conclusion: what America needed was strong, powerful praying, preaching, and dynamic leadership. "Do you know," concluded Falwell, "why the wave of eastern religions is creeping over this continent? Do you know why transcendental meditation, called TM, is infesting this republic? Because we don't have any praying preaching leaders crying out against it and calling it vulgar humanism in its lowest form."[94]

The closest to Falwell's ideal of a president was Ronald Reagan, whom he identified as "the best thing to happen to America in at least twenty years"; the best thing, not only because Reagan came out against abortion and homosexuality, but also because now America was not taking any "guff from its enemies." The United States shot down Libyan planes that attacked American aircraft over the Mediterranean Sea, liberated Granada, attacked Khadafy in Libya, and approved the Israeli attack on the Baghdad nuclear reactor. Falwell called Begin to congratulate the Israelis on the raid. Said Falwell: "Mr. Prime Minister, I want to congratulate you for a mission that made us very proud that we manufacture those F-16s. In my opinion you must've put it right down the smokestack."[95]

The dilemma of sorts was that predecessor Jimmy Carter, a failure in Falwell's eyes, was a "born-again Christian" and Reagan was not. Falwell had said that the ideal was to have a man in the White House who was a born-again Christian. No doubt sensing the inconsistency, Falwell emphasized that that was the *ideal*. "But if I've got to have a man who is a born-again Christian who doesn't follow Godly and Biblical principles, and an unsaved man who does, I'll take him [the unsaved man]."[96] The phenomenon at work here was called "transtolerance," a term used by Peter Vierck to mean that one was willing to overlook a candidate's wrong theology for his right politics, a phenomenon that occurred in the 1950s when some separatist fundamentalists supported the Roman Catholic Joseph McCarthy.[97]

Regardless of the occupant in the White House, however, for Falwell prayer for leaders was paramount since prayer put divine pressure on the leader's heart, "and he makes decisions God's Way, because he's been prayed for, though he himself may not be aware of what he's doing."[98] It was all so clear and simple, identifying and describing the malady of society and prescribing the antidote.

But behind the seeming focused sense of the malady and remedy for America lay a fundamental angst. James Davison Hunter has observed that "Fundamentalism . . . is not born out of great confidence and bravado but out of genuine fear about survivability" in a sin-sick society.[99] Added to that is a theology of eternal hell fire which awaits those who die outside of Christ. And, further in the mix of tension, as George Marsden observes, is the conflict between "insider" and "outsider" traditions within fundamentalism. "Outsiders" are those who see the world going straight to destruction, culminating in the end of the present dispensation. Therefore, to get socially involved in reforming society is merely to rearrange the deck chairs on the Titanic. The "insiders" are those who "had a political agenda that was a revival of the Old Puritan agenda to build a New Israel, based on God's law." This group revived when it sensed in the 1970s that it was getting closer to power.[100]

Falwell represents all these tensions in American Protestant fundamentalism. Theologically he is an "outsider" with his dispensational theology that tells us the end is near. Functionally, he is an "insider" influencing the president of the United States himself and the Republican party. Recently he has retreated somewhat toward the middle, preferring to emphasize pastoral ministry and the nurturing of Liberty University.[101] And the anxieties represented in a hell-fire dispensational theology and the anxiety that the decadence of society will make fundamentalist survival increasingly difficult appear to result in two kinds

of response by Falwell. On the one hand, he appears to almost fran-
tically vacillate in the search for answers, reflecting the inner tension
between outsider/insider conflicts within fundamentalism, and, on
the other hand, he offers a more focused response to anxiety with a
single-minded diagnosis and prescription for society. In either case
Falwell's theology of anxiety and his nationalism of anxiety appear
closely linked.

But in a broader sense Falwell comes off as a caricature of much
that is American. As for anxiety in the American psyche, Alexis de
Tocqueville detected this tendency 150 years ago. Said he: "In America
I saw the freest and most enlightened men placed in the happiest circumstances that the world affords; it seems to me as if a cloud habitually hung upon their brow, and I thought them serious and almost sad,
even in their pleasures." Laying the blame for this condition of anxiety
on materialism, he noted the citizens frantic in possessions. "One
would suppose the [American] was constantly afraid of living long
enough to enjoy [possessions]. There was the maddening pace of daily
life."[102] Toqueville apparently detected an anxiety rooted in the
material and perhaps observed a fear in Americans that the prosperity
enjoyed was all too good to be true and an anxiety that it could all be
lost as well.

Falwell effectively appeals to this built-in anxiety in many Americans by using American myths to suggest the past was better than the
present—that Americans of the past were God-fearing and prosperous
because of their reverence. Because the values of the past were being
shunted aside America was in danger of losing her moral leadership in
the world and her material prosperity.

There can be something of value in the use of myth as the standard by which the present is evaluated. Falwell appeals to myths (he
wouldn't call them myths) which, while not historically true, are
perhaps conceptually true. The Washington cherrytree story is not
true historically, but conceptually honesty is essential for a society to
survive and thrive, and an ideal for which to strive. The myth of
prayer at the Constitutional Convention is probably not historically
true. Yet the call for prayer is conceptually useful in recognizing
human fallibility and the danger of the arrogance of power. Perhaps
appreciation of American myth tells one that society is in trouble—
that there is cause for anxiety over the national situation. And perhaps
liberal and conservative can at least agree that there is a problem.

In another sense, too, Falwell comes off as a caricature of much
that is American. When, or if, one is amused at his vacillations, one
should be amused at the society as a whole. Falwell reflects perhaps in

the extreme the American and perhaps human tendency of wanting it both ways. Boldly announcing the virtues of free enterprise, capitalism, and individualism, the noisy exponents of these traditional American values howl in protest at any threat to fossilized subsidies, tax credits, and price supports, all justified on the so-called basis of national interest. Americans boldly proclaiming individualism as the great American trait, expect, even demand the safety net of government to cushion the fall, if not gently lower them for an angelic descent, before, of course, elevating them again. Anxiety can indeed bring almost frantic vacillations in life philosophy and methodology in the search for answers to perplexing problems.

Fear/anxiety can also be positive in motivating turn-around, whether for an alcoholic, an institution, or a nation. It is to be hoped that the frantic activity so often associated with anxiety be avoided as the nation seeks to resolve the serious crises that plague it.

CHAPTER 11

Conclusion

I remember reading many years ago the following advice in the "Humor" section of a church pamphlet serial.

> Keep your eyes on the stars, your nose to the grindstone and your ear to the ground. Now try and work that way.

This is like the advice delivered to the American people by the diverse Protestant leadership throughout the twentieth century. Taken as a whole, it is a message of contradictions that can only confuse the American people in the attempt to find national identity and role and mission in the world. The message can also be seen as merely a collection of Protestant leaders who reflect these societal contradictions. Whether Protestant leadership contributed to this confusion or merely reflected it is not the subject of this study. Either scenario is not pretty. Both possibilities do not say much for leadership, either as an incoherent force for direction or as merely reflecting societal chaos.

Exacerbating the scene, not only have there been conflicting perceptions of American identity, some of which could potentially represent diverse parts of the whole were there good will, but often the conflicting perceptions have led to outright hostility, a culture war. A liberal Protestant minister was called "a whited wall, a sepulcher full of all uncleanness . . . a child of Satan . . . on [his] way to Hell on a bobsled" by a fundamentalist minister. Using a verbal sledge hammer on this driveled insult, the liberal reciprocated the compliment that he would "not for the sake of questionable unity, join hands with these people [fundamentalists]." They are "neanderthal types who spread their poisonous vapor and hate in the name of Jesus." They are "human dinosaurs [who] sympathize with their perverted brethren in the Southern states who believe in, and practice segregation." They utter "sanctimonious belching [with] sickening slogan." One has more in common "with a Radhakrishnan of India, a Martin Buber of Israel, and

191

even a Bertrand Russell than . . . with those whose fanaticism would make God in their own puny image." One must oppose these "lilliputian creatures whose arrogance and one-sidedness would reduce everyone to the level of an ant heap."[1] Whatever the distance between people, and it is great, one thing is certain and that is there will never be any hope of "living with our deepest differences" with such talk.

The bitterness of these conflicts has permeated the political process as well. A newspaper reported that "Pat Buchanan brought 2,000 Christian conservatives to their feet . . . with a fiery defense of the Republican Party's anti-abortion stance and a vow to rebuff GOP moderates and never 'raise a white flag in the cultural war.'" The speech continued with an "attack on 'multiculturalism,' scoffing at those who say the world's many cultures are equal. 'Our culture is superior,' Buchanan said, 'our culture is superior because our religion is Christianity, and that is the truth that makes men free.'"[2]

Turning from the rabid, one can hear the sobering analysis of it all from a Clifford Geertz who warned: "The primary question, for any cultural institution anywhere, now that nobody is leaving anybody else alone and isn't ever again going to, is not whether everything is going to come seamlessly together or whether, contrariwise, we are all going to persist sequestered in our separate prejudices. It is whether human beings are going to continue to be able, in Java or Connecticut, through law, anthropology, or anything else, to imagine principled lives they can practicably lead."[3] Describing the nature of the growing dilemma, Geertz continued: "What has been well called the long conversation of mankind may be growing so cacophonous that ordered thought of any sort, much less the turning of local forms of legal sensibility into reciprocal commentaries, mutually deepening, may be impossible. But however that may be, there is, so it seems to me no choice."[4]

In the realm of theology and history, William Dean described the dilemma in similar terms: "The monistic world view underlying exceptionalist arguments has been replaced, on the whole, with a pluralistic world view denying any nation an absolute identity, allowing an identity only relative to a nation's own history, and confusing any talk of a nation's manifest destiny in the community of nations."[5]

The American nation should be so lucky to have that much of an identity as sociologist James Davison Hunter described cultural conflict in America as "political and social hostility rooted in different systems of moral understanding. . . . Our most fundamental ideas about who we are as Americans are now at odds." The source of conflict, continued Hunter, could be traced to the "matter of moral authority" which is "the basis by which people determine whether something is good or bad, right or wrong, acceptable or unacceptable."[6] Specifically, Hunter defined the conflict between orthodoxy, defined as "commitment by adherents to an external definable, and transcendent authority . . . a consistent, unchangeable measure of value, purpose, goodness . . . that is sufficient for all time," versus a cultural progressivism whereby "moral authority tends to be defined by the spirit of the modern age, a spirit of rationalism and subjectivism. . . . All progressivist world views," continued Hunter, "share in common the tendency to resymbolize historic faiths according to the prevailing assumptions of contemporary life."[7]

This distinction helps in defining the nature of the American identity confusion and crisis. But even identifying this dichotomy does not explain the depth of the problem. Some of the most bitter, most deadly conflicts in history have been waged over what represents definable transcendent authority. Monotheistic religions have the tendency to insist on one culture, one point of view, with the tendency to impose the one "true" way on others. Harvey Cox wrote a most revealing and insightful article on "Understanding Islam" in which he suggests that the "principle source of the acrimony underlying the Christian-Moslem relationship is a historical equivalent of sibling rivalry. Christians somehow hate to admit that in many ways their faith stands closer to Islam than to any other world religion."[8] Dante in a sense helped to set the tone with his view of Mohammed as that of a "schismatic deserving of punishment to include an eternal chopping in half of his body from chin to anus with entrails and excrement spilled at Satan's door."[9] The wars of the Reformation, which represented a conflict between antagonists of an even closer theological affinity, were not waged between adherents of orthodoxy versus those affirming cultural progressivism, to use Hunter's model. Nor were the adversaries in the American Civil War lined up in such a fashion. Rather, one question was whose God's transcendent authority, whose natural law, whose theological correctness?

This issue underlies much of the current culture war. And it is the thesis of this study that the current crisis of identity and lack of consensus in the American experience is not some recent phenomenon beginning in the turbulent 1960s with Vietnam and Watergate, as though consensus existed before the 1960s. Rather, the culture war was inherent in the American experience from the very beginning,[10] and the current crisis was an accident waiting to happen. Vietnam and Watergate simply served as a trip wire that exposed the fissures always present below the surface. Certainly inherent fissures that reflected societal divisions existed among Protestant leadership from the very beginning of the twentieth century to the current time.

All the figures in this study affirmed a transcendent authority. But this, on the face of it, is about as significant as affirming motherhood. And, to further confuse the issue, all the figures under study, in varying degrees, employed a combination of transcendent authority and cultural progressivism in determining the "good or bad, right or wrong, acceptable or unacceptable." That is, they all proposed to apply their perception of transcendent authority by resymbolizing their historic faiths "according to the prevailing assumptions of contemporary life." Some, such as Conwell, Rauschenbusch, Niebuhr, Hocking, and ultimately the editors of *Christianity Today*, were aware of the relativity of their application of transcendent authority to their respective contemporary conditions. Some, Rice, Falwell, and Machen, confused prevailing assumptions of contemporary life with an expression of transcendent authority. Those three would adamantly reject this statement, but the fact remains that miraculously capitalism and only capitalism was literally in holy writ for them. The editors of *Christianity Today* in the early days of the publication also confused a politically conservative agenda with the transcendent but later became not only sensitive to the danger, but even repentant for connecting the two. Even Edminster displayed a combination of transcendent authority and cultural progressivism with his numerological determinism and his surprising concern about environmental deterioration. Why he should have cared is beyond me since he thought it was all going to be over with in 1986 anyway.

But even with all this, the most critical time of confusion and conflict over the American identity and its role and mission to the world has yet to be considered. For all the figures in this study not only defining transcendent authority but also appropriately applying this authority to societal needs was divisive and confusing.

For Falwell, transcendent authority included everything from verbal inerrancy of the Bible, belief in human depravity, the Trinity, salvation by faith alone, the imminent Second Coming of Christ, and everlasting blessedness of the saved and everlasting damnation of the lost, to the dress code at Liberty University. Rice and Machen, fundamentalists of earlier generations going back to the turn of the century would have agreed. As a matter of emphasis, Machen included decentralization of nation, state, and church in the list of applications, and Rice, fully with the spirit of the times in the 1950s, applied the transcendent to the fight against Communists in every conceivable institution and especially in the National Council of Churches.

A contemporary with all three and as opposite in complexion was William Ernest Hocking. While affirming a transcendent authority with standards of reason and right applicable to all, Hocking maintained this authority did not reside exclusively in one religion or culture. Rather, at the core of the world's great religions was a nucleus of religious truth, and the insights of other religions could often provide additional insights into one's own religion and enrich one's own faith. Likewise, the sum total of economic, social, or political truth was not to be found in capitalism or Communism. Each had something to teach the other.

This was not to say that all religions or all social, political, economic systems were equal, because for Hocking they were not. The goal of "achieving the highest material and moral good for mankind" was the standard to be applied collectively not only in judging members in the family of nations, but also in the process of legitimating proposed nationhood and self-determination of Third World applicants. It was also a standard to be applied to the relative contributions of the world's religions to the spiritual and material well-being of humankind. Celebrating the uniqueness of each culture, race, religion, and political orientation, Hocking urged a diversity in unity for the nation and the world. His concept made our three fundamentalist brethren retch.

Reinhold Niebuhr could hardly buy into the Hocking perception of transcendent authority and its application to society either, but for different reasons. Hocking was much too idealistic for Niebuhr, who posited that all human collectives are evil, that some are more evil than others, and that the less evil ones through power must contain the more evil ones. With such a perpetual condition of mate and checkmate, history could only be fulfilled outside of time. In the meantime, the United States as a collective less evil than the Soviet Union had the God-ordained mission to head off Soviet aggression and international anarchy. To carry out this mission, Niebuhr wanted to make moral claims consistent with Christian values relevant to international politics. In attempting to apply Christian values to international politics, he appeared at times to link the God-ordained mission to Western interests. Western individualism and culture, for example, was the standard by which to judge other cultures. While tending to make this kind of linkage he often warned against the peril of misplacing perceptions of national chosenness. He insisted that institutions be evaluated according to their usefulness to human life consistent with Christian values. In this sense his perception of the American mission sounded similar to that expressed by Hocking. He appeared, however, unable to accept the extent of Hocking's affirmation that the core of all the world's great religions contained religious truth and that other religions could provide additional insights into one's own religion and enrich one's own faith. Only later in his career was he able to affirm as much, relative to the Jewish faith. And, he was not one to buy into Hocking's optimistic assessment that capitalism and Communism were drifting together out of mutual self-interest, or that the United States should take the initial risk in reaching out to the Soviet Union based on such an optimistic assumption.

As for a pessimistic view of the human condition, *Christianity Today* was at one with Niebuhr. However, *Christianity Today*, in contrast to Niebuhr, asserted not only that a distinctive Christian social morality was possible for the regenerate individual and for the community of evangelical faith but also that the same saving dynamic could transform society. Social sin was individual sin. Save enough individuals for Christ and the social problem would be solved. This was *Christianity Today's* formula for achieving social justice. For Niebuhr, social justice was achieved through the pressure of organized opinion exerted by a less evil collective upon a more evil one. Social strategy did not depend on individual regeneration, and the significance of spiritual revival was minimal. For *Christianity Today* this strategy was flawed because it was not based on "rational revelation" and hence had no absolute basis for the ethical positions it advocated. Rather, it attempted to enlist Christian commitment and action "for temporary imperatives as if they were in fact the will of God."

But asserting a "rational revelation" and a divine Judeo-Christian norm by which every individual action and every institution stood under judgment did not spare *Christianity Today* from confusion in application. For Carl Henry and the *Christianity Today* editors, fact and faith were one, which meant that the divine norm sanctioned free enterprise, private property, and the profit motive. Individual regeneration would affirm capitalism. And it was the responsibility of the regenerated individual and evangelical community to press the society to return to these so-called traditional American values. Only later did the journal admit that capitalism was probably not the only legitimate means of applying the divine normative to American society.

The journal also had to eat crow incrementally when its initial tub-thumping support for intervention in Vietnam, pro-Israel stance, opposition to Red China in the United Nations, and its press for prayer and bible reading in the public schools appeared to be built on a foundation of sand rather than on the rock of ages. Sobered in the attempt to apply transcendent authority to its vision of America, *Christianity*

Today became increasingly aware of the danger of attributing the divine will to transitory issues.

For Conwell, Protestant Christianity manifested transcendent authority that justified the early-twentieth-century American drive to democratize and Christianize the world. Clearly, America had been chosen, not to bask in luxury, power, and greed but to serve mankind, spreading the good news of the Gospel through education, medicine, technology, and the military, if necessary. This new, most powerful nation in the world was divinely mandated to defend people who suffered oppression anywhere in the world and to discipline any floundering and inept system of government. And so Mexico was a "disgrace" needing United States intervention to straighten it out. Puerto Rico and the Philippines were candidates for ultimate Christian home rule. Cuba needed to be liberated and nurtured for eventual statehood. As a noisy supporter of America's entrepreneurs—Captains of industry—Conwell was equally noisy in supporting open immigration to America's shores, excoriating the restrictive immigration laws of the 1920s as unworthy of the United States as a nation of nations. Of course, this high-sounding sentiment for unrestricted immigration provided a source of cheap labor for captains of industry.

This very issue caused Walter Rauschenbusch to oppose unrestricted immigration, a position that puzzles many until his opposition is understood. Championing the working classes, this divinity school professor saw the surge of immigrants on American shores as playing into the hands of entrepreneurs eager to inhale this mass of cheap labor for their sweat shops. The wages and living conditions of the pathetic workers already mired in hopelessness would be further undermined.

However, while known and revered by liberals for his Social Gospel, Rauschenbusch revealed some mixed signals concerning America's role and mission in the world. On the one hand he admired of the "yellow-haired" Custer, the Indian fighter, and supported Anglo-Saxon Protestant America's crusade against decadent Catholic Spain. On the other hand, there was his pacifism and agony over the Great War that pitted Teuton against Teuton in which he feared that the Anglo-Saxon leadership of the world was threatened by this ethnic civil war. While the good he accomplished through his theology of a Social Gospel must not be forgotten or unappreciated, the explanation for the unsavory aspects of his career cannot be entirely passed off as mere consistency with his times. One has to wonder if his pacifism by the time of World War I would have held had the players been different with the "yellow peril" rather than the "Hun." And, in his own Baptist denomination, there was opposition to the acquisition of the

Philippines since America had not handled its own Indian problem well, and hence was in no morally superior position to tutor the Philippines.

More in keeping with universal Protestant hopes amid the growing non-Protestant, non-Christian pluralism was Rauschenbusch's interpretation of the Sermon on the Mount as a mandate for a "national evangelism which would dominate the [American] society and allow by sufferance [toleration] the existence of . . . Roman Catholics, Mormons, and Judaism."[11] His ideal was to achieve a "noncoercive [Christian] messianic theocracy,"[12] hardly an endorsement of religious and ethnic pluralism.

This brings us to a point of particular relevance to this study that the one issue tying together in varying degrees all of the subjects in this study, except one, was their rejection of, or nervousness with, cultural and religious pluralism in American society. All, whether fundamentalist, evangelical, neo-orthodox, or liberal, with the exception of William Ernest Hocking, wanted to play at the game of pluralism but on a field tilted to the disadvantage of the opposition. But beyond this surface level of consensus, they gave no consistent direction on how to respond to growing American pluralism.

Similarly, all the figures in the study believed in the necessity of foreign missions. But the goals and methodology of missions ranged from an aggressive "killing with kindness" whereby the strategy was to feed, clothe, and heal accompanied by a Western and Christian commercial, to mere preaching of the Word unrelated to any physical well-being, to missions that sought the truth with adherents of other religions, learning about and integrating with the local culture.

In a similar manner, all these leaders reveled in the glory of national greatness tempered by warnings of dire consequences should the nation go against the will of God. Who cannot agree that the United States is great without agreeing on "why?" or "how?" But again this was only an easy but surface consensus which crumbled upon definition of greatness and identification of peril to the nation. One hears Conwell excoriate the nation for its hubris, Edminster for its trashing of the environment, and Rauschenbusch for its exploiting of the poor, certain that social sin must be attacked in large part by government social action. Machen is just as certain that such government bureaucratic centralized social meddling is heading the nation toward inevitable ruin, while *Christianity Today* and Falwell wail about moral deterioration. Niebuhr scoffs at the errors of soft-headed idealism, while Hocking the great idealist laments the national paranoia of diversity. John R. Rice simplifies the whole mess and dumps the load onto Communist infiltration into every American institution, secular and sacred. "Now try and work that way."

Of course, Americans unified to save the world from Kaiserism. And it was easy for them to hang together amid the horrifying threat of a Hitler or a Pearl Harbor catastrophe. At first, even the Korean War was a fairly clear-cut issue with an invasion unifying the American people. But with Vietnam came the personification of ambiguity and Americans fell apart. The real condition of inherent diversity was drawn to the surface. With subtlety came ambiguity of mission and identity. This is part of the story of America—always needing a jump start provided by some stupid tactic from a foreign power that did not understand the American psyche and how to divide and conquer it. American identity appears healthy when all goes well or when there is an enemy that lacks subtlety.

But the confusion about national identity and its role and mission reflected in twentieth-century Protestant leadership, I would suggest, goes even further back into the nineteenth century. While this aspect is not part of this study in any systematic fashion, this confusion of identity seems to be inherently rooted in the American experience, and most graphically and violently within the American Protestant experience. To reiterate, some of history's most violent, acrimonious, and ugly conflicts have occurred among "sibling rivals" within a religion. This is most certainly true within the American Protestant experience in American history manifested in the Civil War, or if one prefers, the War between the States—one of the most violent and destructive wars in modern history, and a war not between Islam and Christianity, or between Communism and capitalism, or between Protestantism and Catholicism; not between black and white; not only between white and white, but between evangelical Protestant and evangelical Protestant. This is a bitter reality that seems to be consistently overlooked in current analyses whether they be attempts to understand the current polarization of American society[13] or recent studies that emphasize excessively "This nation under God" that somehow is able to overlook the continuing polarizing fallout from the civil conflict.[14]

Even in the general societal picture of nineteenth-century America the presence of polarization and upheaval was much the same. "If one were born in 1856 . . . one would have lived through an era marked by the assassination of three American presidents, the impeachment of a fourth, . . . a stolen election by a fifth," and a sixth sired a child out of wedlock before becoming president. "The country's population, number of foreign-born, suicides, industrial laborers, divorces, gross national product, and white-collar workers all doubled."[15] And this is the age that so many who call for a return to the values of the past that made America great want to return to.

Whatever surface consensus—which one observer called "pan Protestant piety"[16]—existing among Protestants into the twentieth century until about 1950 was insignificant compared to the underlying fissures inherent in the Protestant experience. One has only to read C. C. Goen's *Broken Churches, Broken Nation* to feel the depth of division in nineteenth-century American society. Goen reveals with moving power the degree to which acrimonious bitterness between evangelical Protestants influenced the coming of the American Civil War. Baptists, Methodists, and Presbyterians, who made up 90 percent of the churches in the South, fought the civil war fifteen years before the Union and Confederacy, a tragedy which both Daniel Webster and John C. Calhoun acknowledged as an ominous forecast of the Union's future. And the depth of the division is revealed in the unlikely place of David Thorp's study of *The Moravian Community in Colonial North Carolina*. The end of his study of antebellum Moravians has the effect of a stun gun: "And when north and south went to war in 1861, dozens of [Moravian] young men marched out of Salem [North Carolina] to fight for the Confederacy, while four hundred miles to the north their [Moravian] Brethren in Bethlehem [Pennsylvania] donned the blue and marched out to meet them."[17]

In a sense, too, Hunter, while effectively identifying America's current culture wars, also plays down the inherent nature of these cultural conflicts. He correctly identifies the "contemporary culture war [as] ultimately a struggle over national identity—over *the meaning of America*, who we have been in the past, who we are now, and perhaps most important, who we, as a nation, will aspire to become in the new millennium."[18] However, Hunter suggests that prior to this "contemporary culture war" there were only "disagreements from time to time about matters of community interest and even in public policy. [But] these are to be expected. Yet a 'culture war' in America? The very thought or possibility of a deeply rooted and historically pivotal cultural conflict in America strains our imagination."[19]

This perception partially accounts for the contemporary problem Hunter speaks of. Americans have been caught off guard by years of consensus happy talk ignoring fundamental, inherent cleavages in American values throughout the nation's history. This study attempts in a small way to set the record straight. However, not only did Protestant leadership express confusion over the meaning of America and how that meaning should play out at home and abroad, but also within individual players there was confusion, contradiction, and bifurcation. It is a record of confusion throughout the twentieth century that extends into the nineteenth century to include the Civil War and earlier. John M. Murrin expressed the dilemma concisely that "Tension between secular humanist and orthodox or evangelical values has been an active part of American public life for two centuries. It shows no signs of abating."[20] Students of American religious, social, and cultural history will invariably acknowledge this but the failure to transfer this acknowledgment to one's interpretation of the American experience appears to confirm the biblical observation that "hearing they do not hear and seeing they do not see." At best, one may argue that culture wars are not apparent on the surface. But clearly they are deeply rooted in the American experience from the very beginning. They have the characteristic of an eternal changeless condition that has only been revealed at points in time in American history with the current "culture war" being one of the most serious revelations of inherent societal division. Reminiscent of Stanley Elkins' thesis that American slavery was the worst form of slavery partly because no single institutional voice in America took the part of the slave, I argue that Protestantism was unable throughout the twentieth century—to say nothing of the years preceding the Civil War in the nineteenth century—to give strong, consistent, institutional support for a clear understanding of American identity.

The open question from this may be taken from Michael Hunt's observation that nationalistic ideas are "expressions of a civic religion formulated to hold an ethnically, racially, regionally, and religiously diverse country together."[21] If that is the role of nationalism, and yet there is such diversity of American nationalistic vision among white Anglo-Saxon Protestant leadership in the twentieth century, how then hold the nation together in harmony when thrown into the mix are all the social, cultural, racial, religious, ethnic elements that make up the American scene?

Is there any hope for resolution? As an opener, the current national identity crisis is a clarion call to demythologize early on in a person's education an insipid and unrealistic image that makes national founders bigger than life and motives and behavior of a people always liberating, whether it be in the context of the American Revolution, the Constitutional Convention, America's wars, the "winning of the West," the Cold War, or all the other usual topics used to create unrealistic images and expectations concerning the American experience and its capacity for honorable accomplishments.

So often, as it currently stands, I find students coming to the college classroom shaken when they learn what the Boston Massacre really was, or read the letter written by President Lincoln to Horace Greeley that he would be willing to keep slavery if that were necessary to save the Union, or read Frank Freidel's *The Splendid Little War*. Forrest G. Wood's piece, *The Arrogance of Faith: Christianity and Race in America* comes as a shock, if it does not provoke disbelief. How the West was really won from a Native American perspective is often greeted with outrage—outrage from some who are angry that such a perspective is presented—outrage from others for whom the material is new, shocking, and disgusting. Such perspectives along with other angles need to be part of the education process.

Such an emphasis, containing elements of deconstruction, would serve to emphasize that the American experience does consist of warts and beauty marks in its quest for unity and security—that there is much to praise and much to improve as a society—that national motives are not always altruistic but often times sordid—that far too much has been left out of the historical narrative, justifying the accusation by Derrida that history is a scandal. To understand the American experience, one must be given a more complete picture. Such an approach, if done with sensitivity, invariably leads to a deeper appreciation for the American experience rather than the cynicism which so often accompanies one's awareness of current societal trends. After studying the scurrilous political campaign of 1884 one student remarked, "We've actually made some improvements as a people over the years." Awareness of the sordid as well as the heroic teaches that we as a people, including our leadership past and present, are very human, subject to behavior ranging beneath the animal to the angelic.

Obviously, many school boards are not inclined to buy into such an approach, and thousands of public school teachers across the land chaff at the official and unofficial strictures on what can be taught in the classroom concerning the nation's history and the many other sensitive moral issues that divide the nation. Leading with the chin will hardly bring about the needed demythologizing which amounts to cultural change. The remedy suggested by *Christianity Today* is hardly the answer either, when it recommended that "we need to do exactly what a football coach does when he sees his fair young hopefuls pushed around by an opponent: schedule some sessions in fundamentals. America needs a drill in right thinking and right acting according to God's Word."[22] Theologically correct and hence politically correct? *Christianity Today* preempted the idea twenty-five years before the present-day exponents of political correctness, although how each side would now define the term would reveal the depth of American polarization. Present exponents of political correctness, like their opposites, could use a history lesson on previous, not too distant past examples of "political correctness." Not that the ideals embodied in political correctness are bad—that human beings need to become sensitive to the dangers of "desecralization" of another's sacred. But the *term* "politically correct" or "theologically correct" contains within itself an implied rigidity that precludes discussion between adversaries, and hence defeats the very thing it attempts to sponsor. Such rigidity, if pressed, is as much a recipe for disaster as theological correctness was in the past. But ultimately after much trauma, death, intimidation, came the discovery again that diversity is better than devastation, not a pleasant road to accommodation but one likely to be traveled again.

Hunter expands the discussion by speculating on how to achieve public agreement to disagree over the moral differences that divide the society. While he sees a mere agreement to not kill each other over differences as a start, such accommodation does not create mutual respect, encourage serious public argument, raise the quality of public debate, resolve public policy disputes, or provide a mechanism for deciding on a national agenda.[23] On the other hand, he seems to recognize a Kantian solution that "civil conflict can and should eventually lead to more substantial forms of political agreement,"[24] a kind of unsocial sociableness. He agrees that helping people recognize that different positions have roots in the very beginnings of the republic and hence were legitimate positions for patriots of the past, is useful but effective argument mainly for intellectuals. Furthermore, such an argument ignores the problem of power, wherein some traditions are linked to political authority "which are themselves capable of undermining the legitimacy of other opposing traditions."[25] What is needed, he suggests, is a change in the environment of public discourse which provides a genuine forum of debate before the same audience that witnesses all the debate. "The very context of genuine debate," argues Hunter, "predisposes actors to rhetorical moderation and forbearance."[26]

Certainly any change that cuts the rhetoric on talk shows or news interviews/debates in which individuals cannot allow a person to finish a sentence or who hog the conversation by interminable babbling would be a welcome change in the quest for intelligent public discourse. However, even with such a utopian condition, the problem, as sociologist Robert Wuthrow discovered, was that the more conservatives knew about liberals the less they liked them, and vice versa.[27] In other words, in sound public discourse the probability is that I may hear and understand clearly what my opponent is saying and disagree as much or perhaps even more than before. If issues of ultimate reality make up the substance of the debate, the possibilities of resolution virtually disappear.

Offering additional conditions for resolving moral differences, Hunter suggests that democracy depends on hearing many voices, for without this "there is no basis for making public compromises. There is not even the will to make the effort."[28] Upon hearing the many voices there must be a recognition of the "sacred" within different moral communities. The "sacred" is non-negotiable and defines the limits of what will be tolerated. Therefore, suggests Hunter, "All parties need to recognize that their own particular action can be so offensive to their opposition . . . that it spurs the opposition to a reaction that really does present a vital threat to the community, namely the use of violence."[29] There must be common recognition of what constitutes a "vital threat" for the opposition. Recognizing that will induce opposing factions to pursue "a measure of prudence and caution."[30]

Such a recognition and result would be refreshing; however, what one community views as obscene, murder, or "desecralization," another views as a constitutional right. This is seen recently in the rap controversy which has divided the African-American community, to say nothing of the division it has caused within the broader society. Also, being constantly aware of what constitutes a "vital threat" causes people to be gun shy in discourse for fear of inadvertent desecration of the sacred. The quagmire of interpreting First Amendment rights is thus brought into play.

Finally, Hunter suggests that contending communities recognize "the inherent weaknesses, even dangers in their own moral commitments."[31] He was not suggesting compromise of convictions. Rather, along with his other suggestions for resolution, he was leading into the call for "a principled pluralism and a principled toleration, . . . not the bland arithmetic means of what everyone in a society believes, nor tolerance the obligation to make one's deepest beliefs tolerable to others." Rather, it is the condition where "all contenders, however much they may disagree with each other on principle, do not kill each other over these differences, do not desecrate what the other holds sublime, and do not eschew principled discourse with the other."[32]

Again, a principled pluralism and toleration is a key to the creative survival of a sharply divided society. However, the very act of principled pluralism and principled toleration itself violates the non-negotiable for some. Moreover, Hunter's statement could have been applied to the slavery issue, and we know what happened on that score. Furthermore, these suggestions, while admirable, strike me as equally inadequate, using Hunter's own rationale that recognizing the rootage of differing positions falls short because they are arguments only for intellectuals. Is it likely that "activists who occupy the trenches of cultural warfare, much less ordinary citizens [who] either do not have the time or economic incentive (since their job is to 'win') to decode the traditions they oppose"[33] will take the time and effort to avoid desecrating what another holds sacred?

Hunter admits that this call for principled pluralism and principled toleration "might be unrealistic." But, ever hopeful, he observes that "Our founders faced similarly imposing historical odds in forging the public philosophy that established the American experiment in democracy in the first place."[34] While this is true indeed, included in the political mix that helped create the miracle of the Constitution was the three-fifths compromise, which only postponed the "irrepressible conflict," the Civil War.

Are there, then, any plausible suggestions to bring resolution in America's growing culture war beyond the heroic search for solutions suggested by Hunter? While I have great respect for, and agree with the strategies for resolution suggested by Hunter, it is my sense, given the human condition, that the more likely scenario will be that American society will continue to limp along, fortunate that the polarization of society is not regional as it was in the mid-nineteenth century. This certainly does not preclude decades of conflict in which it becomes increasingly difficult to govern the Union. However, history does provide some interesting precedents for conflict resolution. Even as a conflict of absolutes between reformers versus reformers and reformers versus the Roman Catholic church led to a century and a half of conflict only to end in exhaustion and the realization that the joys of life can be achieved by living and letting live, overcoming the logic of action of one's absolutes, so it may be that an extended period of conflict and bloodshed may need to be endured until at last the moral imperatives of one's life are set aside for the sake of peace. This is not a desirable way to solve problems. It is, however, a fairly common one. The Religious Peace of Augsburg, 1555, which established the religion of the prince as the religion of the state, may become a model for accommodation, with moral policy established by respective states instead of by a particular state religion. In a sense this is already becoming somewhat evident as state governments have varying laws regarding abortion rights. The nature of the Union could again be an issue with something similar to the concept of popular sovereignty being granted to states regarding various moral issues. Ultimately on the strength of centuries of religious conflict over absolutes, the founders of the republic opted for diversity rather than devastation. In more recent times, fortunately, in a peaceful resolution of conflict the United States overcame the logic of action based on its absolutes during the Nixon administration, of all things, with the opening of Red China for trade and cultural exchange. Profits could be made by setting aside ideological absolutes.

Another possible scenario for resolution which has ample historical precedent is accepting authoritarianism to end conflict, ambiguity, and confusion. Continuing on a theme of religion and politics, the Counter Reformation of the sixteenth and seventeenth centuries is a prime example. After so much debate with increasing confusion, the time came for the Church to essentially declare an end to debate with a statement concerning theological correctness. It may be that down the road of continuing social and cultural war that the day would come in which people would welcome a force capable of ending such strife. None of these scenarios are desirable or pleasant to contemplate.

Law professor Michael J. Perry has obviously struggled with this issue in his *Love and Power: The Role of Religion and Morality in American Politics*, extending the process of attempted resolution to include love and power. After dismissing the ideal of "neutral politics" posited by Bruce Ackerman in his work, *Social Justice in the Liberal State*, and Thomas Nagel's concept of "impartial" political justification[35] as ideals that cannot work, Perry calls for a "political community in which love *(agape)* and power—*political* love and *political* power—are intimately connected" in the resolution process. The ideal for Perry is the "political community in which love both inspires and inhibits the exercise of political power (including power exercised *against* the state, as in civil disobedience, as well as power exercised *by* the state), in which the exercise of political power, and the decision not to exercise it, are, at best, acts of love."[36]

Careful to define his use of "love" as *agape* love, Perry notes that such love does not romanticize the "Other." It in fact sees the "Other" "in all [of its] fallenness and even perversity." By the same token, an act of love can be misguided which is why "love should inhibit as well as inspire the exercise of political power."[37] The practical aspect of this ideal would be to know, love, and respect those with whom one disagrees, while engaging in vigorous dialogue. But the bottom line is that when dialogue fails to bring resolution, power, comprising of the "unruly practices of campaigning, advertising, lobbying, bartering, strikes, even civil disobedience" may be resorted to as an appropriate response "to oppressive ideologies whether religious or secular."[38] Perry suggests that while on the one hand such use of power may end dialogue, on the other hand it may be the catalyst that reinitiates and complements dialogue.

Of course, such advice can be taken as seriously by opposite sides in any disagreement over transcendent authority. The very definition of "oppressive ideologies" draws controversy. Perry would naturally have identified his candidates of oppression and after failing to convince the opposition of being like-minded would recommend the employment of power in love. Considering the Protestant leadership figures in this study and their varying and sometimes antithetical perceptions of the meaning of America and their prescriptions for national healing, we all will have our preferences for those who represent our own values and hopes for the nation. "Warts and beauty marks" is a very subjective designation in judging the relative merit of a person's perception of the meaning of America. Beauty, it is said, is in the eye of the beholder. We all make our choices and I no less than anyone. Unless one were to advocate ethnic cleansing or legal or de facto discrimination based on race, creed, or sexual orientation, which would surely lead to societal devastation, it seems there is no alternative to diversity which accepts pluralism itself as an inherent ideal/value system in its own right.

Combining the emphases of two Protestant leaders in this study seems to me to be plausible in implementing diversity in American society and could encompass Perry's ideal of applying love and power in the search for resolution. The two are Reinhold Niebuhr and William Ernest Hocking. This may seem a strange combination since their concepts of the state as a collective were quite at odds as were their perceptions of the proper United States role in the Cold War. But a mixture of Hocking's idealism with Niebuhr's advocacy of the use of power, given the brutal nature of politics and the place of power as the driving force that protects and ensures cultural values and mores, seems to be appropriate and potentially effective. This is not to say that Niebuhr lacked idealism nor Hocking realism. Niebuhr's social philosophy resembled in its ideals the Social Gospel of the early twentieth century, but lacked the optimism of inevitable evolutionary progress characteristic of much Social Gospel thinking. Rather, Niebuhr believed in the need for power blocks to fight for social justice in the political cauldron. And Hocking was ever aware of the practical dangers that accompanied his advocacy of risktaking to break the cycle of mutual fear between the United States and the Soviet Union in the Cold War. But Niebuhr did not have the same vision as Hocking in regard to a social, cultural, and religious pluralism in which diversity is not to be feared or endured but in fact welcomed wholeheartedly as an inherent value. Americans must accept this principle if the nation is to creatively live with its deepest differences. And it will take the wise, judicious use of power to massage the American people to an acceptance of this value system.

To play off of the words of Clifford Geertz, America is a various place, various between fundamentalists and liberals, various between believer and skeptic, various between pro-life and pro-choice, and much is to be gained by confronting that reality rather than dreaming up insipid consensus theories (although not overlooking areas of agreement), or praying for winds of evaporation. The question for Americans is whether in their diversity they can accept the principle of pluralism itself as a key American principle of identity, willingly crawl into the skin of the adversary, and enter genuine dialogue, thus making pluralism America's blessing rather than her bane.

Notes

1. Introduction

1. William Hutchison, *Errand to the World* (Chicago and London: The University of Chicago Press, 1987), 208.

2. Louis Snyder, *Varieties of Nationalism* (Hinsdale, Ill: The Dryden Press, 1976), 201–10.

3. Snyder, 202.

4. Russell B. Nye, *The Almost Chosen People* (East Lansing: Michigan State University Press, 1966), 172.

5. Michael H. Hunt, *Ideology and U.S. Foreign Policy* (New Haven and London: Yale University Press, 1987), 162.

6. Hutchison, 208.

7. Snyder, 206.

8. Robert R. Ergang, *Herder and the Foundations of German Nationalism* (New York: Octagon Books, 1966), 154.

9. Gordon A. Craig, *The Germans* (New York: New American Library Press, 1982), 30.

10. Robert Jewett, *The Captain America Complex* (Santa Fe: Bear & Company, 1984), 49.

11. Nye, 174.

12. Ibid., 202.

13. Ibid., 177.

14. Hunt, 106.

15. Ibid., 116

16. Ibid., 117

17. *New York Times*, 19 February 1991.

18. Hunt, 123.

19. lbid.

20. Ibid., 107.

21. Hutchison, 111.

22. Gerald Strober and Ruth Tomzak, *Jerry Falwell: A Flame for God* (New York: Thomas Nelson Publishers, 1979), 169.

23. Clyde Edminster, *The Deliverance of Israel and the Kingdom Age by 1986* (Ranier, Wash.: Christ is the Answer Publications, 1975), 2.

2. Bifurcated Nationalism

1. Walter Rauschenbusch, "The Contribution of Germany to the National Life of America," commencement address to Rochester Theological Seminary, 1902 (Doris Robinson Sharpe, Walter Rauschenbusch Collection, Box 20, Colgate Rochester Divinity School, hereinafter referred to as Sharpe Collection), 6.

2. Ibid., 1–2.

3. Ibid., 4

4. Ibid., 7–8

5. Ibid., 10–11.

6. Ibid., 19.

7. Ibid., 21.

8. Gordon Craig, *The Germans* (New York: Putnam, 1982), 31.

9. Rauschenbusch, "The Present and the Future," Thanksgiving sermon delivered to Rochester Baptists, and printed in its entirety in the *Rochester Post-Express* (25 November 1898), 50.

10. Ibid.

11. David Alan McClintock, "Walter Rauschenbusch: The Kingdom of God and the American Experience," (Ph.D. diss., History, Case Western Reserve, 1975), 356.

12. Rauschenbusch, "The Present and the Future," 51.

13. Ibid., 50–51.

14. Rauschenbusch, "Decoration Day Thoughts," no date (Sharpe Collection, Box 20, Colgate Rochester Divinity School), 4.

15. Ibid., 4

16. Rauschenbusch, "Decoration Day Thoughts," no date; "Why We Can Be Proud of Our Country," 30 June 1903; "The Duty of the Church to the Nation," 30 June 1904; "Fourth of July Address," 3 July 1904.

17. Rauschenbusch, "Be Fair to Germany: A Plea for Open-Mindedness," September 1914 (Sharpe Collection, Box 19), 1. This article was published in *The Congregationalist*, 15 October 1914.

18. Charles F. Aked and Walter Rauschenbusch, "Private Profit and the Nation's Honor: A Protest and a Plea," *The Standard* (31 July 1915), 1486–87.

19. Rauschenbusch, "Be Fair to Germany."

20. Paul M. Minus, *Walter Rauschenbusch: American Reformer* (New York, London: Macmillan, 1988), 108,

21. John R. Aiken, "Walter Rauschenbusch and Education for Reform," *Church History* 35 (4 December 1967), 456–69.

22. Ibid., 465.

23. Ibid., 460.

24. Ibid., 469

25. McClintock, 362.

26. Rauschenbusch, "The Service of the Church to Society" in "Treasury," September 1899 as quoted by Doris Robinson Sharpe, *Walter Rauschenbusch* (New York: Macmillan, 1942), 323–24.

27. Rauschenbusch, "The Church and Social Questions," *Conservation of National Ideals* (New York: H. Revel Co., 1911), 106.

28. Ibid.

29. Sharpe. Sharpe analyzes Rauschenbusch's impact on Western Christianity and quotes him in Walter Rauschenbusch, *A Theology for the Social Gospel* (New York: Macmillan, 1919), 324.

30. Henry W, Bowden, "Walter Rauschenbusch and American Church History," *Foundations* 9 (July–September 1966), 241.

31. Walter Rauschenbusch, *Christianizing the Social Order* (NewYork: Macmillan , 1914), 191.

32. Bowden, 241 "Professor Bowden says that Rauschenbusch "almost" equated democratizing forces with the Kingdom of God.

33. Rauschenbusch, "The True American Church, Great Christian Groups Which Belong Together," *The Congregationalist* (23 October 1913), 562.

34. Rauschenbusch, "Christian Unity," 1914 (Sharpe Collection, Box 22), 5.

35. Ibid.

36. Rauschenbusch, "The American Church," commencement address to Rochester Theological Seminary, 1917 (Sharpe Collection, Box 22), 27.

37. Ibid.

38. Rauschenbusch, "Christian Unity," 5.

39. Bowden, "Walter Rauschenbusch and American Church History," and McClintock, "Walter Rauschenbusch: The Kingdom of God and the American Experience." Both historians provide evidence that could be used to support the possibility that Rauschenbusch favored organic unity, yet both conclude that he was not interested in this. I prefer to make the distinction between what he believed to be a realistic possibility of cooperation among Protestant churches in his lifetime, and his hope and belief that ultimately organic unity would occur.

40. Rauschenbusch, "The True American Church," 562,

41. Ibid.

42. Ibid.

43. Bowden, "Walter Rauschenbusch and American Church History," 244.

44. Ibid., 245.

45. Ibid., 246.

46. Rauschenbusch, "The True American Church," 562.

47. Rauschenbusch, "The American Church," 32.

48. Ibid., 17.

49. McClintock, 383.

50. Rauschenbusch, "The True American Church," 562.

51. Ibid.

52. McClintock, 394.

53. Ibid., 396.

54. Ibid.

55. Ibid., 395.

56. Ibid., 395–96,

57. Rauschenbusch, *Christianizing the Social Order*, 131.

58. Ibid., 132.

59. Ibid., 131.

60. Ibid., 133.

61. Rauschenbusch, "The Church and Social Questions," 119.

62. Ibid.

63. Rauschenbusch, "The Higher Life of Our Nation." From manuscript of proposed book, 1902 (Sharpe Collection, Box 45), 2.

64. Rauschenbusch, *Christianizing the Social Order*, 134.

65. Ibid., 137.

66. Ibid., 139.

67. Rauschenbusch, "The Higher Life," 15.

68. Rauschenbusch, *Christianizing the Social Order*, 145.

69. Ibid.

70. Ibid., 147.

71. Ibid., 146.

72. Rauschenbusch, "The Higher Life," 32.

73. Ibid.

74. Rauschenbusch, *Christianizing the Social Order*, 148.

75. Ibid., 149.

76. Ibid., 150–51.

77. Ibid., 152.

78. Ibid.

79. Ibid., 153.

80. Ibid., 154.

81. Rauschenbusch, "What Is A Christian Nation?," *The Standard* (23 February 1907), 5.

82. Rauschenbusch, *Christianizing the Social Order*, 155.

83. Winthrop Hudson, "Walter Rauschenbusch and the New Evangelism," *Religion in Life* 30 (1960–61), 423.

84. Ibid., 412.

85. Walter Rauschenbusch, *A Theology for the Social Gospel* (New York: Macmillan, 1919), 4–5.

86. Rauschenbusch, *For God and the People: Prayers of Social Awakening* (Boston, New York, Chicago: The Pilgrim Press, 1909), preface.

87. Ibid., 9.

88. Ibid., 11.

89. Ibid.

90. Rauschenbusch, "The Freedom of Spiritual Religion." Sermon before the Northern Baptist Convention, 8 May 1910.

91. Ibid.

92. Rauschenbusch, "A Task of Evangelization," no date (Sharpe Collection, Box 19), 4.

93. Rauschenbusch, *Christianizing the Social Order*, 197.

94. Michael Hunt, *Ideology and U.S. Foreign Policy* (New Haven, London: Yale University Press, 1987), 17–18.

95. Robert D. Cross, "Catholicism and a Non-Catholic State," in John F. Wilson and Donald L. Drakeman, *Church and State in American History*, 2nd ed. (Boston: Beacon Press, 1987), 144.

96. William R. Hutchison, *Errand to the World* (Chicago, London: University of Chicago Press, 1987), 196.

97. William Graham Sumner, "The Conquest of the United States by Spain," *Yale Law Journal* 8 (January 1899), 192–93.

98. Aiken, "Walter Rauschenbusch and Education," 469.

99. Sidney Mead, *The Old Religion in the Brave New World* (Berkeley: University of California Press, 1977), chapters 1–2.

100. Charles W. Dunn, *American Political Theology* (New York: Prager, 1984), chapters 1–2. The contradictory themes Dunn documents concerns the differing views on the origin of the American republic—deistic liberal vs.

Christian orthodox. At times these two views uneasily coexist in the society, and at other times, the present being one of them, surface in what has been called a "culture war."

101. Hunt, *Ideology*. Hunt traces three ideological principles that were present in the formulation of U.S. foreign policy in the twentieth century: The United States as the greatest democracy in the world must promote liberty everywhere: the Anglo-Saxon race is superior, and has the responsibility to accomplish this, but treats the lesser races with condescension; the United States has the ability and obligation to determine which revolutions are legitimate, and not threatening to principles of liberty, and which ones are not.

102. Hutchison, 111.

3. Foreign Policy through Benediction

1. Russell Conwell, "Mexico," *Temple Review* 27, no. 44 (19 December 1919), 3. (Hereinafter cited as *TR*.)

2. Ibid.

3. Esther 4:14.

4. Henry May, *Ideas, Faiths, and Feelings* (New York and Oxford: Oxford University Press, 1983), 175.

5. *TR* (24 October 1895), 519.

6. Conwell, "America's Danger," *True Philadelphian* 2, no. 3 (24 June 1898), 347.

7. Ibid.

8. Conwell, "Freedom That Is Slavery," *TR* 9, no. 23 (7 March 1902), 481.

9. Ibid.

10. Conwell, "Opportunities in National Unrest," *TR* 27, no. 14 (4 April 1919), 3.

11. Conwell, "The Influence of Our Nation," *TR* 12, no. 9 (27 November 1903), 3.

12. Ibid.

13. Ibid., 4.

14. Ibid.

15. Ibid., 5.

16. Ibid., 14.

17. Conwell, "Patriotic Sons of America," *TR* 17, no. 14 (16 October 1908), 4.

18. Conwell, "Rule of the Majority," *TR* 21, no. 22 (3 April 1913), 6.

19. Conwell, "Thanksgiving for Victories," *True Philadelphian* 2, no. 19 (5 August 1898), 524.

20. Ibid.

21. Ibid.

22. Conwell, "Theodore Roosevelt," *TR* 27, no. 10 (21 November 1919), 1.

23. Conwell, "The Savior at the Panama Canal," *TR* 23, no. 44 (9 December 1915), 3.

24. Matthew 6:29.

25. Russell Conwell, "The Saviour," 4, 5.

26. Ibid., 5.

27. Ibid.

28. Ibid., 6.

29. Russell Conwell, "God's Care of the Nation," *TR* 7, no. 24 (15 March 1901), 523.

30. Russell Conwell, "Mexico," 3.

31. Ibid.

32. Ibid., 4.

33. As an aside, before delivery of this sermon, Conwell reminded the congregation of its responsibility to study the issue of the League and vote accordingly. While Conwell publicly supported woman's suffrage he hardly gave it a ringing endorsement when he declared "Everyone of you women who now *have* the right to vote and everyone of you men who *should* vote must study this question so that you may vote right. Italics mine.

34. Russell Conwell, "An Unfair Partnership," *TR* 31, no. 2 (5 October 1923), 276.

35. Ibid.

36. II Corinthians 6:14.

37. Matthew 28:16–20.

38. Russell Conwell, "An Unfair Partnership," *TR* 31, no. 2 (5, October 1923), 276.

39. Ibid.

40. Ibid., 278.

41. Russell Conwell, "German Indemnity," *TR* 25, no. 43 (14 December 1917), 3–6.

42. Baptist reaction to Turkish massacres is recorded in Robert G. Torbet, *A Social History of the Philadelphia Baptist Association, 1707–1940* (Philadelphia: Westbrook Publishing Co., 1944), 219–20.

43. Russell Conwell, "The Second Battle," *TR* 28, no. 18 (30 April 1920), 2.

44. Ibid., 4.

45. Russell Conwell, "Rule of the Majority," *TR* 21, no. 22 (13 April 1913), 4.

46. Russell Conwell, "Patriotic Hearts," *TR* 25, no. 35 (16 November 1917), 4, 5.

47. Russell Conwell, "Rule," 4.

48. Russell Conwell, "Limits of Liberty," *TR* 30, no. 25 (23 June 1922), 4.

49. Russell Conwell, "Mexico," *TR* 27, no. 44 (19 December 1919), 5.

50. Russell Conwell, "Thanksgiving for Victories," *True Philadelphia*, 2 no. 19 (5 August 1898), 524.

51. Ibid.

52. Ibid., 525.

53. Ibid.

54. Ibid.

55. Clyde Kenneth Nelson, "The Social Ideas of Russell Conwell," (Ph.D. diss., University of Pennsylvania, 1968), 380.

56. Russell Conwell, "Loving One's Other Self," *TR* 31, no. 35 (2 November 1923), 305, 306.

57. Ibid.

58. Russell Conwell, "The Kingdom of God a True Democracy," *TR* 27, no. 6 (18 January 1919), 7.

59. Russell Conwell, "America's Danger," *True Philadelphian* 2, no. 13 (24 June 1898), 353.

60. Russell Conwell, "Church Aid to Patriotism," *TR* 24, no. 4 (27 January 1916), 11.

61. Julius W. Pratt, *Expansionists of 1898* (Glouster, Mass: Peter Smith, 1959), 279–316.

62. Robert G. Torbet, *A Social History of the Philadelphia Baptist Association 1707–1940* (Philadelphia: Westbrook Publishing Co., 1944).

63. Nelson, 358.

64. Ibid., 364.

65. Pratt, 316.

66. Richard Hofstadter, *The Paranoid Style of American Politics* (New York: Alfred A. Knopf, 1965), 150.

67. Martin Marty, *Righteous Empire* (New York: Harper & Row, 1970), 186.

4. One Way, One Truth, One Life

1. Ned B. Stonehouse, *J. Gresham Machen: A Biographical Memoir* (Chestnut Hill, Philadelphia: Westminster Theological Seminary, 1977), 318.

2. Stonehouse, 320.

3. David Wells, *The Princeton Theology* (Grand Rapids: Baker Book House, 1989).

4. Stonehouse, 441 ff.

5. J. Gresham Machen in letter to Franklin Delano Roosevelt, 28 September 1935.

6. Ibid.

7. Ibid.

8. Ibid.

9. J. Gresham Machen, "An Open Letter to President Roosevelt," *The Presbyterian Guardian* 1, no. 2 (21 October 1935), 23.

10. Heywood Broun, "It Seems To Me," *The World Telegram*, New York, 4 October 1935.

11. Ibid.

12. J. Gresham Machen in letter to Heywood Broun, 5 October 1935 in archives at Westminster Theological Seminary, Philadelphia.

13. Machen in letter to Miss Doris Blake, 5 October 1935 in archives at Westminster Theological Seminary.

14. Machen in letter to Mr. Kirkland A. Wilson, 3 October 1935; Mr. H. B. Kane, 25 October 1935; Miss Edith Fancher, 4 October 1935, Westminster archives.

15. Machen in letter to Dr. A. Guyot Cameron, 3 October 1935; Mr. H. B. Maurer, 7 October 1935, Westminster archives.

16. Machen, "Professor Machen Says Child Labor Amendment Would Threaten U.S. With Tyranny Similar to Russia," *Trenton Sunday Times-Advertiser*, 25 January 1925.

17. Ibid.

18. Machen, "A Communication: Child Labor and Liberty," *The New Republic*, 31 December 1924, 145.

19. Ibid., also in *The Woman Patriot 9*, no. 5 (1 March 1925).

20. Machen in letter to Mrs. John Balch, secretary to Sentinels of the Republic, 4 October 1933.

21. Machen in letter to Mrs. John Balch, 16 January 1934.

22. "Program and Policies Adopted by the Sentinels of the Republic" at annual meeting, New York City, 26 January 1934.

23. Ibid.

24. *Sentinels of the Republic*, 1367 National Press Building, Washington, D.C. No date but probably 1934.

25. Machen, Statement submitted at the request of Mr. C. F. Will of the *Philadelphia Record*, 8 January 1934.

26. Machen in letter to Mr. Alexander Lincoln, president of the Sentinels, 9 June 1934.

27. Machen, "Shall We Have a Federal Department of Education?" *The Woman Patriot*, 15 February 1926, and address delivered by Machen to the Sentinels of the Republic, 12 January 1926, 25, 26.

28. Ibid.

29. Ibid.

30. Ibid., 25, also in Machen, "The Necessity of the Christian School," *Forward in Faith* (Convention Year Book, Chicago: Nation Union of Christian Schools, 1934), 2.

31. Ibid., 26.

32. Ibid.

33. Ibid.

34. Machen, testifying before Joint Hearings before Committee on Education and Labor, United States Senate, and the Committee on Education, House of Representatives, 69th Congress, 1st session, on S 291 and HR 5000.

35. Machen, "Shall We Have A Federal Department of Education?"

36. Ibid.

37. Ibid.

38. Ibid.

39. Ibid.

40. Machen, "Shall We Have A Federal Department of Education?," 27.

41. Ibid.

42. Ibid.

43. Machen, "The Necessity of the Christian School," 4, 5.

44. Ibid.

45. Ibid., 13.

46. Ibid.

47. Ibid.

48. Ibid., 15.

49. Machen, "The Christian School: The Hope of America," *The Christian School: The Outflowering of Faith* (Convention papers, Chicago: National Union of Sunday Schools, 1934), 15.

50. Ibid.

51. Ibid., 14.

52. Machen, "The Second Declaration of The Council on Church Union," *The Presbyterian*, 17 March 1924.

53. Stonehouse, 305.

54. Machen, "The Proposed Plan of Union," *The Presbyterian*, 10 June 1920.

55. Ibid.

56. Machen, "The Second Declaration."

57. Machen, "The Proposed Plan of Union."

58. Stonehouse, 248.

59. Ibid.

60. Ibid., 246.

61. Ibid., 244.

62. Ibid., 407.

63. Ibid., 246.

64. Ibid., 247.

65. Ibid., 249.

66. Ibid., 299.

67. Machen, "Against Alien Enrollment," *New York Herald Tribune*, 9 December 1925.

68. Ibid.

69. Machen, "Compulsory Registration," *New York Times*, 13 September 1933, 18.

70. Stonehouse, 304.

71. J. Gresham Machen, *Modernism and the Board of Foreign Missions of the Presbyterian Church in the U.S.A.; Argument of J. Gresham Machen in Support of an Overture Introduced in the Presbytery of New Brunswick at Its Meeting on January 24, 1933, and Made the Order of the Day for the Meeting April 11, 1933* (Philadelphia: J. Gresham Machen), 39.

72. Machen, *Modernism*, 39, 40. The "Auburn Affirmation," signed by over a thousand Presbyterian ministers, was a statement rejecting the action of the General Assembly of the Presbyterian Church in the U.S.A. taken in 1923 which expressed the opinion concerning five doctrinal statements that each one "is an essential doctrine of the Word of God and our standards." The affirmation declared that "On the constitutional ground [of the church] . . . we are opposed to any attempt to elevate tests for ordination or for good standing in the church." The affirmation went on to recognize that the five doctrinal statements in question "are not the only theories allowed by

Scriptures and our standards as explanations of these facts and doctrines of our religion."

73. Ibid., 41.

74. Machen, in letter to Rev. Clarence E. Macartney, D.D. minister, First Presbyterian Church, Pittsburgh, 8 April 1933.

75. Machen, "Is Pearl Buck a Christian?," *The Evening Sun*, 16 May 1933.

76. Ibid.

77. William Ernest Hocking, *Re-Thinking Missions: A Layman's Inquiry after One Hundred Years* (New York: Harper & Brothers, 1932).

78. Machen, "Tentative Form of a Report of Any Committee of Any Presbytery on Foreign Missions" (abbreviated). Drafted 7 January 1933.

79. Machen, *Modernism and the Board*, 42.

80. Machen, "Tentative Form."

81. Ibid.

82. Robert Speer, *Re-Thinking Missions Examined* (New York: Fleming H. Revelle, Co., 1933), 31.

83. Ibid.

84. Ibid., 32.

85. Ibid., 35.

86. Machen in letter to Rev. Clarence E. Macartney, D.D. First Presbyterian Church, Pittsburgh, 12 April 1933.

87. Stonehouse, 245.

88. Ibid., 406.

89. Francis Schaeffer, *The Great Evangelical Disaster* (Westchester, Ill.: Crossway Books, 1984), 23, 32.

90. Francis Schaeffer, *A Christian Manifesto* (Westchester, Ill.: Crossway Books, 1981), 61, 62.

91. Walter Capps, *The New Religious Right* (Columbia: University of South Carolina Press, 1990), 86, 87.

5. The Face of Egalitarian Nationalism

1. William Ernest Hocking, *The Spirit of World Politics* (New York: Macmillan, 1932), 168.

2. William Ernest Hocking, *Strength of Men and Nations* (New York: Harper & Brothers, 1959), 172.

3. Hocking, *The Spirit of World Politics*, 186, 164.

4. Ibid., 185.

5. Hocking, *Strength of Men and Nations*, 11.

6. Ibid., 188.

7. William Ernest Hocking, *Man and the State* (New Haven: Yale University Press, 1926), 401, 402.

8. Ibid.

9. Ibid.

10. Hocking, *The Spirit of World Politics*, 169, 166.

11. Ibid., 167.

12. Ibid., 189, 190, 192.

13. William Ernest Hocking, "Christianity and the Non–Christian Religions," *Drew University Bulletin*. An address delivered at Drew University, Madison, New Jersey, 19 October 1933.

14. William Ernest Hocking, *Re-Thinking Missions: A Laymen's Inquiry after One Hundred Years* (New York: Harper & Brothers, 1932), 19.

15. Ibid.

16. Hocking, "Christianity and Non–Christian Religions," 21.

17. William Ernest Hocking, *The Coming World Civilization* (New York: Harper & Brothers, 1956), 140, 141.

18. Ibid., 58.

19. Hocking, "Christianity and the Non-Christian Religions," 21, 22.

20. Hocking, *The Coming World Civilization*, 134.

21. Ibid., 134, 135.

22. Hocking, *Re-Thinking Missions*, 93.

23. Hocking, *Strength of Men and Nations*, 14. Also in a letter to Eugene Exman, editor of Harper & Brothers, Hocking explained his main argument of *Strength*, indicating appeasement is out, but rigid "stand–pat–ism wholly infantile" and equally rejected.

24. Hocking, *Strength of Men and Nations*, 34.

25. Ibid., 35.

26. Ibid., 54, 55.

27. Ibid.

28. Hocking, *Strength of Men and Nations*, 47. In a letter to Eugene Exman, 29 September 1958, Hocking explained the central thesis of his book, *Strength of Men and Nations*. "I am repudiating war as indeed we must indicating that revolution always a matter of violence however justified in earlier days, has now become a criminal procedure." Furthermore, "the idea of world–revolution embedded in Marxian classics is being abandoned in the USSR. With the right analysis we can definitely promote this abandonment— that is my thesis."

29. Ibid., 211.

30. Hocking, *Re-Thinking Missions*, 31, 84.

31. Ibid., 31, 87. `

32. Ibid., 30.

33. Ibid., 141. Also see William Ernest Hocking, "The Ethical Basis Underlying the Legal Right of Religious Liberty as Applied to Foreign Missions," *Principles of Religious Liberty* (London, New York: International Missionary Council, October 1931), 19. Hocking discusses the potential problems faced by the convert even in situations where the government of the host country gives its official approval of missionary activity.

34. Hocking, *Re-Thinking Missions*, 16, 17.

35. Ibid., 6, 27, 254, 34.

36. Hocking, "The Ethical Basis Underlying the Legal Right of Religious Liberty as Applied to Foreign Missions," 12.

37. Ibid.

38. Ibid., 19. It was established that the purpose of religious propaganda was to bring about "first of all on minor change" which then "works outward into society." The further the development gets from this inner and spiritual center, the more entangled it gets with other considerations such as public policy, property and diplomacy.

39. Hocking, "The Ethical Basis Underlying the Legal Right of Religious Liberty as Applied to Foreign Missions," 16.

40. Hocking, *Re-Thinking Missions*, 51.

41. Ibid., 53.

42. Ibid., 69, 83, 89.

43. Hocking, *The Coming World Civilization*, 169.

44. Ibid., 169, 170.

45. Ibid., 136.

46. Ibid., 168.

47. Hocking, *Strength of Men and Nations*, 179, 192.

48. Ibid., 187.

49. Hocking, *Strength of Men and Nations*, 204. In a letter to Eugene Exman, 28 February 1959, Hocking revealed just how much tension can be felt in recommending the "creative risk" in rapprochement to the Soviet Union. He did not take lightly this giving of advice.

50. In a letter to Mr. James Best, editor, Harper & Brothers, 2 August 1958, Hocking wrote of his alarm at the growth of statism in the United States. "Rapidly we are getting to the place where criticism of government gets retributive action as quickly as in the totalitarian state; we must assume government is 100% right—no citizen should question national policy."

51. Hocking, *Strength of Men and Nations*, 186, 187, 81.

52. Ibid., 148.

53. Hocking, *The Spirit of World Politics*, 212.

54. Ibid., 165.

55. Hocking, *Strength of Men and Nations*, 205.

56. Hocking, "Christianity and the Non–Christian Religions," and *Re-Thinking Missions*, 34.

57. Letter to William Ernest Hocking from Charles J. Ewald, secretary, National Committee for the Presentation of the Laymen's Foreign Missions Inquiry, 10 October 1933.

58. Description of mass rally held 20 March 1933 against the Laymen's Report held at Calvary Baptist Church, New York City, reported by a Mr. Ward N. Madison and Miss Ebsen of the Laymen's Foreign Missions staff.

59. George H. Sabine review of *The Spirit of World Politics* in *International Journal of Ethics* 44, 1933, 140, 141.

60. Letter to William Ernest Hocking from Charles Malik, 24 July 1961.

61. Letter to Eugene Exman, 29 September 1958.

6. Nationalism and the Sword

1. Fred M. Barlow, *Dr. John Rice, Giant of Evangelism* (Murfeesboro, Tenn.: Sword of the Lord Publishers, 1983)

2. Ibid., 7.

3. Ibid., 24.

4. Warren L. Vinz, "The Politics of Protestant Fundamentalism in the 1950s and 1960s," *Journal of Church and State* 14 (Spring, 1972), 244.

5. Ibid.

6. Kenny McComas, "America's Most Degrading Disaster," *The Sword of the Lord*, (Hereafter cited as *SL*.) 17 October 1980, 13.

7. Genesis 14:12–16.

8. McComas, 13.

9. Luke 14:28–32.

10. McComas, 13.

11. Ezekiel 16:32–37.

12. McComas, 13.

13. Capt. G. Russell Evans, USCG (Ret.), "Panama Canal," *SL*, 17 August 1979, 1.

14. Ibid., 16.

15. Vinz, 242, 243.

16. John B. Ashbrook, "The Bible and Abortion," *SL*, 1 November 1974, 8.

17. Ibid., 1.

18. Hugh Pyle, "Let's Start an Avalanche," *SL*, 1 July 1977, 1.

19. Ibid.

20. Dr. Don Boys, "Public Education A Poisoned Pot," *SL*, 27 February 1981, 4.

21. Ibid.

22. Ibid.

23. Vinz, 242.

24. Ibid., 243.

25. Ibid., 244.

26. Deuteronomy 22:9–11 is the basis of the *Sword's* practice of separation.

27. John R. Rice, "No Mixed Seed, Mixed Teams, Mixed Mates, Mixed Garments, " *SL* (21 October 1977), 10.

28. Ibid.

29. Rice, "Romanist Still Claim Right to Burn Heretics," *SL*, 18 June 1954, 5.

30. Ibid.

31. Vinz, 248.

32. Ibid., 249.

33. Ibid., 250.

34. Ibid., 251.

35. Ibid.

36. Ibid., 247.

37. Ibid.

38. I Corinthians 3:19.

7. Nationalim and Realism

1. Reinhold Niebuhr, *Moral Man and Immoral Society* (New York: Charles Scribner's Sons, 1960), xx.

2. Reinhold Niebuhr, *The Irony of American History* (New York: Charles Scribner's Sons, 1952), 88.

3. Niebuhr, *Moral Man*, xxiii.

4. Niebuhr, *Irony*, 37.

5. Niebuhr, *Moral Man*, 94.

6. Ibid., 95.

7. Ibid., 97.

8. Ibid.

9. Niebuhr, *Irony*, 39.

10. Ronald H. Stone, *Reinhold Niebuhr: Prophet to Politicians* (New York: University Press of America, 1981), 50.

11. Reinhold Niebuhr, *The Nature and Destiny of Man* (New York: Charles Scribner's Sons, 1949), 121.

12. Niebuhr, *Irony*, 63.

13. Stone, 203.

14. Henry R. Davis and Robert C. Good, eds., *Reinhold Niebuhr on Politics* (New York: Charles Scribner's Sons, 1960), 328.

15. Stone, 199.

16. Reinhold Niebuhr, *Christian Realism and Political Problems* (New York: Charles Scribner's Sons, 1953), 17.

17. Reinhold Niebuhr, "Our Dependence is on God," *The Christian Century* 71 (1 September 1954), 1034.

18. Stone, 117.

19. Barney Grey Barnhouse, *Eternity*, February 1957, 9.

20. Ibid.

21. Reinhold Niebuhr, "The Christian Faith and the World Crisis," *Christianity and Crisis* 1 (10 February 1941), 4–6.

22. Niebuhr, *Irony*, 38.

23. Ibid., 75.

24. Ibid.

25. Reinhold Niebuhr, *Christianity and Power Politics* (New York: Charles Scribner's Sons, 1940), 65.

26. Reinhold Niebuhr, "The Anatomy of American Nationalism," *New Leader* 38, no. 9 (28 February 1955), 16–17.

27. Reinhold Niebuhr, "The Alternative to Communism," *New Republic*, (1 October 1962).

28. Niebuhr, *Irony*, 22.

29. Reinhold Niebuhr, "The Condition of Our Survival," *Virginia Quarterly Review* 26 (Autumn 1956), 181–82.

30. Niebuhr, *Irony*, 126.

31. Ibid., 125–26.

32. Ibid., 127.

33. Ibid., 129.

34. Reinhold Niebuhr, "American Power and World Responsibility," *Christianity and Crisis* 3 (5 April 1943), 2.

35. Stone, 40–41.

36. Reinhold Niebuhr, "Anglo–Saxon Destiny and Responsibility," *Christianity and Crisis* 3 (4 October 1943), 2.

37. Reinhold Niebuhr, "The Death of the President," *Christianity and Crisis* 5 (30 April 1945), 14.

38. Reinhold Niebuhr, "America's Eminence," *Christianity and Society* 13 (Summer 1948), 4.

39. Reinhold Niebuhr, "Hazards and Resources," *Virginia Quarterly Review* 34 (Spring 1949), 201–2.

40. Stone, 191.

41. Ibid., 187.

42. Ibid., 188.

43. Kenneth Thompson, "Europe's Crisis and America's Dilemma," *Christianity and Crisis* 16 (7 January 1957), 184.

44. Niebuhr, "Anglo-Saxon Destiny," 2–3.

45. Ibid.

46. Niebuhr, "America's Eminence," 3–4.

47. Reinhold Niebuhr, "The Peril of Complacency in Our Nation," *Christianity and Crisis* 14 (8 February 1954), 1.

48. Reinhold Niebuhr, "American Pride and Power," *American Scholar* 17 (Autumn 1948), 394.

49. Niebuhr, *Irony*, 24.

50. Ibid., 35.

51. Reinhold Niebuhr, "Pretense and Power," *The New Leader* 47 (1 March 1965), 6–7.

52. Amos 5:21, 23–24.

53. Reinhold Niebuhr, "The Cuban Missile Crisis in Retrospect," *The New Leader* 45 (10 December 1962), 8–9.

54. Stone, 243; and Reinhold Niebuhr, "The Presidency and the Irony of American History," *Christianity and Crisis* 30 (13 April 1970), 72.

55. Reinhold Niebuhr, "The Social Myths of the Cold War," *Journal of International Affairs* 21 (1967), 54–55.

56. Niebuhr, *Irony*, 141.

57. Ibid., 123.

58. Ibid., 124.

59. Stone, 176.

60. Niebuhr, *Irony*, 79.

61. Stone, 86.

62. Gabriel Fackre, *The Promise of Reinhold Niebuhr* (Philadelphia, New York: J. B. Lippincott Co., 1970), 25.

63. Niebuhr, *Irony*, 124.

64. Reinhold Niebuhr, "Can Democracy Work?" *The New Leader* 45 (28 May 1962), 8–9.

65. Stone, 115.

66. Ibid.

67. Niebuhr, "Can Democracy Work?," 8–9.

68. Reinhold Niebuhr, "The Eisenhower Doctrine," *The New Leader* 40 (4 February 1957), 9.

69. Niebuhr, "The Eisenhower Doctrine," 8.

70. Stone, 199.

71. Ibid., 177.

72. Ibid., 173.

73. Reinhold Niebuhr, "The Limits of American Power," *Christianity and Society* 17 (Autumn 1952), 5.

74. Niebuhr, "Can Democracy Work?," 9.

75. Niebuhr, "The Dilemma of American Power," *The New Leader* 46 (25 November 1963), 11–12.

76. Kenneth W. Thompson, *Political Realism and the Crisis of World Politics* (Princeton: Princeton University Press, 1960), 50–61, and Niebuhr, "The Dilemma of U.S. Power," 11–12.

77. Charles W. Kegley, *Politics, Religion and Modern Man* (Quezon City: University of the Philippines Press, 1969), 21.

78. Ibid., 33.

79. Fackre, 29.

8. The Nationalism of Moderation

1. Herein after *Christianity Today* will be referred to as *CT*.

2. Edward Dobson, "Goals of Evangelical Political Involvement: A Fundamentalist Perspective," Evangelical Political Symposium, Calvin College, Grand Rapids, Michigan, 18 October 1986.

3. Herein after referred to as NCC, the liberal voice of so-called Protestant mainline churches.

4. Editor, "Where Are We Drifting?," *CT* (22 December 1958), 21.

5. Editor, "Will to Greatness in Russia and America," *CT* (13 October 1958), 22. Also Editor, "America's Future: Can We Salvage The Republic?," *CT* (3 March 1958).

6. Editor, "America's Future," 3.

7. Editor, "Will to Greatness," 22.

8. Editor, "Where Are We Drifting?," 21.

9. Ibid.

10. Ibid.

11. Editor, "What of Tomorrow?," *CT* (3 March 1958), 22.

12. Editorials, "God Make Us Great," *CT* (22 June 1962), 20.

13. Editor, "America's Future," 3.

14. Ibid., 3, 6.

15. Editorials, "The Crisis in Education," *CT* (12 May 1958), 21.

16. Editorials, "God Make Us Great," 21.

17. Editorials, "The American Malaise," *CT* (20 June 1960), 20.

18. Carl F. H. Henry, "Perspectives for Social Action" Part I, *CT* (19 January 1959), 9–11.

19. Editor, "Uncle Sam or Big Brother?," *CT* (25 June 1962), 20–21.

20. Carl F. H. Henry, "Perspectives for Social Action" Part II, *CT* (2 February 1959), 13.

21. Ibid.

22. Ibid., 15.

23. Ibid.

24. Editorials, "Can We Weather the Storm?," *CT* (23 November 1962), 26–27; "Low Tide in the West," *CT* (24 December 1956), 20–24; "Government Service as a Christian Vocation," *CT* (24 June 1957), 21–22; "The American Malaise," *CT* (20 June 1960), 20–21; "Light Out of Darkness," *CT* (20 December 1963), 20–21; "National Need—Righteousness," *CT* (6 December 1963), 26–27; "Freedom and Morality," *CT* (17 January 1964), 26–27; "A World Short of Breath," *CT* (6 November 1964), 28; "A National Day of Humiliation," *CT* (27 October 1972), 29.

25. Editorials, "God Make Us Great," 20.

26. Editorials, "Christian Faith and National Power," *CT* (2 July 1965), 20.

27. Ibid.

28. Editorials, "Human Rights in an Age of Tyranny," *CT* (4 February 1957), 20–21.

29. Editorials, "The American Malaise," 21; "Financing Murder," *CT* (29 January 1971), 72; "Twisted Logic," *CT* (22 December 1972), 24–25.

30. Editorials, "The American Malaise," 21.

31. Ibid.

32. Carl F. H. Henry, "Christian Education on Culture," *CT* (10 November 1958), 3.

33. Ibid.

34. Ibid., 5.

35. Editor, "Do We Need A Christian University?," *CT* (9 May 1960), 3.

36. Carl F. H. Henry, "Religion in the Public Schools," *CT* (30 August 1963), 30–32.

37. Editorials, "NCC, God and the Schools," *CT* (8 June 1959), 21. Also Editorials, "Stating the Case for Religion in Public Schools," *CT* (9 May 1960).

38. Editor, "Evolution: Theory or Dogma?," *CT* (5 January 1973), 28–29.

39. Editorials, "The Trumpet of the Lord," *CT* (10 June 1957), 21; "Fallout Shelters and Their Spiritual Application," *CT* (19 January 1962), 25–26.

40. Editor, "The Christian's Duty in the Present Crisis," *CT* (5 January 1959), 22.

41. Editor, "Christ and the Atom Bomb," *CT* (2 September 1957), 21.

42. Ibid.

43. Said originally by Pope Innocent III.

44. Carl F. H. Henry, "Christianity and Communism," *CT* (24 April 1961), 12–13.

45. Editorials, "The Trumpet of the Lord," 20–22.

46. Editor, "Where Are We Drifting?," *CT* (4 December 1964), 31.

47. Editorials, "Red's Red After All," *CT* (4 December 1964), 31.

48. Editorials, "The Christian Citizen in the World Conflict," *CT* (27 October 1958), 21.

49. Editorial, "The Ground of Freedom," *CT* (3 July 1964), 20.

50. Editorial, "UN Town Meeting, or Tragedy?," *CT* (1 April 1957), 21–22.

51. Editorial, "The Ground of Freedom," 20–21.

52. Editor, "Christian Criticism and Labor's Big Stick," *CT* (10 December 1956), 23–25; "Natural Law and Revelation," *CT* (24 June 1957), 20–21; "In Defense of Property Rights," *CT* (11 September 1964), 32; "Capitalism and Communism," *CT* (13 February 1971), 34–35; Carl F. H. Henry, "The World Council and Socialism," *CT* (8 July 1966), 3–7; Henry, "The Judgment of America," *CT* (8 November 1974), 22–24.

53. Editorial, "The Church and Public Relations," *CT* (14 April 1958), 20–22.

54. Editor, "Even the Devil Wears a Smile," *CT* (2 February 1959), 22–23.

55. Editor, "The Spirit of Foreign Policy," *CT* (29 April 1957), 22.

56. Editorials, "The Gospel in Modern Asia," *CT* (28 September 1959), 21.

57. Editor, "Diversity in Unity: Report on New Delhi," *CT* (22 December 1961), 3.

58. Editorials, "The Gospel in Modern Asia," *CT* (28 September 1959), 21.

59. Editor, "Diversity in Unity," 3–5.

60. Editor, "The Demands of Detente," *CT* (29 August 1975, 26).

61. Ibid.

62. Editorial, "The Christian as Patriot," *CT* (22 June 1973), 22.

63. Editor, "NCC World Order Policy Softens on Red China," *CT* (22 December 1958), 23.

64. Editor, "The Peking Gambit," *CT* (6 August 1971), 24.

65. Ibid.

66. Editor, "Red China and World Morality," *CT* (10 December 1956), 21.

67. Editorial, "Next Year in the New Jerusalem?," *CT* (7 July 1967), 21; "Realignment of Nations in the Middle East," *CT* (3 March 1958), 23; "War Sweeps the Bible Lands," *CT* (23 June 1967), 20–21; Carl F. H. Henry, "Israel: Marvel Among the Nations," Part I, *CT* (11 September 1961), 13–16.

68. Editorial, "Israeli–Egyptian Peace Treaty," *CT* (20 April 1979), 8.

69. Editor, "Still the Evil Empire?," *CT* (15 July 1988), 14.

70. Ibid.

71. Ibid.

72. Editor, "No More Bad Guys?," *CT* (12 May 1989), 16.

73. Editor, "Exporting Democracy," *CT* (8 November 1974), 29.

74. Editorial, "The Difference CT Means to Make," *CT* (2 January 1981), 12–13.

75. Editorials, "The Crisis in Education," *CT* (12 May 1958), 21–22.

76. Ibid., 22.

77. Ibid.

78. Ibid.

79. Ibid., 21.

80. Editorials, "Supreme Court Ban: Where Will It Lead?," *CT* (20 July 1962), 25–26.

81. Editor, "Prayer in the Schools," *CT* (23 June 1967), 23; "Church and State: Playing Fair with Prayer," *CT* (6 June 1980), 12–13; Editorials, "Supreme Court Prayer Ban: Where Will It Lead Us?," *CT* (20 July 1962), 25–26.

82. Editorials, "Is the Supreme Court on Trial?," *CT* (1 March 1963); "Compulsory Devotions Banned: The Bible Retains Classroom Value," *CT* (5 July 1963), 26; "Religion in Public Schools," *CT* (30 August 1963), 30; "What Johnny Should Read," *CT* (31 January 1975), 19.

83. Carl F. H. Henry, "Christian Responsibility in Education," *CT* (27 May 1957), 11–14.

84. Editorial, "The Supreme Court Ban: Where Will It Lead?," *CT* (20 July 1962), 26.

85. Editor, "Of Evolution and Creation and the Space Between," *CT* (7 May 1982), 12–13.

86. Editorial, "Halting Red Aggression in Viet Nam," *CT* (23 April 1965), 32.

87. Editorial, "The Ground of Freedom," *CT* (3 July 1964), 20–21.

88. Editorials, "Ignorance Often Has a Loud Voice," *CT* (12 February 1965), 35.

89. Editorial, "A Time To Speak," *CT* (21 May 1965), 26.

90. Ibid.

91. Ibid.

92. Editorial, "Dodging the Draft," *CT* (5 November 1965), 36.

93. Editorial, "The New Spirit of Defiance," *CT* (23 December 1966), 19–20.

94. Editorial, "Halting Red Aggression in Viet Nam," *CT* (23 April 1965), 32.

95. Editor, "Viet Nam: Where Do We Go From Here?," *CT* (7 January 1966), 31.

96. Ibid.

97. Editorial, "The Church and the Viet Nam Bound Soldier," *CT* (13 May 1966), 30–31. "Are Churchmen Failing Servicemen in Viet Nam?," *CT* (18 August 1967), 30–31.

98. Editorial, "Honesty in Government," *CT* (26 March 1971), 25.

99. Editor, "The Right to Know," *CT* (16 July 1971), 22–23.

100. Editor, "The Calley Verdict," *CT* (23 April 1971), 27.

101. Editorial, "Shutting Down the Government," *CT* (21 May 1971), 35.

102. Editor, "Viet Nam—Continuing Impasse," *CT* (6 August 1971), 25.

103. Editor, "The Viet Nam Pact," *CT* (16 February 1973), 34.

104. Editor, "The Indo-China Fiasco," *CT* (25 April 1975), 27.

105. Editor, "What to Remember about Viet Nam," *CT* (23 May 1975), 45–46.

106. Ibid., 46. Italics mine.

9. The Nationalism of Survival

1. Clyde Edminster, *The Manchild—The Birth of America* (Rainier, Wash.: Christ Is The Answer Publications, 1976), 1. Interview on site with Clyde Edminster, 25 June 1982.

2. Edminster, *Manchild*, 2.

3. Leviticus 26:27–28. This and all other scripture passages to follow represent Edminster's use of scripture in developing his thesis.

4. According to Edminster, one "time" is 360 years even as one year is 360 days. 360 days was the original length of a year until the great flood occurred which caused a year to be lengthened by 5 days.

5. Revelation 12:14; II Samuel 7:10; Edminster, *Manchild*, 3.

6. Edminster, *Manchild*, 3.

7. Genesis 35:10–11.

8. Edminster, *Manchild*, 4.

9. Ibid., 7.

10. Genesis 41–46.

11. Deuteronomy 33:13–17.

12. Clyde Edminster, *The Deliverance of Israel and the Kingdom Age by 1986* (Rainier, Wash.: Christ Is The Answer Publications, 1975), 4.

13. Edminster, *Deliverance*, 4.

14. Ibid.

15. Matthew 23:1–39; John 8:44; Edminster, *Manchild*, 4.

16. Edminster, *Deliverance*, 4.

17. Ibid., 9.

18. Ibid., 10.

19. Ibid.

20. Exodus 1; Jashar 66:9–31.

21. Edminster, *Deliverance*, 22.

22. Jashar 81:4. The book of Jashar is a source used extensively by Edminster. It is an ancient book of songs, religious and secular, that describe the epic events of the nation of Israel. This book is occasionally quoted in the Old Testament itself.

23. Edminster, *Deliverance*, 2.

24. Ezekiel 38:1–7.

25. Edminster explained in interview that Palestine could never be the place for Armageddon since no Israelites are in Palestine—only Jews, i.e., Reds. Only the United States has Israelites—the New Israel.

26. Description of flash and results are perceived to be in Matthew 24:27–28 and Zechariah 14:12–15.

27. Edminster, *Deliverance*, 50.

28. Psalms 91:1–11.

29. Isaiah 1:18–29; Joel 3:12–17.

30. Joel 2:15–20.

31. Ezekiel 39:11–12.

32. Isaiah 10:26–27.

33. Ezekiel 39:11–16.

34. Edminster, *Deliverance*, 52.

35. Emil J. Trautman, "Soviet Shift Winter Weather to U.S.A.," *Christ Is The Answer* 15 (April 1982), 7–9.

36. Clyde Edminster, *America's Four Sore Judgments!* (Rainier, Wash: Christ Is The Answer Publications, 1981), 13.

37. Ibid., 25.

38. Jimmy L. Sabin, "What Really Constitutes the Christian Israel Belief?" *Christ Is The Answer* 14 (June 1981), 11–12.

39. Edminster even identifies specific people who have been in our government as a "type and shadow" of specific people in the ancient past. For example in Jasher 67:8–11: "Balaam, son of Beor fled from the land of Chittini, which was an Esau—red controlled and dominated country. He came to the Pharaoh Melol in Egypt and he was immediately made advisor to the King. The modern-day sequel is Dr. Henry Kissinger, a Jew, a refugee from red socialist dominated Germany. After a short schooling in the "world

planners' ivy league college, he was exalted as chief advisor to our president." *Deliverance*, 12.

10. The Nationalism of Anxiety

1. Edward G. Dobson, "Goals of Evangelical Political Involvement: A Fundamentalist Perspective," Evangelical Political Symposium, Calvin College, Grand Rapids, Michigan, 18 October 1986.

2. Eric Fromm, *Escape from Freedom* (New York: Farrar and Rinehart, Inc., 1941).

3. The term "zealous nationalism" is taken from Robert Jewett, *Captain America Complex: The Dilemma of Zealous Nationalism* (Santa Fe, N.M.: Bear and Co.).

4. W. Wesley Hurd, "Liberty University: Fortress in the War For a Christian America," (Ph.D. diss., Division of Education Policy and Management, Graduate School, University of Oregon, 1988), 214.

5. Jerry Falwell, *Listen America* (Garden City, N.Y.: Doubleday, 1980), 265.

6. Ibid., 24.

7. Dobson, "Goals."

8. Ibid.

9. Dinesh D'Souza, *Falwell, Before the Millennium: A Critical Biography* (Chicago: Regnery Gateway, 1984), 190.

10. Falwell, *Listen America*, 106.

11. Jerry Falwell, "Our Citizenship as Americans," sermon, 7 March 1976, 5, 6.

12. Dean Fadley and Ralph Hamlett, "The Three Faces of Falwell." Paper delivered to the Annual Convention of the Speech Communication Association, Washington, D.C., 10–13 November 1983. Also in *Moral Majority Capitol Report*, August 1979.

13. Falwell, *Listen America*, 7.

14. Falwell, "Our Citizenship as Americans," 5.

15. Falwell, *Listen America*, 106.

16. Ibid., 99–104.

17. Ibid., 98.

18. Edward M. Berckman, "'The Old-Time Gospel Hour' and Fundamentalist Paradox," *Christian Century*, 29 March 1978.

19. Ibid.

20. Merril Simon, *Jerry Falwell and the Jews*, (New York: Jonathan David Publishers, 1984), 53.

21. Berckman, "'The Old Time Gospel Hour'."

22. D'Souza, 188.

23. Ibid., 186.

24. *Liberty University Undergraduate Student Catalogue, 1987–1988*, Lynchburg, Va.

25. D'Souza, 191.

26. Ibid., 186.

27. *Liberty University Undergraduate Student Catalogue, 1987–1988*.

28. Falwell, *Listen America*, 102.

29. Ibid., 15.

30. Falwell, "Our Citizenship as Americans," 14.

31. Ibid., 2.

32. Falwell, "Our Citizenship as Americans," 12.

33. Falwell, "Our Citizenship as Americans," 5. Also see Walter Capps, *The New Religious Right* (Columbia: University of South Carolina Press, 1990), 35, 36. In response to the question, Is the United States the New Israel?, Nelson Keener, a Falwell associate, stated that while Falwell didn't want the nation to be a theocracy and was aware of the problems connected to calling the United States a Christian nation, wanted to affirm that the United States stands in a position of special favor with God because of the principles and convictions upon which it was founded.

34. Jerry Falwell "An Interview with the Lone Ranger of American Fundamentalism," *Christianity Today*, 4 September 1981, 24. Also see Simon, *Jerry Falwell and the Jew*, 115, 116. Falwell, as quoted by Simon remarked, "It is as ridiculous to assume that America can be Christianized as to believe that it can be Judaized." America was distinctive as a melting pot, and "while America is predominantly Judeo–Christian, there is also room for the Moslem. There is room for the Hindu. There is room for the atheist" (p. 115). There "is no biblical basis for believing that the majority of the population of this nation or any nation at any time in history will ever be Christian" (p. 116).

35. Capps, 56.

36. Simon, 35–47.

37. Gerald Strober and Ruth Tomczak, *Jerry Falwell: Aflame for God* (New York: Thomas Nelson Publishers, 1979), 167.

38. Capps, 55, 56.

39. Ibid., 39. Similar views were expressed in a sermon by Falwell, "God Bless America, Please." "That flag, old glory, is more than just a symbol of the United States of America and our sovereignty. It's a symbol of freedom, liberty, the kind of liberty that has allowed us in 205 years not only to become the greatest nation on earth, but from within this great nation through the churches we've been able to preach the saving gospel of Christ to the world" (p. 3).

40. Fadley and Hamlett, "The Three Faces of Falwell." Fadley and Hamlett identify the exhortatory audience as one which "demands a strong emotional experience to induce the political action desired by Falwell. The mimetic audience is already convinced and needs only to have the conviction reflected and confirmed by the discourse." Falwell provides the "emotional experience and the convictional confirmation satisfying the exhortatory and mimetic type audiences" (p. 11).

41. Ibid., and in Falwell, *Listen America*, 74, 217.

42. Fadley and Hamlett, p. 11, and quotes from letter to Fadley and Hamlett from Falwell, 11 March 1982, 2.

43. These terms are collected from Fadley and Hamlett, "The Three Faces"; Falwell, *Listen America*; Falwell, "Mobilizing the Moral Majority" Jerry Falwell, *America Can Be Saved* (Murfreesboro, Tenn.: Sword of the Lord Publishers, 1979); Strober and Tomczak, *Jerry Falwell*; and Capps, *The New Religious Right*.

44. Strober and Tomczak, 186.

45. Fadley and Hamlett, 15, 16, and in Falwell, "Mobilizing."

46. Jerry Falwell, "Inside The Cup," *The Old Time Gospel Hour*, 12 September 1982, 20.

47. Ibid., 16.

48. Ibid., 17.

49. Fadley and Hamlett, 18, and Falwell, "Mobilizing."

50. Ibid., The Three Faces...," 18.

51. Ibid., 19.

52. C. C. Goen.

53. Jerry Falwell, *America Can Be Saved!*, 34.

54. Falwell, "Our Citizenship as Americans," 13. See also Jerry Falwell, *The Fundamentalist Phenomenon: The Resurgence of Conservative Christianity* (Garden City, N.Y.: Doubleday, 1981), 212, 213.

55. Capps, 29.

56. Falwell, "Our Citizenship as Americans," 1.

57. Ralph Clark Chandler, "Worshiping a Past That Never Was," *Christianity and Crisis*, 15 February 1982, 20.

58. James Davison Hunter, *American Evangelicalism: Conservative Religion and the Quandary of Modernity* (New Brunswick, N.J.: Rutgers University Press, 1983), 113.

59. Capps, 27.

60. Chandler, 20.

61. Falwell, "God Bless America, Please." The seven principles that made America great according to Falwell were:

> The principle of the dignity of human life,
> The principle of the traditional monogamous family,
> The principle of common decency,
> The principle of the work ethic,
> The principle of the Abrahamic covenant,
> The principle of God–centered education,
> The principle of Divinely Ordained establishment
>   A. The home
>   B. State or civil government
>   C. Religious institutions

62. Strober and Tomczak, 183–85. Falwell is quoted as saying that God directly punishes people for their sins. After the shooting of the San Francisco mayor and city supervisor Falwell said: "Without question, San Francisco is undergoing the judgment of God today. I am sorry that San Francisco has become, in the words of a former mayor of that city, an 'open city' where everybody, regardless of their sexual orientation, is welcome. . . . What he was really saying is that it doesn't matter to us what God thinks about it, we have endorsed what God condemned whether He likes it or not. . . . The people of San Francisco had better awaken to the fact that the judgment, the wrath that is falling upon the city, is of divine origin. . . . Did you know that the homosexuals in San Francisco jokingly call Frisco 'Sodom and Gomorrah'? This is a way of flaunting their arrogance in the face of Almighty God."

63. *Spokesman Review*, 11 January 1909.

64. Roy H. Abrams, *Preachers Present Arms* (Scottdale, Pa.: Herald Press, 1933, revised 1969), 112, and *Watchman Examiner* 6, no. 16 (18 April 1918), 503.

65. Strober and Tomczak, 167. Falwell believed in an inexorable connection between the well-being of Israel and the United States, and the end of time. At Alon Moreh God promised Abraham, Genesis 12:3, "I will bless them that bless thee, and curse him that curseth thee." Strobe and Tomczak said of Falwell, "He thought with anticipation of the day when civilization which had begun in that sacred spot would consummate there" (166, 167). Explicitly, Falwell stated, "I believe that if we fail to protect Israel, we will cease to be important to God." 167. These thoughts also in "An Interview with the Lone Ranger of America," *Christianity Today*, 4 September 1981, 26.

66. Strober and Tomczak, 157.

67. Hurd, 192.

68. D'Souza, 192, 193.

69. Hurd, 200.

70. Dobson.

71. Lisa Solod, "Jerry Falwell," *Nutshell* 1981–82, 37–41. Also in Fadley and Hamlett, 21.

72. Strober and Tomczak, 177.

73. D'Souza, 203.

74. Strober and Tomczak, 169.

75. Ibid., 170.

76. Ibid.

77. Ibid.

78. Ibid., 171.

79. Hurd, 235.

80. *Liberty University Undergraduate Studies Catalogue*, 1987–1988, 71.

81. Falwell, *The Fundamentalist Phenomenon*, 175.

82. Jeffrey Hadden and Anson Shupe, *Televangelism, Power and Politics* (New York: Henry Holt and Company, 1988), 176.

83. Hurd, 142.

84. *Liberty University Undergraduate Studies Catalogue*, 1987–1988, 82.

85. Ibid., 68.

86. Hurd, 235.

87. Berckman

88. Falwell, *America Can Be Saved!*, 32.

89. Ibid., 33.

90. Ibid.

91. Ibid.

92. Ibid., 35.

93. Ibid., 35, 36.

94. Ibid., 36.

95. Capps, 38.

96. Falwell, "Mobilizing."

97. Warren L. Vinz, "The Politics of Protestant Fundamentalism in the 1950s and 1960s," *Journal of Church and State* 14, no. 2, (1972), 235–60.

98. Falwell, "Our Citizenship as Americans."

99. James Davison Hunter, "Fundamentalism in Its Global Contours," in Norman Cohn, ed., *The Fundamentalist Phenomenon* (Grand Rapids: Eerdmans, 1990), 70.

100. George M. Marsden, "Defining American Fundamentalism," in Cohn, *The Fundamentalist Phenomenon*, 29.

101. Dobson.

102. William Packard, *Evangelism in America: From Tents to TV* (New York: Paragon House, 1988), 219.

11. Conclusion

1. Editorials, *Christianity Today*, 4 December 1964, 31.

2. "Buchanan Stirs Up Support," *Idaho Statesman*, 12 September 1993, 2.

3. Clifford Geertz, *Local Knowledge* (New York: Basic Books, 1983), 234.

4. Ibid.

5. William Dean, *History Making History* (Albany: State University of New York Press, 1988), 25.

6. James Davison Hunter, *Culture Wars: The Struggle to Define America* (New York: Basic Books, 1991), 42.

7. Ibid., 44.

8. Harvey Cox, "Understanding Islam," *The Atlantic Monthly*, January 1981.

9. Ibid.

10. Charles W. Dunn, *American Political Theology* (New York: Praeger Publishers, 1984). Dunn documents the nature of the "theological tension and the founding of the American government" in this volume and continues the theme throughout till the 1980s.

11. David Alan McClintock, "Walter Rauschenbusch: The Kingdom of God and the American Experience" (Ph.D. diss., History, Case Western Reserve, 1975), 394.

12. Ibid.

13. Robert Wuthrow, *The Struggle for America's Soul* (Grand Rapids: William B. Eerdman Publishing Company, 1989). Wuthrow does refer to the Civil War in the sense that American society is more polarized at the present than at any other time since the Civil War. He does not attempt to show any ongoing polarization from that civil conflict but rather primarily uses it to show by comparison the seriousness of the present crisis of societal division.

14. Barry A. Kosmin and Seymour P. Lachman, *One Nation Under God* (New York: Harmony Books, 1993). This latest work while comprehensive and informative gives the general impression that because a majority of American people believe in God that somehow this serves as a unifying force in American society.

15. Thomas J. Schlereth, *Victorian America: Transformation in Everyday Life, 1875–1915* (New York: Harper Collins, 1991), xi.

16. Robert F. Drinan, S.J., "The Advocacy Role of Religion in American Politics," in James E. Wood, Jr. and Derek Davis, eds., *The Role of Religion in the Making of Public Policy* (Waco, Tex.: Baylor University, 1991), 223.

17. Daniel Thorp, *The Moravian Community in Colonial North Carolina* (Knoxville: The University of Tennessee Press, 1989), 206.

18. Hunter, 50.

19. Ibid., 34.

20. John M. Murrin, "Religion and Politics in America from the First Settlements to the Civil War," in Mark A. Noll, ed., *Religion and American Politics from the Colonial Period to the 1980s* (New York: Oxford University Press, 1990), 36.

21. Michael Hunt, *Ideology and U.S. Foreign Policy* (New Haven: Yale University Press, 1987), 189.

22. Editorial, "God's Judgment on the Summit," *Christianity Today*, 6 June 1960, 21.

23. Hunter, 318.

24. Ibid., 319.

25. Ibid., 319, 320.

26. Ibid., 320.

27. Wuthrow, 24.

28. Hunter, 322.

29. Ibid.

30. Ibid.

31. Hunter, 322.

32. Ibid., 325.

33. Ibid.

34. Ibid.

35. Michael J. Perry, *Love and Power: The Role of Religion and Morality in American Politics* (New York: Oxford University Press, 1991), 10.

36. Ibid., 145.

37. Ibid., 207–8.

38. Ibid., 144.

Bibliography

Articles

Aiken, John R. "Walter Rauschenbusch and Education for Reform." *Church History* 35 (4 December 1967), 456–69.

Aked, Charles F., and Walter Rauschenbusch. "Private Profit and the Nation's Honor: A Protest and a Plea." *The Standard*, 31 July 1915, 1486–87.

Ashbrook, John B. "The Bible and Abortion." *Sword of the Lord*, 1 November 1974, 8.

Bowden, Henry W. "Walter Rauschenbusch and American Church History." *Foundations* 9 (July–September, 1966), 241.

Boys, Don. "Public Education A Poisoned Pot." *Sword of the Lord*, 27 February 1981, 4.

Broun, Haywood. "It Seems To Me." *The World Telegram*, 4 October 1935.

Chandler, Ralph Clark. "Worshiping a Past That Never Was." *Christianity and Crisis*, 15 February 1982.

Conwell, Russell. "The Savior at the Panama Canal." *Temple Review* 23, no. 44 (9 December 1915), 3.

———. "Thanksgiving for Victories." *True Philadelphian* 2, no. 19 (5 August 1898), 524.

———. "God's Care of the Nation." *Temple Review* 7, no. 24 (15 March 1901), 523.

———. "Patriotic Sons of America." *Temple Review* 17, no. 14 (16 October 1908), 4.

———. "The Influence of Our Nation." *Temple Review* 12, no. 9 (27 November 1903), 3.

———. "America's Danger." *True Philadelphian* 2, no. 3 (24 June 1898), 347.

———. "Mexico." *Temple Review* 27, no. 44 (19 December 1919), 3.

———. "An Unfair Partnership." *Temple Review* 31, no. 2 (5 October 1923), 276.

———. "Church Aid to Patriotism." *Temple Review* 24, no. 4 (27 January 1916), 11.

———. "German Indemnity." *Temple Review* 25, no. 43 (4 December 1917), 3–6.

———. "The Kingdom of God a True Democracy." *Temple Review* 27, no. 6 (18 January 1919), 7.

Editor. "Christ and the Atom Bomb." *Christianity Today*, 2 September 1957, 21.

———. "Will to Greatness In Russia and America." *Christianity Today*, 13 October 1958, 22.

———. "Diversity in Unity: Report on New Delhi." *Christianity Today*, 22 December 1961, 3.

———. "Still the Evil Empire?" *Christianity Today*, 15 July 1988, 14.

———. "No More Bad Guys?" *Christianity Today*, 12 May 1989, 16.

———. "Exporting Democracy." *Christianity Today*, 8 November 1974, 29.

———. "Viet Nam: Where Do We Go From Here?" *Christianity Today*, 7 January 1966, 31.

———. "Viet Nam: Continuing Impasse." *Christianity Today*, 6 August 1971, 25.

———. "The Viet Nam Pact." *Christianity Today*, 16 February 1973, 34.

———. "The Indo–China Fiasco." *Christianity Today*, 25 April 1975, 27.

———. "Jack and Jill." *Christianity Today*, 31 August 1962, 20.

———. "The Christian's Duty in the Present Crisis." *Christianity Today*, 5 January 1959, 22.

———. "Even the Devil Wears a Smile." *Christianity Today*, 2 February 1959, 22–23.

———. "What to Remember About Viet Nam." *Christianity Today*, 23 May 1975, 45–46.

Editorials. "The American Malaise," *Christianity Today*, 20 June 1960, 20.

———. "God Make Us Great." *Christianity Today*, 22 June 1962, 20.

———. "Christian Faith and National Power." *Christianity Today*, 2 July 1965, 20.

———. "NCC, God and the Schools." *Christianity Today*, 8 June 1959, 21.

———. "Stating the Case for Religion in Public Schools." *Christianity Today*, 9 May 1960, 26.

———. "Red's Red After All." *Christianity Today*, 4 December 1964, 31.

———."UN Town Meeting, or Tragedy?" *Christianity Today*, 1 April 1957, 21–22.

———. "The Christian as Patriot." *Christianity Today*, 22 June 1973, 22.

———. "God's Judgement on the Summit." *Christianity Today*, 6 June 1960, 21.

———. "The Crisis in Education." *Christianity Today*, 12 May 1958, 21–22.

———. "Halting Red Aggression in Viet Nam." *Christianity Today*, 23 April 1965, 32.

Evans, Captain G. Russell, USCG (Ret.) "Panama Canal." *Sword of the Lord*, 17 August 1979, 1.

Fadley, Dean and Humlett, Ralph. "The Three Faces of Falwell." Paper delivered to the Annual Convention of the Speech Communication Association, Washington, D.C., 10–13 November 1983.

Henry, Carl F. H. "Christianity and Communism," *Christianity Today*, 24 April 1961, 12–13.

———. "Religion in the Public Schools." *Christianity Today*, 30 August 1963, 30–32.

———. "Christian Education on Culture." *Christianity Today*, 10 November 1958, 3.

———. "Christian Responsibility in Education." *Christianity Today*, 27 May 1957, 11–14.

———. "Perspectives for Social Action," Part II. *Christianity Today*, 2 February 1959, 13.

———. "Perspectives for Social Action," Part I. *Christianity Today*, 19 January 1959, 9–11.

Hocking, William Ernest. "Christianity and Non–Christian Religions." *Drew University Bulletin*. An address delivered at Drew University, Madison, New Jersey, 19 October 1933.

Machen, J. Gresham. "The Necessity of the Christian School." *Forward in Faith* (Convention Year Book, Chicago: National Union of Christian Schools, 1934), 2.

———."Shall We Have a Federal Department of Education?" *The Woman Patriot*, 15 February 1926.

———. "A Communication: Child Labor and Liberty." *The New Republic*, 31 December 1924, 145.

———. "Is Pearl Buck a Christian?" *The Evening Sun*, 16 May 1933.

———. "Professor Machen Says Child Labor Amendment Would Threaten U.S. With Tyranny Similar to Russia," *Trenton Sunday Times-Advertiser*, 25 January 1925.

———. "Compulsory Registration." *New York Times*, 13 September 1933, 18.

———. "An Open Letter to President Roosevelt." *The Presbyterian Guardian* 1, no. 2 (21 October 1935), 23.

McComas, Kenny. "America's Most Degrading Disaster." *Sword of the Lord*, 17 October 1979, 13.

Murrin, John M. "Religion and Politics in America From the First settlements to the Civil War." In Mark A. Noll, ed., *Religion and American Politics From the Colonial Period to the 1980s*. New York: Oxford University Press, 1990, 36.

Niebuhr, Reinhold. "American Pride and Power." *American Scholar* 17 (Autumn 1948), 394.

———. "The Peril of Complacency in Our Nation." *Christianity and Crisis* 14 (8 February 1954), 1.

———. "America's Eminence." *Christianity and Crisis* 13 (Summer 1948), 4.

———. "Anglo-Saxon Destiny and Responsibility." *Christianity and Crisis* 3 (4 October 1943), 2.

———. "American Power and World Responsibility." *Christianity and Crisis* 3 (5 April 1943), 2.

———. "The Condition of Our Survival." *Virginia Quarterly Review* 26 (Autumn 1956), 181–82.

———. "The Anatomy of American Nationalism." *New Leader* 38, no. 9 (28 February 1955), 16–17.

———. "America's Precarious Eminence." *Virginia Quarterly Review* 23 (Autumn 1947), 481–82.

———. "The Christian Faith and the World Crisis." *Christianity and Crisis* 1 (10 February 1941), 4–6.

———. "Our Dependence is on God." *The Christian Century* 71 (1 September 1954), 1034.

———. "Can Democracy Work?" *The New Leader* 45 (28 May 1962), 8–9.

———. "Pretense and Power." *The New Leader* 47 (1 March 1965), 1–7.

———. "The Limits of American Power." *Christianity and Society* 17 (Autumn 1952), 5.

Rauschenbusch, Walter. "The True American Church, Great Christian Groups Which Belong Together." *The Congregationalist*, 23 October 1913, 562.

———. "Be Fair to Germany: A Plea for Open-Mindedness." September, 1914 (Sharpe Collection, Box 19), 1.

———. "Decoration Day Thoughts." Sermon delivered 31 June 1903 (Sharpe Collection, Box 20, Colgate Rochester Divinity School), 4.

———. "The Present and the Future." Thanksgiving sermon delivered to Rochester Baptists, and printed in its entirety in the *Rochester Post-Express*, 25 November 1898, 50.

———. "What Is A Christian Nation?" *The Standard*, 23 February 1907, 5.

———. "The Higher Life of Our Nation." From manuscript of proposed book, 1902 (Sharpe Collection, Box 45), 2.

Rice, John R. "No Mixed Seed, Mixed Teams, Mixed Mates, Mixed Garments." *The Sword of the Lord*, 21 October 1977, 10.

———. "Romanists Still Claim Right to Burn Heretics." *Sword of the Lord*, 18 June 1954, 5.

Sabin, Jimmy L. "What Really Constitutes the Christian Israel Belief?" *Christ Is The Answer* 15 (June 1981), 11–12.

Trautman, Emil J. "Soviets Shift Winter Weather to U.S.A." *Christ Is The Answer* 15 (April 1982), 7–9.

Vinz, Warren. "The Politics of Protestant Fundamentalism in the 1950s and 1960s." *Journal of Church and State* 14 (Spring 1972), 242–44.

Books

Abrams, Roy H. *Preachers Present Arms*. Scottdale, Pa.: Herald Press, 1933, revised 1969.

Barlow, Fred M. *Dr. John Rice, Giant of Evangelism.* Murfeesboro, Tenn.: Sword of the Lord Publishers, 1983.

Cajyes, Walter. *The New Religious Right.* Columbia: University of South Carolina Press. 1990.

Cohn, Norman. *The Fundamentalist Phenomenon.* Grand Rapids: Eerdmans, 1990.

Craig, Gordon A. *The Germans.* New York: New American Library Press, 1982.

D'Souza, Dinesh. *Falwell, Before the Millennium: A Critical Biography.* Chicago: Regnery Gateway, 1984.

Davis, Henry and Robert C. Good, eds. *Reinhold Niebuhr on Politics.* New York: Charles Scribner's Sons, 1960.

Dean, William. *History Making History.* Albany: State University of New York Press, 1988.

Dunn, Charles W. *American Political Theology.* New York: Prager. 1984.

Edminster, Clyde. *The Manchild—The Birth of America.* Rainier, Wash.: Christ Is The Answer Publications, 1976.

———. *America's Four Sore Judgements!.* Rainier, Wash.: Christ Is The Answer Publications, 1981.

———. *The Deliverance of Israel and The Kingdom Age by 1986.* Rainier, Wash.: Christ Is the Answer Publications, 1975.

Ergang, Robert R. *Herder and the Foundations of German Nationalism.* New York: Octagon Books. 1966.

Fackre, Gabriel. *The Promise of Reinhold Niebuhr.* Philadelphia, New York: J. B. Lippincott Co., 1970.

Falwell, Jerry. *America Can Be Saved!* Murfreesboro, Tenn.: Sword of the Lord Publishers, 1979.

———. *Listen America!* Garden City, New York: Doubleday, 1980.

———. *The Fundamentalist Phenomenon: The Resurgence of Conservative Christianity.* Garden City, N.Y.: Doubleday, 1981.

Fromm, Eric. *Escape from Freedom.* New York: Farrar and Rinehart, 1941.

Geertz, Clifford. *Local Knowledge.* New York: Basic Books, 1983.

Hadden, Jeffrey, and Anson Shupe. *Televangelism, Power, and Politics.* New York: Henry Holt and Company, 1988.

Hocking, William Ernest. *The Coming World Civilization.* New York: Harper & Brothers, 1956.

————. *Re-Thinking Missions: A Laymen's Inquiry after One Hundred Years.* New York: Harper & Brothers, 1932.

————. *Man and the State.* New Haven: Yale University Press, 1926.

————. *Strength of Men and Nations.* New York: Harper & Brothers, 1959.

————. *The Spirit of World Politics.* New York: The Macmillan Co., 1932.

Hofstadter, Richard. *The Paranoid Style of American Politics.* New York: Alfred A. Knopf. 1965.

Hula, Erich. *Nationalism and Internationalism: European and American Perspectives.* New York: University Press of America, 1984.

Hunt, Michael. *Ideology and U.S. Foreign Policy.* New Haven, London: Yale University Press. 1987.

Hunter, James Davison. *Culture Wars: The Struggle to Define America.* New York: Basic Books, 1991.

————. *American Evangelism: Conservative Religion and the Quandry of Modernity.* New Brunswick, N.J.: Rutgers University Press, 1983.

Hurd, W. Wesley. "Liberty University: Fortress in the War For a Christian America." Ph.D. dissertation, Division of Education Policy and Management, Graduate School, University of Oregon. 1988.

Hutchison, William R. *Errand to the World.* Chicago, London: University of Chicago Press, 1987.

Jewett, Robert. *The Captain America Complex.* Sante Fe: Bear & Company, 1984.

Kegley, Charles W. *Politics, Religion and Modern Man.* Quezon City: University of the Philippines Press. 1969.

Machen, J. Gresham. *Modernism and the Board of Foreign Missions of the Presbyterian Church in the U.S.A.; Argument of J. Gresham Machen in Support of an Overture Introduced in the Presbytery of New Brunswick at Its Meeting on January 24, 1933, and Made the Order of the Day for the Meeting April 11, 1933.* Philadelphia: J. Gresham Machen.

Marty, Martin E. *Righteous Empire.* New York: Harper & Row, 1970.

————. *Modern American Religion: The Noise of Conflict, 1919–1941.* Chicago: University of Chicago Press, 1991.

May, Henry. *Ideas, Faiths, and Feelings.* New York and Oxford: Oxford University Press, 1983.

McClintock, David Alan. "Walter Rauschenbusch: The Kingdom of God and the American Experience." A Ph.D. dissertation, History, Case Western Reserve, 1975.

Mead, Sidney. *The Old Religion in the Brave New World*. Berkeley: University of California Press, 1977.

Minus, Paul M. *Walter Rauschenbusch: American Reformer*. New York, London: Macmillan, 1988.

Nelson, Clyde Kenneth. "The Social Ideas of Russell Conwell." Ph.D. dissertation, University of Pennsylvania, 1968.

Niebuhr, Reinhold. *Christian Realism and Political Problems*. New York: Charles Scribner's Sons, 1953.

———. *The Nature and Destiny of Man*. New York: Charles Scribner's Sons, 1949.

———. *Moral Man and Immoral Society*. New York: Charles Scribner's Sons, 1960.

———. *The Irony of American History*. New York: Charles Scribner's Sons, 1952.

———. *Christianity and Power Politics*. New York: Charles Scribner's Sons, 1940.

Nye. Russell B. *This Almost Chosen People*. East Lansing: Michigan State University Press, 1966.

Packard, William. *Evangelism in America: From Tents to TV*. New York: Paragon House, 1988.

Perry, Michael J. *Love and Power: The Role of Religion and Morality in American Politics*. New York: Oxford University Press, 1991.

Pratt, Julius W. *Expansionists of 1898*. Glouster, Mass.: Peter Smith, 1959.

Rauschenbusch, Walter. *A Theology for the Social Gospel*. New York: Macmillan, 1919.

———. *Christianizing the Social Order*. New York: Macmillan, 1914.

———. *For God and the People: Prayers of Social Awakening*. Boston, New York, Chicago: The Pilgrim Press, 1909.

Schaffer, Francis. *The Great Evangelical Disaster*. Westchester, Ill.: Crossway Books, 1984.

———. *A Christian Manifesto*. Westchester, Ill.: Crossway Books, 1981.

Simon, Merril. *Jerry Falwell and the Jews*. New York: Jonathan David Publishers, Inc. 1984.

Snyder, Louis. *Varieties of Nationalism*. Hinsdale, Ill.: Dryden Press. 1976.

Stober, Gerald and Tomczak. *Jerry Falwell: Aflame for God*. New York: Thomas Nelson Publishers, 1979.

Stone, Ronald H. *Reinhold Niebuhr: Prophet to Politicians*. New York: University Press of America, 1981.

Stonehouse, Ned B. *J. Gresham Machen: A Biographical Memoir*. Philadelphia: Westminster Theological Seminary, 1977.

Thompson, Kenneth W. *Political Realism and The Crisis of World Politics*. Princeton: Princeton University Press, 1960.

Torbet, Robert G. *A Social History of the Philadelphia Baptist Association 1707–1940*. Philadelphia: Westbrook Publishing Co. 1944.

Wells, David. *The Princeton Theology*. Grand Rapids: Baker Book House, 1989.

Wuthrow, Robert. *The Struggle for America's Soul*. Grand Rapids: William B. Eerdman Publishing Company, 1989.

Index

Roman Catholics
  Conwell, acceptance of, 55, 58, 59
  included in moral majority, 183
  tolerated by Protestants, 198
Roosevelt, Theodore, 4, 5, 46, 48, 112
Roosevelt, Franklin D., 62, 63, 65,
  66, 115, 127

Saltenstall, Leverett, influenced by
  William Ernest Hocking, 107
Schaeffer, Francis, influenced by J.
  Gresham Machen, 83, 84, 180
Schaeffer, Francis, *A Christian
  Manifesto*, used in Falwell's
  *God Bless America Survival
  Kit*, 180
Schwarz, Fred C., Christian Com-
  munism Crusade, early influence
  on *Christianity Today*, 14
Sentinels of the Republic, purpose of,
  66–68
Seventeenth Amendment, alleged
  tool of Zionism, 163
Smith, Wilber, fundamentalist
  influenced by J. Gresham
  Machen, 4, 83
Snyder, Louis, *Varieties of
  Nationalism*, 2
Social Gospel, 141, 207
  contribution of Christianity to
  world religions, 97
  early linkage with evangelicals, 59,
  60
  evils of, 65, 115, 180
  naivete of, 133
  Rauschenbusch and the, 15, 20,
  24, 37, 40, 41, 42, 197
Social Security
  accepted by Jerry Falwell, 186
  rejected by J. Greshan Machen, 63
socialism
  evils of, 84, 115, 118, 139, 163,
  177–81
  international socialism, Rauschenbusch a microcosm of, 40

Soviet Union
  "Evil empire," 12, 146, 148, 179
  God will destroy, 172, 173
  Great Red Dragon, 163
  imposing their will, 102
  manipulators of climate, 166
  moderation toward, 151
  more evil collective than U.S., 14,
  125, 126, 195
  moving closer to U.S., 15, 16,
  90–92
Spanish-American War, 15, 24, 55
Speer, Robert B., versus J. Gresham
  Machen, 78–81
Stonehouse, Ned, biographer of J.
  Gresham Machen, 61, 77
Sumner, William Graham, support of
  American Anti-Imperialism
  League, 41
Sunday, Billy, his nationalism, 104,
  180
Sword of the Lord, zealous
  nationalism of, 109–19

Taiwan
  potential war over, 107
  alleged abandonment by U.S., 111
Taoism, views on, 97
Teuton/Teutonic, destined by God to
  civilize the world, 4, 19, 20–25,
  197
Third World
  Communist woo, 126
  nationalism, 87, 131–34
  poverty of, 130
  Western superiority over, 4, 128,
  195
Thorp David, *The Moravian
  Community in Colonial North
  Carolina*, 200
Trudeau, Gary, American
  judgmental skills, 9
Trueblood, Dr. Elton, observation of
  Mohammed's birth, 149